First World War
and Army of Occupation
War Diary
France, Belgium and Germany

2 DIVISION
Divisional Troops
483 Field Company Royal Engineers
23 December 1914 - 31 August 1919

WO95/1332

The Naval & Military Press Ltd
www.nmarchive.com
Published in association with The National Archives

Published by

The Naval & Military Press Ltd

Unit 10 Ridgewood Industrial Park,

Uckfield, East Sussex,

TN22 5QE England

Tel: +44 (0) 1825 749494

www.naval-military-press.com

www.nmarchive.com

This diary has been reprinted in facsimile from the original. Any imperfections are inevitably reproduced and the quality may fall short of modern type and cartographic standards.

© Crown Copyright
Images reproduced by permission of The National Archives, London, England, 2015.

Contents

Document type	Place/Title	Date From	Date To
Heading	BEF 2 Div Troops 483 Fld Coy R.E		
Heading	2nd Division War Diaries 1st East Anglian Field Coy R.E. From December 1914 To December 1915		
Heading	2nd Division 1st East Anglian Field Coy RE Vol I 23.12.14-30.4.15		
War Diary	Bury St Edmunds	23/12/1914	23/12/1914
War Diary	Southampton	23/12/1914	24/12/1914
War Diary	Harve	25/12/1914	29/12/1914
War Diary	St Omer	30/12/1914	30/12/1914
War Diary	Heuringham	30/12/1914	04/01/1915
War Diary	Guarbeique	04/01/1915	05/01/1915
War Diary	Locon	05/01/1915	17/01/1915
War Diary	Rue De Bois	17/01/1915	17/01/1915
War Diary	Locon	17/01/1915	17/01/1915
War Diary	Le Hamel	17/01/1915	31/01/1915
War Diary	Rue De Dois	17/01/1915	24/01/1915
War Diary	Rue De L'Epinette	24/01/1915	30/01/1915
War Diary	Le Hamel	01/02/1915	01/02/1915
War Diary	Vendin-Lez-Bethune	01/02/1915	01/02/1915
War Diary	Annequin	01/02/1915	01/02/1915
War Diary	Vendin-Lez-Bethune	03/02/1915	03/02/1915
War Diary	Le Quesnoy	03/02/1915	28/02/1915
War Diary	Annequin	01/02/1915	06/02/1915
War Diary	Cuinchy	06/02/1915	12/03/1915
War Diary	Givenchy	10/03/1915	11/03/1915
War Diary	Cuinchy	12/03/1915	12/03/1915
War Diary	Le Quesnoy	12/03/1915	23/03/1915
War Diary	Cuinchy	23/03/1915	31/03/1915
Heading	2nd Division 1st East Anglian Field Coy R.E Vol II 1-31.5.15		
War Diary	Cuinchy	01/04/1915	02/05/1915
War Diary	Le Quesnoy	02/05/1915	05/05/1915
War Diary	Cuinchy	06/05/1915	12/05/1915
War Diary	Le Casan	12/05/1915	16/05/1915
War Diary	La Couture	16/05/1915	16/05/1915
War Diary	Rue De L'Epinette	16/05/1915	16/05/1915
War Diary	La Couture	18/05/1915	18/05/1915
War Diary	Rue De L'Epinette	18/05/1915	18/05/1915
War Diary	La Couture	19/05/1915	19/05/1915
War Diary	Rue De L'Epinette	19/05/1915	20/05/1915
War Diary	La Couture	20/05/1915	20/05/1915
War Diary	Rue De L'Epinette	21/05/1915	22/05/1915
War Diary	Allouagne	22/05/1915	30/05/1915
War Diary	Les Brebis	31/05/1915	31/05/1915
Heading	2nd Division 1st East Anglian Field Coy R.E Vol III 1-27.6.15		
War Diary	Alles Brebis	01/06/1915	09/06/1915
War Diary	Les Brebis	06/06/1915	09/06/1915
War Diary	Noyelles	10/06/1915	10/06/1915
War Diary	Al Noyelles	10/06/1915	18/06/1915

War Diary	Novelles	18/06/1915	18/06/1915
War Diary	Al Cuinchy	18/06/1915	05/07/1915
War Diary	Cuinchy	22/06/1915	27/06/1915
Heading	2nd Division 1/1 E. Anglian Field Coy. RE Vol IV July & August 15		
War Diary	Cuinchy	01/07/1915	05/07/1915
War Diary	Gorre	05/07/1915	31/08/1915
Diagram etc	Diagram		
Diagram etc	Section of Trench Mono-Rail With Stretcher July 1915		
Heading	2nd Division 1/1st East Anglian Field Coy RE Sep 15		
War Diary	Gorre	01/09/1915	30/09/1915
Heading	2nd Division 1st Fd Co East Anglian R.E. Oct 1915 Vol VI		
War Diary	Annequin	01/10/1915	03/10/1915
War Diary	Beuvry	03/10/1915	08/10/1915
War Diary	Annequin	11/10/1915	22/10/1915
War Diary	Le Preol	22/10/1915	27/12/1915
War Diary	La Miquellerie	27/12/1915	31/12/1915
Heading	2nd Division Divl Engineers 1-1st East Anglian Field Coy. R.E Jan-Dec 1916		
Heading	2nd Divisional Engineers 1/1st East Anglian Field Company R.E. January 1916		
War Diary	La Miquellerie	01/01/1916	17/01/1916
War Diary	Le Touret	17/01/1916	31/01/1916
Heading	2nd Divisional Engineers 1/1st East Anglian Field Company R.E. February 1916		
War Diary	Le Touret	01/02/1916	17/02/1916
War Diary	La Miquellerie	17/02/1916	25/02/1916
War Diary	Gonnehem	26/02/1916	26/02/1916
War Diary	Fosse 10	27/02/1916	27/02/1916
War Diary	Bully Grenay	29/02/1916	29/02/1916
War Diary	Bully Grenay & Calonne	27/02/1916	29/02/1916
Heading	2nd Divisional Engineers 1/1st East Anglian Field Company R.E. March 1916		
War Diary	Calonne Bully Grenay	01/03/1916	31/03/1916
Heading	2nd Divisional Engineers 1/1st East Anglian Field Company R.E. April 1916		
War Diary	Calonne Bully Grenay	01/04/1916	30/04/1916
Heading	2nd Divisional Engineers 1/1st East Anglian Field Company R.E. May 1916		
War Diary	Calonne Bully Grenay	01/05/1916	17/05/1916
War Diary	Cite Jeanne D'Arc	18/05/1916	22/05/1916
War Diary	Grand Servin	25/05/1916	25/05/1916
War Diary	Gour Servins	26/05/1916	31/05/1916
Heading	2nd Divisional Engineers 1/1st East Anglian Field Company R.E. June 1916		
War Diary	Gour Servins	01/06/1916	30/06/1916
Heading	2nd Divisional Engineers 1/1st East Anglian Field Company R.E. July 1916		
War Diary	Gour Servins	01/07/1916	15/07/1916
War Diary	Bajus	15/07/1916	18/07/1916
War Diary	Grossart	18/07/1916	20/07/1916
War Diary	Ville Sous Corbie	21/07/1916	23/07/1916
War Diary	Sandpit	23/07/1916	24/07/1916
War Diary	Carnoy Happy Valley	25/07/1916	25/07/1916
War Diary	Carnoy	25/07/1916	31/07/1916

Map	Map		
Heading	2nd Divisional Engineers 1/1st East Anglian Field Company R.E. August 1916		
War Diary	Carnoy	01/08/1916	07/08/1916
War Diary	F.23.b.2.9	08/08/1916	08/08/1916
War Diary	Happy Valley	09/08/1916	12/08/1916
War Diary	Meaulte	13/08/1916	13/08/1916
War Diary	La Chausse	14/08/1916	16/08/1916
War Diary	Vignacourt	17/08/1916	17/08/1916
War Diary	Beaumetz	18/08/1916	18/08/1916
War Diary	Sarton	20/08/1916	20/08/1916
War Diary	Courcelles Au Bois	20/08/1916	31/08/1916
Heading	2nd Divisional Engineers 1/1st East Anglian Field Company R.E. September 1916		
War Diary	Courcelles Au Bois	01/09/1916	30/09/1916
Heading	2nd Divisional Engineers 1/1st East Anglian Field Company R.E. October 1916		
War Diary	Courcelles-Au-Bois	01/10/1916	03/10/1916
War Diary	Englebelmer	03/10/1916	04/10/1916
War Diary	Mailly-Maillet	04/10/1916	10/10/1916
War Diary	Puchevillers	10/10/1916	17/10/1916
War Diary	P 11d-Sheet 57d	17/10/1916	30/10/1916
Heading	2nd Divisional Engineers 1/1st East Anglian Field Company R.E. November 1916		
War Diary	Beaussart-Mailly Road P.11.d. Sheet 57d	01/11/1916	19/11/1916
War Diary	Longuevillette	20/11/1916	21/11/1916
War Diary	Candas	22/11/1916	23/11/1916
War Diary	Longvillers	24/11/1916	24/11/1916
War Diary	Cornehotte	25/11/1916	25/11/1916
War Diary	Caours	26/11/1916	27/11/1916
War Diary	Conteville	28/11/1916	30/11/1916
Map	Map		
Heading	2nd Divisional Engineers 1/1st East Anglian Field Company R.E. December 1916		
War Diary	Prouville	01/12/1916	01/12/1916
War Diary	Beauval	02/12/1916	02/12/1916
War Diary	Aveluy	03/12/1916	20/12/1916
War Diary	Puchvillers Aveluy	21/12/1916	21/12/1916
War Diary	Bernatre Beaumetz	21/12/1916	22/12/1916
War Diary	Bernatre	22/12/1916	31/12/1916
Heading	2nd Division Divl. Engineers 483rd Field Company R.E Jan-Dec 1917		
Heading	2nd Divisional Engineers 483rd Field Company R.E. January 1917		
War Diary	Bernatre	01/01/1917	09/01/1917
War Diary	Bernaville	09/01/1917	11/01/1917
War Diary	Rubempre	11/01/1917	12/01/1917
War Diary	Senlis	12/01/1917	13/01/1917
War Diary	Wolseley Huts	13/01/1917	13/01/1917
War Diary	Wolseley Huts W.18b	15/01/1917	20/01/1917
War Diary	Wolfe Huts X9c	20/01/1917	31/01/1917
Heading	2nd Divisional Engineers 483rd Field Company R.E. February A 1917		
War Diary	Wolfe Huts X.9.c	01/02/1917	06/02/1917
War Diary	Wolseley Huts W.18.b	06/02/1917	16/02/1917
War Diary	Wolfe Huts X.9.c	16/02/1917	28/02/1917

Heading	2nd Divisional Engineers 483rd Field Company R.E March 1917		
War Diary	Wolfe Huts X.9.c	01/03/1917	14/03/1917
War Diary	Dyke Valley M.14.d.1.1	14/03/1917	18/03/1917
War Diary	No.1 Sectn Sapignies	18/03/1917	18/03/1917
War Diary	Dyke Valley (M.14.d.1.1) Sapignies	19/03/1917	19/03/1917
War Diary	No.1 Sectn (Sapignies Mory)	19/03/1917	19/03/1917
War Diary	Dyke Valley (M.14.d.1.1)	20/03/1917	20/03/1917
War Diary	No.1 Sectn Mory Dyke Valley	20/03/1917	20/03/1917
War Diary	Dyke Valley (M.14.d.1.1)	21/03/1917	21/03/1917
War Diary	Wolfe Huts X.9.c	21/03/1917	21/03/1917
War Diary	Warloy-Baillon	21/03/1917	25/03/1917
War Diary	La Vicogne	26/03/1917	27/03/1917
War Diary	Neuvillette	27/03/1917	28/03/1917
War Diary	Sibiville (La Mont Joie Farm)	28/03/1917	30/03/1917
War Diary	Antin	30/03/1917	30/03/1917
Heading	2nd Divisional Engineers 483rd Field Company R.E. April 1917		
War Diary	Antin	01/04/1917	07/04/1917
War Diary	Ourton	07/04/1917	10/04/1917
War Diary	Ecoivres "X" Huts Map Ref F.19th Sheet 51c	10/04/1917	10/04/1917
War Diary	Maroeuil	11/04/1917	16/04/1917
War Diary	Anzin	16/04/1917	26/04/1917
War Diary	Ecurie	27/04/1917	30/04/1917
Heading	2nd Divisional Engineers 483rd Field Company R.E. May 1917		
War Diary	Ecurie	01/05/1917	31/05/1917
Heading	2nd Divisional Engineers 483rd Field Company R.E. June 1917		
War Diary	Ecurie	31/05/1917	31/05/1917
War Diary	Advanced Billets	01/06/1917	13/06/1917
War Diary	Billet Anzin	14/06/1917	19/06/1917
War Diary	Beuvry Billet F.21.a.5.2	20/06/1917	30/06/1917
Heading	2nd Divisional Engineers 483rd Field Company R.E. July 1917		
War Diary	Beuvry Billets F.21.a.5.2	01/07/1917	31/07/1917
Heading	2nd Divisional Engineers 483rd Field Company R.E. August 1917		
Heading	483rd (E.A) Field Coy R.E War Diary August 1917		
War Diary	Beuvry F.21.a.5.2	01/08/1917	24/08/1917
War Diary	Le Touret	25/08/1917	31/08/1917
Miscellaneous	O/s 66		
Miscellaneous	O/S 65		
Heading	2nd Divisional Engineers 483rd (East Anglian) Field Company R.E. September 1917		
War Diary	Le Touret	01/09/1917	19/09/1917
War Diary	Beuvry	20/09/1917	20/09/1917
War Diary	Beuvry F.21.a.5.2	21/09/1917	30/09/1917
Miscellaneous	C.R.E. 2nd Division	06/09/1917	06/09/1917
Miscellaneous	Handing Over Report 483rd (E.A) Fd Coy R.E to 465th Fd Coy R.E		
Miscellaneous	Copy of Report to 99th Inf Bde		
Miscellaneous	General Condition of Trenches		
Miscellaneous	List Of Documents	23/08/1917	23/08/1917
Miscellaneous	List Of Plans Drawings & Details of the Cambrin Sector Handed over is the 465th Field Co R.E	24/08/1917	24/08/1917

Heading	2nd Divisional Engineers 483rd Field Company R.E October 1917		
War Diary	Beuvry	01/10/1917	05/10/1917
War Diary	Busnettes	05/10/1917	31/10/1917
Heading	2nd Divisional Engineers 483rd Field Company R.E November 1917		
War Diary	Busnettes	01/11/1917	04/11/1917
War Diary	Poperinghe	04/11/1917	05/11/1917
War Diary	Brielen	05/11/1917	06/11/1917
War Diary	Brielen B.30.c.10.90	06/11/1917	18/11/1917
War Diary	Poperinghe	19/11/1917	19/11/1917
War Diary	Winnezeele	20/11/1917	20/11/1917
War Diary	Winnezeele J.3.c.3.3	21/11/1917	22/11/1917
War Diary	Esquelbecq	23/11/1917	23/11/1917
War Diary	Basatre	24/11/1917	24/11/1917
War Diary	Doignies	25/11/1917	28/11/1917
War Diary	Beaumetz J.20.b Sheet 57c N.E	29/11/1917	30/11/1917
Heading	2nd Divisional Engineers 483rd Field Company R.E. December 1917		
War Diary	Beaumetz J.20.b	01/12/1917	03/12/1917
War Diary	Bertincourt P.1.d	04/12/1917	06/12/1917
War Diary	Beaumetz J.20.b	07/12/1917	11/12/1917
War Diary	Bertincourt P.1.d	12/12/1917	31/12/1917
Heading	2nd Division 483rd Field Company R.E January To December Late 1/E Anglian 1918		
Heading	2nd Divisional Engineers 483rd Field Company R.E January 1918		
War Diary	Bertincourt	01/01/1918	04/01/1918
War Diary	Rocquigny	05/01/1918	15/01/1918
War Diary	Bertincourt P.1.d.6.4	16/01/1918	21/01/1918
War Diary	Metz	23/01/1918	29/01/1918
War Diary	Metz (H.Q Q.19b.3.3)	30/01/1918	31/01/1918
Heading	2nd Divisional Engineers 483rd Field Company R.E. February 1918		
War Diary	Metz H.Q. Q.19.b.3.3	01/02/1918	27/02/1918
Heading	2nd Divisional Engineers 483rd Field Company R.E March 1918		
War Diary	Metz	01/03/1918	21/03/1918
War Diary	Royaulcourt	22/03/1918	22/03/1918
War Diary	Beaulencourt	23/03/1918	23/03/1918
War Diary	Geudecourt	24/03/1918	24/03/1918
War Diary	Miraumont	25/03/1918	25/03/1918
War Diary	Bertrancourt	26/03/1918	27/03/1918
War Diary	Lealvillers	28/03/1918	31/03/1918
Miscellaneous	Narration of Events 483rd (E.A) Field Company R.E	07/04/1918	07/04/1918
Miscellaneous	To O.C 483rd Fd Coy R.E	07/04/1918	07/04/1918
Diagram etc	Diagram		
Miscellaneous	Demolition Of Bore Hole At Beaulencourt		
Diagram etc	Demolition Of Bore Hole At Beaulencourt		
Miscellaneous	V Corps Line Night Of 24th / 25th March 1918	08/04/1918	08/04/1918
Miscellaneous	To O.C 483rd Fd Coy R.E	03/04/1918	03/04/1918
Miscellaneous	O.C. 5th Field Co R.E	06/03/1918	06/03/1918
Miscellaneous	C.R.E 2nd Divn		
Operation(al) Order(s)	Orders By Lieut-Colonel P.K. Betty, D.S.O., R.E Commanding Royal Engineer, 2nd Division Order No. 104	10/03/1918	10/03/1918

Miscellaneous	O.C. 483rd (E.A.) Field Co R.E.	21/03/1918	21/03/1918
Miscellaneous	A Form Messages And Signals		
Miscellaneous			
Miscellaneous	O.C. 483rd Field Coy R.E	23/03/1918	23/03/1918
Miscellaneous	A Form Messages And Signals		
Miscellaneous	Appendix M	27/03/1918	27/03/1918
Miscellaneous	A Form Messages And Signals		
Miscellaneous	Appendix O	28/03/1918	28/03/1918
Miscellaneous	Appendix P	29/03/1918	29/03/1918
Miscellaneous	Appendix Q	30/03/1918	30/03/1918
Miscellaneous	Appendix R.	30/03/1918	30/03/1918
Miscellaneous	Appendix S	31/03/1918	31/03/1918
Miscellaneous	Appendix T	31/03/1918	31/03/1918
Miscellaneous	Appendix U	01/04/1918	01/04/1918
Heading	2nd Divisional Engineers 483rd Field Company R.E. April 1918		
War Diary	Lealvillers	01/04/1918	02/04/1918
War Diary	Hurtebise Farm	04/04/1918	04/04/1918
War Diary	Honval	05/04/1918	10/04/1918
War Diary	Sombrin	11/04/1918	11/04/1918
War Diary	La Herliere	12/04/1918	13/04/1918
War Diary	Ransart	14/04/1918	30/04/1918
Miscellaneous	C Form Messages And Signals		
Miscellaneous	2nd Division No. G.S. 1543/27	04/04/1918	04/04/1918
Miscellaneous	O.C. 483rd Field Coy R.E	01/04/1918	01/04/1918
Miscellaneous	O.C. 483rd Field Coy R.E Appendix B	02/04/1918	02/04/1918
Miscellaneous	O.C. 483rd Field Coy R.E Appendix C	03/04/1918	03/04/1918
Operation(al) Order(s)	99th Infantry Brigade Order No. 231	11/04/1918	11/04/1918
Miscellaneous	March Table Issued With 99th Inf. Brigade Order No. 231		
Operation(al) Order(s)	99th Infantry Brigade Order No.232	12/04/1918	12/04/1918
Miscellaneous	March Table Issued With 99th Inf. Bde Order No.232		
Miscellaneous	Appendix H		
Miscellaneous	A Form Messages And Signals		
Miscellaneous	Copies to:-		
Heading	2nd Divisional Engineers 483rd Field Company R.E. May 1918		
War Diary	Ransart	01/05/1918	11/05/1918
War Diary	Laherliere	12/05/1918	31/05/1918
Miscellaneous	Orders By Lieut. Colonel P.K. Betty, D.S.O., R.E C.R.E. 2nd Division	09/05/1918	09/05/1918
Miscellaneous	Appendix B	09/05/1918	09/05/1918
Miscellaneous	Appendix C		
Miscellaneous	O.C. 483rd (E.A.) Field Co R.E.	17/05/1918	17/05/1918
Miscellaneous	Programme or Morning Work For The Training Of Royal Engineers At 2nd Divisional Wing	19/05/1918	19/05/1918
Miscellaneous	OC 483 Field Co R.E.	21/05/1918	21/05/1918
Operation(al) Order(s)	99th Infantry Brigade Order No. 240	22/05/1918	22/05/1918
Miscellaneous	Appendix H	23/05/1918	23/05/1918
Miscellaneous	2nd Divisional Wing Massed Sports	26/05/1918	26/05/1918
Miscellaneous	2nd Division "G"	30/05/1918	30/05/1918
Miscellaneous	2nd Divisional Wing Result of Massed Sports		
Heading	2nd Divisional Engineers 483rd Field Company R.E. June 1918		
War Diary	Laherliere	01/06/1918	07/06/1918
War Diary	E.11c.15.43	07/06/1918	30/06/1918

Operation(al) Order(s)	C.R.E's Order No. 113	04/06/1918	04/06/1918
Miscellaneous	CRE 2nd Divn	10/06/1918	10/06/1918
Heading	2nd Divisional Engineers 483rd Field Company R.E. July 1918		
War Diary	E.11c.15.43	01/07/1918	31/07/1918
Heading	2nd Divisional Engineers 483rd Field Company R.E. August 1918		
War Diary	E.11.c.15.43	01/08/1918	19/08/1918
War Diary	W.25.6.4.3	19/08/1918	19/08/1918
War Diary	E.4.c.2.4	20/08/1918	20/08/1918
War Diary	E.4.c.15.43	21/08/1918	21/08/1918
War Diary	F.9.a.4.5	23/08/1918	28/08/1918
War Diary	A.16.a.7.0	28/08/1918	28/08/1918
War Diary	A.22.d.7.2	28/08/1918	31/08/1918
War Diary	E.11.c.15.43	02/08/1918	19/08/1918
War Diary	W.25.b.4.3	20/08/1918	20/08/1918
War Diary	E.11.c.15.43	22/08/1918	22/08/1918
War Diary	F.9.a.7.5	23/08/1918	23/08/1918
War Diary	A.16.d.7.0	30/09/1918	30/09/1918
Heading	2nd Divisional Engineers 483rd Field Company R.E September 1918		
War Diary	B.29.d To I.4.c.3.2	01/09/1918	15/09/1918
War Diary	B.24.b.7.6	16/09/1918	27/09/1918
War Diary	J.29.c.2.8	27/09/1918	28/09/1918
War Diary	K.14.a.7.8	28/09/1918	28/09/1918
War Diary	L.14.a.2.6	28/09/1918	30/09/1918
Heading	2nd Divisional Engineers 483rd Field Company R.E October 1918		
War Diary	Seranvillers	18/10/1918	20/10/1918
War Diary	Boussieres	21/10/1918	22/10/1918
War Diary	St Hilaire	23/10/1918	24/10/1918
War Diary	Ferme De Rieux	25/10/1918	31/10/1918
War Diary	Flesquieres L.14.a.2.6	01/10/1918	14/10/1918
War Diary	Seranvillers	15/10/1918	19/10/1918
Heading	2nd Divisional Engineers 483rd Field Company R.E November 1918		
War Diary	Farm-De-Rieux	01/11/1918	02/11/1918
War Diary	Villers Pol	05/11/1918	17/11/1918
War Diary	Villers Pol to Farm-Les-Motte (Longueville)	18/11/1918	18/11/1918
War Diary	Longueville (Farm-Les-Motte)	19/11/1918	19/11/1918
War Diary	Vieux Reng	23/11/1918	23/11/1918
War Diary	Vieux Reng to Ressaix	24/11/1918	24/11/1918
War Diary	Ressaix to Marchienne-Du-Pont	25/11/1918	25/11/1918
War Diary	Marchienne-Du-Pont	26/11/1918	27/11/1918
War Diary	Chatelet to Sart St Laurent	29/11/1918	29/11/1918
Heading	2nd Divisional Engineers 483rd Field Company R.E. December 1918		
War Diary	Sart St Laurent	01/12/1918	02/12/1918
War Diary	Sart St Laurent Marche-Les-Dames	04/12/1918	04/12/1918
War Diary	Marche-Les-Dames Seilles	05/12/1918	05/12/1918
War Diary	Seilles to Barse	06/12/1918	06/12/1918
War Diary	Bares to Mont	07/12/1918	07/12/1918
War Diary	Mont to Hestroumont	09/12/1918	09/12/1918
War Diary	Mont to Hestroumont Bernister	11/12/1918	11/12/1918
War Diary	Bernister Elsenborn Lager	12/12/1918	12/12/1918
War Diary	Elsenborn Lager Huppenbroach	13/12/1918	13/12/1918

War Diary	Huppenbroach Thum	14/12/1918	14/12/1918
War Diary	Thum Ellen	19/12/1918	24/12/1918
War Diary	Ellen Angelsdorf	27/12/1918	27/12/1918
War Diary	Angelsdorf Vanikum	28/12/1918	31/12/1918
War Diary	Wald	01/08/1919	31/08/1919

BEF
2 DIV TROOPS

483 FLD COY RE

(Box 1004)

2nd Division.

War Diaries

1st East Anglian Field Coy. R.E.

From December 1914 To December 1915

121/53144

2nd Division

1st East Anglian Field Coy RE.

Vol I 23.12.14 —— 30.4.15

1/1 E.O.Y.R.Y. Army Form C. 2118.

WAR DIARY
or
INTELLIGENCE SUMMARY.
(Erase heading not required.)

DECEMBER.

Instructions regarding War Diaries and Intelligence Summaries are contained in F. S. Regs., Part II. and the Staff Manual respectively. Title pages will be prepared in manuscript.

Hour, Date, Place			Summary of Events and Information	Remarks and references to Appendices
9 A.M.	23/12/14.	Bury St. Edmunds	Left for Southampton.	
7.30 P.M.	28/12/14.	Southampton.	Arrived	
Night	28/12/14	Ditto	Rest Camp.	
11 A.M. to 5 P.M.	24/12/14	Ditto	Commenced loading and Embarking	
6.30 P.M.	Do.	Do.	Sailed from	
6 A.M.	25/12/14.	Harve.	Disembarked. (Very Loody December.)	
25/12/14 to 29/12/14.		Do.	No 2 Camp (Very wet from the 26th)	
2.30 P.M.	29/12/14.	Do.	Left. (By Rail)	
10.15 A.M.	30/12/14.	St Omer.	Arrived (Offrs leaving Bury St Edmunds every possible assistance was willingly given to the Unit by all R.T.O, M.L.O. up to its destination (at St Omer.)	
3 P.M.	30/12/14.	Do.	Left. (By Road)	
5 P.M.	30/12/14.	Heuringham	Arrived	
30/12/14 to 4/1/15.		Do.	Billeted in small farms - awaiting instructions.	

WAR DIARY or INTELLIGENCE SUMMARY.

Army Form C. 2118.

(Erase heading not required.)

JANUARY.

Hour, Date, Place		Summary of Events and Information	Remarks and references to Appendices
30/12/14 to 4/1/15.	HEURINGHAM.	Bulleted. Lot. on Instructor Duties	
10 A.M.	4/1/15.	D°. Left (By Road)	
6 P.M.	4/1/15.	QUARBEIQUE Arrived	
9.30 AM	5/1/15.	D°. Left (By Road)	
6.30 PM	5/1/15.	LOCON. Arrived. (Roads in a very bad condition)	
5/1/15 to 10/1/15.	D°.	Billeted in MESPLAUX. Redoubt commenced 1 mile East of Junction of RUE DE BOIS, and RUE DE L'EPINETTE. Work carried out in Front Line also.	
10/1/15.	RUE DE BOIS.	One SAPPER wounded.	
4 P.M.	14/1/15.	LOCON. Left By. Rd.	
7.30 P.M.	14/1/15.	LE HANEL Arrived	
14/1/15 to 31/1/15.	D°.	Carried on Redoubt and work in Front Line	
17/1/15.	D°.	Take over Civilians working at FESTUBERT on the construction of Intermediate Line. Two Reports from LOWLAND F² C° R.E.	
17/1/15.	RUE DE BOIS	One SAPPER wounded. Two SAPPERS Killed	
24/1/15.	D°.	Handed over Civilians at FESTUBERT to 11th F.D.C° R.E.	
D°.	RUE DE L'EPINETTE	One SAPPER Killed	
D°. 30/1/15.	D°.	" D°. — " D°. — 2ND LIEUT. E.J. MUNBY Killed.	G.W.

(D 29 6) W 3332—1107 100,000 10/13 H W V Forms/C. 2118/10.

WAR DIARY
or
INTELLIGENCE SUMMARY.
(Erase heading not required.)

Army Form C. 2118.

FEBRUARY

Hour, Date, Place	Summary of Events and Information	Remarks and references to Appendices
2.30 PM 1/2/15. LE HAMEL	Company left. (Headquarters but both)	
1/2/15 VENDIN-LEZ-BETHUNE	Headquarters and two Sections arrived. Take out Rubble	
" ANNEQUIN	Two Sections arrive.	
1/2/15 - 3/2/15. VENDIN-LEZ-BETHUNE	Two Sections and Headquarters Billeted here.	
10.30 AM 3/2/15 — D°—	Two Sections and Headquarters leave for —	
12.30 PM 3/2/15. LE QUESNOY	Two Sections and G.H.Q. arrive & take out Rubble and Fascines	
3/2/15 — 2/2/15. — D°—	Headquarters and Transport with two sections Billeted	
1/2/15 — 5/2/15. ANNEQUIN	Two Sections Billeted. Work carried out in PONT FIXE	
6/2/15. — D°—	& strong point round PONT FIXE. Two Sections leave for	
6/2/15. CUINCHY	Two Sections arrive and Billets here and carry on the work	
6/2/15 to 28/2/15. — D°—	Working in GIVENCHY area, Repair and Drainage of Trenches. The Drainage was a very difficult problem owing to the very wet weather conditions & certain parts of the high ground is full of Natural Springs.	47/

WAR DIARY
or
INTELLIGENCE SUMMARY.
(Erase heading not required.)

Army Form C. 2118.

FEBRUARY

Hour, Date, Place	Summary of Events and Information	Remarks and references to Appendices
3 P.M. 14/2/15. CUINCHY.	2ND LIEUT O.H. KEELING arrived	
19/2/15. Do	One Sapper Wounded.	
11-11.0 A.M. 26/2/15. Do	An attack was made on the German trenches in front of DUCKS BILL GIVENCHY to ascertain whether the Enemy were moving towards our trenches after a preliminary Bombardment two small columns consisting of parties of 1st Royal Berks. 2nd S. Staffs and Glasgow Highlanders, and Two Officers & 2 N.C.Os & Sappers of our Coy. succeeded in bombarding the trench and afterwards gained it was found that the Enemy were not moving. The head was evacuated and party returned. Two Sapper 6. Killed Two Missing Eight Wounded.	
24/2/15. Do	1st LIEUT C.H. HUMPHREYS Wounded	
	One Sapper Wounded	
3.30 P.M. 24/2/16. Do	1st LIEUT E.T. BRADDELL arrived.	

WAR DIARY or INTELLIGENCE SUMMARY

Army Form C. 2118.

MARCH

Hour, Date, Place	Summary of Events and Information	Remarks and references to Appendices
1/3/15 to 12/3/15 GUINCHY	Work carried out in GUINCHY area which consisted of general repair of trenches. The drainage was a very important problem owing to the very wet weather conditions.	
4 A.M. 10/3/15 GIVENCHY.	Attack made on the German trenches after a heavy bombardment by our artillery. This attack was in connection with the main attack which was delivered at NEUVE CHAPELLE, but owing to the width of front of German trenches being left intact no ground was gained. Our Coy was working with the S. STAFF. REGT two sections furnishing blocking parties, and the other two in Reserve. A second attack was made at 2 PM. on same day with same result. (Weather - rainy with rain falling better half Day) 5 SAPPERS Killed. 18 Wounded.	
3/3/15. — Do —	LIEUT. A.T. BERRY Wounded II Lieut. CH. HUMPHREYS. Awarded M.C. 11 Cpl. H. BRYAN. — " — D.C.M.	
11/3/15 — Do —	Coy in Reserve with 10th BRIGADE pending a counter attack by the Germans.	
3 P.M. 12/3/15 GUINCHY. 11.30 P.M. 12/3/15 LE QUESNOY	Left Qrs. Arrived — Billeted with Coy HD QRS	
13/3/15 to 23/3/15 — Do —	Resting. Some work done for 4th BDE on dugouts of 18.19 & 20. Watering Road at ANNEQUIN.	

Army Form C. 2118.

Army Form C. 2118.

WAR DIARY
or
INTELLIGENCE SUMMARY

(Erase heading not required.)

MARCH

Hour, Date, Place	Summary of Events and Information	Remarks and references to Appendices
1 P.M. 18/3/15 Le Quesnoy	2ND Lieut R.H.Pearsall and draft of 30 Sappers arrive. Two Sappers wounded.	
3 P.M. 21/3/15 Do	Lieut L.H.Kent. arrived.	
4 P.M. 22/3/15 Do	Left for	
5.30 P.M. 23/3/15 Cuinchy	Arrived	
23/3/15 to 31/3/15 Do	Busied behind firing line. Work carried out in Cuinchy area consisting of general repair of trenches and erection of barbed wire entanglements. (Weather conditions fairly good)	E.V.S.

121/5/25

2nd Division

1st East Anglian Field Co. RE.

Vol III 1 — 31.5.15

WAR DIARY
or
INTELLIGENCE SUMMARY

(Erase heading not required.)

Army Form C. 2118.

APRIL

Hour, Date, Place		Summary of Events and Information	Remarks and references to Appendices
1/4/15.	30/7/15 GIVENCHY.	Work carried out with the 6TH BDE. General repairs of trenches and construction of barbed wire entanglement.	
18/4/15	30/4/15. —Do.—	Work carried out with 11TH BDE in GIVENCHY area. Repairs of trenches and construction of Dug Outs.	
3 P.M.	9/4/15 —D°—	Draft of 11 SAPPERS, and 6 DRIVERS. Arrived. One SAPPER wounded.	
	10/4/15 —D°—	Three —D°— —D°—	
11 A.M.	14/4/15. —D°—	30 SAPPERS, & 10 DRIVERS. Draft Arrived.	
	20/4/15. —D°—	1 SAPPER Wounded.	
	25/4/15 —D°—	Civilian Labour taken over at FESTUBERT from 5TH FDCY. Construction of roads through the Majorities.	

WAR DIARY or INTELLIGENCE SUMMARY

Army Form C. 2118.

MAY 1915

Hour, Date, Place	Summary of Events and Information	Remarks and references to Appendices
1/5/15 Ouvrelu	Coy Working with 6th Bde in Ouvrelu sector	
31M 2/5/15 — do —	Unit off to return to H.Q. D Billet at Le Quesnoy	
2 5/15 — 5/5/15 Le Quesnoy	at rest. Coy Resting.	
5 PM 4/5/15 — do —	Three Drivers followed 6th heavy van	
3 PM 5/5/15 — do —	Unit returned to Ouvrelu Coy B4 D section	
6 5/15 – 10/5/15 Ouvrelu	Work carried out in Ouvrelu & Gwendelu sectors with HQ Guards Bde	
	Enemy mail well down behind firing line, there were still minefield owing to embarcation of the Boy	
	for sector. Weather Fine.	
9/5/15 — do —	Heavy Bombardment heard. No R.E. work asked	
	continued the work as usual	
3 PM 12/5/15 — do —	Unit left Ouvrelu for Le Quesnoy	
	Arrived Coy at Le Quesnoy 8½ 2½	
7/5/15 9/5/15 Le Carbon	Arrived Le Cairn. Embare Dorking on Breakwater	
	at Boulogne, en route at Armgur. Landed now to 9/5 H. a BO M field Coy R.E.	

WAR DIARY
or
INTELLIGENCE SUMMARY
(Erase heading not required.)

Army Form C. 2118.

Instructions regarding War Diaries and Intelligence Summaries are contained in F.S. Regs., Part II. and the Staff Manual respectively. Title pages will be prepared in manuscript.

Hour, Date, Place	Summary of Events and Information	Remarks and references to Appendices
Night 13/14.11/15 Le Caser	Two Sections working on Boot Factory at Richebourg. Orders & Covers for 2nd Divl. Operators	
14.11/15. —do—	One Section working in Rue du Bois Area	
11.30 PM 15/11/15. —do—	Dawlor Sector work nearly done. "B" Coy in Reserve with 4th Guards Bde stand to	
4 AM 16.11/15 —do—	Left Le Caser for La Couture	
5.30 AM 16.11/15. La Couture, Estrue & Bullet Hare.		
16.11/15. Rue de l'Epinette	Roads and Tracks in construction & communication cabling traced from British Breastwork to German Breastwork after attack by 6th Bde.	
10 AM 16.11/15. La Couture	One Section & 3 Officers join R.E. Nights Park	
3.10 PM 18.11/15. —do—	One Section & 1 Coy left to join the Bde at Rue de l'Epinette	
18.11/15. Rue de l'Epinette	A Section in construction of new road in ground gained by 4th Guards. Also in communication cabling and cables German Breastwork Communication trench from an enemy Breastwork to British Breastwork.	

WAR DIARY or INTELLIGENCE SUMMARY

Army Form C. 2118.

Instructions regarding War Diaries and Intelligence Summaries are contained in F.S. Regs., Part II. and the Staff Manual respectively. Title pages will be prepared in manuscript.

(Erase heading not required.)

Hour, Date, Place	Summary of Events and Information	Remarks and references to Appendices
19/5/15 La Couture	One Sapper wounded.	
19/5/15 Rue du l'Epinette	Information Communication trench from Front line French to German Bastires Captured. Movements of Communication trenches from German Bastires Opposite to	
19 " do	British Headquarters.	
" do	One Sapper Killed.	
	Examined Communication trench from Front line to Captured German Aircrafts. Two Companies alternate Bastires employed from Point Pickwick to German Bastires to Sighland Sub Sec R.E. Conducting the Officer i/c	
20/5/15 La Couture	round the position. Section returned from R.E. House Park.	
21/5/15 Rue de l'Epinette	Continued improvements to communication trenches as above. Reconnaissance of ground with a view to construction of new trench in advance of British Line Near Rue du Caillout and to Mother Road. This was found impracticable. Construction of new Bridges. Weather 19/21 5/15 Wet.	

WAR DIARY
or
INTELLIGENCE SUMMARY

(Erase heading not required.)

Army Form C. 2118.

Instructions regarding War Diaries and Intelligence Summaries are contained in F.S. Regs., Part II. and the Staff Manual respectively. Title pages will be prepared in manuscript.

Hour, Date, Place	Summary of Events and Information	Remarks and references to Appendices
22.5/15. Rue de l'Epinette	Continued improvement of Communication trenches.	
5 AM 22/5/15 — do —	Photo Section leave for La Couture to enforce the Unit left for Allouagne. Two Officers & N.C.O's left to assist 1st Highland Fd Coy R.E. who were taking over this Sector.	
11.15 AM 22.5/15 Allouagne	Arrived.	
22 – 30. 5/15 — do —	Coy. Working with 6 Cav. Bde on Dut. Reed, Decker. Conditions beautiful.	
23. 5/15 — do —	The two Officers & Men who were left at Rue de l'Epinette Returned to Unit	
26.5/15 — do —	Inspection of Unit by C.R.E. 2nd Div. Experiments carried out with Parachute Rocket Lights with a view to carrying a line for haulage of Ammunition etc over open ground.	
11AM 26/5/15 — do —	Photoed by Bedali Factory. Unit left for Le Pretrie.	
5.30 PM 30/5/15 Le Pretrie	Arrived & Billeted here.	
1 AM 31/5/15 — do —	Coy Working with 6th Cav. Bde. took over Sectors W.1 W.2 W.3 from French R.E.	
31 5/15.		

2nd Division.

1st East Anglian Field Co RE.

Vol III 1 – 27.6.15.

131/6093

MEA
GP

JUNE 1915 WAR DIARY / 2/1 A.F.Co. R.E.(T) Army Form C. 2118.
or
INTELLIGENCE SUMMARY

(Erase heading not required.)

Instructions regarding War Diaries and Intelligence Summaries are contained in F. S. Regs., Part II. and the Staff Manual respectively. Title pages will be prepared in manuscript.

Hour, Date, Place	Summary of Events and Information	Remarks and references to Appendices
1/6/15 to 9/6/15 AT LES BREBIS	Company employed on work in front line with 6th Infantry Brigade. General work in the trenches was also carried on, and a map of the position taken over from the French was prepared.	
6/6/15 LES BREBIS	1 Lieut E.T. BRADDELL was accidentally wounded during a bomb throwing demonstration and evacuated to Hospital	
7/6/15 LES BREBIS	1 Sapper was wounded	
9/6/15 11. P.M. LES BREBIS	Company marched from LES BREBIS via MAZINGARBE to NOYELLES & billeted at that place	
10/6/15 NOYELLES	Two sections marched to VERMELLES & billeted there.	
10/6/15 to 18/6/15 AT NOYELLES	Company employed in work in front line with 6th Infantry Brigade and in general work in trenches. Maps of the position were prepared and strong points in rear of front line in sections held by 6th & 8th Bdes were constructed & repaired.	

1247 W 3299 200,000 (E) 5/14 J.B.C. &A. Forms/C. 2118/11.

WAR DIARY or INTELLIGENCE SUMMARY

Army Form C. 2118.

(Erase heading not required.)

Hour, Date, Place	Summary of Events and Information	Remarks and references to Appendices
18/6/15 NOVELLES. 9.30 P.M.	Company marched to HARLEY STREET, CUINCHY & billeted there. H.Q. & No. 2 & 3 section lorries were sent back to the park out at LE QUESNOY.	
19/6/15 to 21/6/15 AT CUINCHY.	Work on front line with 6th Inf. Bde. The Company was also employed in funeral vaults in trenches, & maps of the position were prepared.	
22/6/15 CUINCHY.	Lieut A.M. MATTHEWS joined the Company from Reserve Company in England.	
24/6/15 CUINCHY.	1 Sergeant wounded	
25/6/15 CUINCHY.	2/C Gillick of the Company was killed. M.O.H. KEELING was wounded. One Sapper was killed & 4 other ranks wounded.	
27/6/15 CUINCHY.	Lieut. L.H. KENT left the Company on being ordered to England for work at Messrs Vickers Fuze works.	

Command,
Capt for Major
1st Field Company,
East Anglian Divl. Royal Engineers.

2nd/15/woven

131/89

2/1 E. Anglian Field Coy: RE.

Vol IV

July & August / 15

WAR DIARY or INTELLIGENCE SUMMARY

Army Form C. 2118.

July 1915

Hour, Date, Place	Summary of Events and Information	Remarks and references to Appendices
July 1st to July 1st 1915 CUINCHY.	General work in Front Line & Support Lines with 6th Infantry Brigade.	
July 2nd CUINCHY.	One Sapper Wounded.	
" 5th — do —	The Boy. Left CUINCHY & billeted at GORRE.	
6th to July 31st GORRE.	The Coy took over the working & supervision of the 2nd Line Defence Scheme — now ore "the Village Line" support from at CAMERIN TONT FIXE & WINDY CORNER (which already existed but had become into a bad state of repair). Were reconstructed a new tooltsmade. Deep dug out were reconstructed. Walls of "Forto concrete" walls & roofs were constructed. Walls of sand bags around were loopholed & barricaded work road bags & second roofs of two storeys to the Cellar were made. The Cellars where the level of floors to a — while & white designed to loopholes for Rifle & Machine Guns. The houses on the CAMERIN TONTINE ROAD & the TONT FIXE WINDY CORNER ROAD were also defended in a similar manner to the above. A new trench was constructed from HERTFORD STREET to CUINCHY KEEP.	

1247 W 3200 200,000 (E) 8/14 J.B.C. & A. Forms/C. 2118/11.

WAR DIARY or INTELLIGENCE SUMMARY

Army Form C. 2118.

July 1915

Hour, Date, Place	Summary of Events and Information	Remarks and references to Appendices
GORRE. July.	A portable device of Monorail was erected in HERTFORD STREET trench in the CUINCHY area from No.1, HARLEY STREET to CUINCHY SUPPORT POINT. By means of Gantries the Monorail found its design of the rail were that it could be erected in any good communication trench & would carry any load the tramrails dimensions not exceeding 250 lb. at a fast walking speed & little labour. The most usual loads were found to be dixies, rations, ammunition, bombs, sandbags & wounded men. A special stretcher was devised for the latter to overcome the difficulty of conveyance. Sitting wounded would transfer. A special chair was also designed for the same purpose. It could be adjusted to any angle according to the requirements of the wounded. The chair could be handled by one man. The rail was taken across WILSON ROAD & across blocking up the road fifteen feet of rail were socketed to a specially designed gateway. The increase of speed & reduction of labour are very most marked. One Sapper Wounded One Sapper Wounded	
July 15		

Commanding,
1st Field Company,
East Anglian Divl. Royal Engineers.
Major.

Army Form C. 2118.

WAR DIARY
or
INTELLIGENCE SUMMARY

(Erase heading not required.)

August 1915

Instructions regarding War Diaries and Intelligence Summaries are contained in F. S. Regs., Part II. and the Staff Manual respectively. Title pages will be prepared in manuscript.

Hour, Date, Place	Summary of Events and Information	Remarks and references to Appendices
GORRE. Aug 1st to 5th	Continuation of "Village Line" Works & Moore Rd as in Lieu.	
Aug 6/15	One Sapper killed at CUINCHY	
" 24th	A draft of 4 Sappers arrived from E/15. E.A. F.d Co. R.E.	
" 31st	"	

Commanding
5th Field Company.
East Anglian Div. Royal Engineers.

1247 W 3299 200,000 (E) 8/11 J.B.C. & A. Forms/C. 2118/11.

Army Form C. 2118.

WAR DIARY
or
INTELLIGENCE SUMMARY
(Erase heading not required.)

Instructions regarding War Diaries and Intelligence Summaries are contained in F. S. Regs., Part II. and the Staff Manual respectively. Title pages will be prepared in manuscript.

Hour, Date, Place	Summary of Events and Information	Remarks and references to Appendices

SECTION OF TRENCH MONO-RAIL WITH STRETCHER
JULY 1915

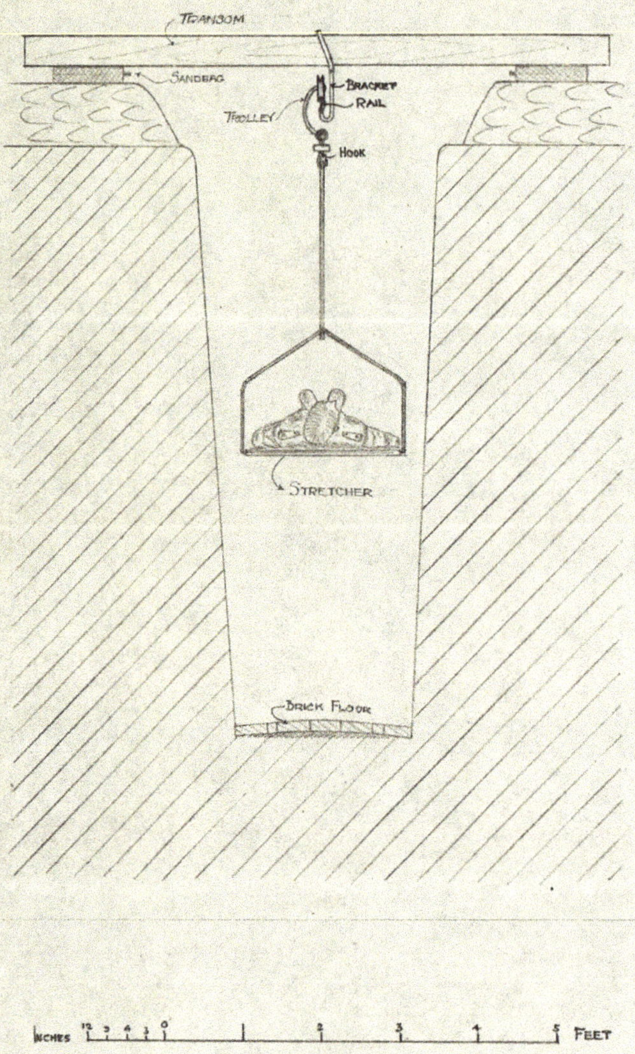

TRANSOM
SANDBAG
BRACKET
RAIL
TROLLEY
HOOK
STRETCHER
BRICK FLOOR
INCHES
12
0
1
2
3
4
5
FEET

SCALE - (APPROX)

Commanding,
1st Field Company,
East Anglian Divl. Royal Engineers.

1247 W 3299 200,000 (E) 8/14 J.B.C. & A. Forms/C. 2118/11.

44476
13/7

Pmt Burrow

1/1st East Anglian 70 Co RE.

Sep. 15

Vol II

A5
DTW
M 7/2
IR 6

H

nil
ans.

Army Form C. 2118.

WAR DIARY
or
INTELLIGENCE SUMMARY
(Erase heading not required.)

September 1915

Instructions regarding War Diaries and Intelligence Summaries are contained in F.S. Regs., Part II. and the Staff Manual respectively. Title pages will be prepared in manuscript.

Hour, Date, Place	Summary of Events and Information	Remarks and references to Appendices
Sept. 1st GORRE	Construction of Village Line & Construction of Armed Trolley Railway. Construction of Dug Outs in front line in GIVENCHY Sector.	
" 2nd "	— do —	
" 3rd "	Ditto also construction of Dug Outs in GIVENCHY Sector. Construction of Pontoon Bridge	
" 4.5.6.7.8.9.10th	Out LABASSEE CANAL. Construction of French Trolley Railway. Construction of Dug Outs. General Work at GIVENCHY & CUINCHY	
" 11th	A Stage of 1 N.C.O. & 11 O.R. handed over to unit for searchlight	
" 12th	Station attached from L.E.E.T.	
" 13th "	— do —	
" 14.15.16th "	Construction of Dug Outs in GIVENCHY, CUINCHY & GORRE. 5.N.	
" 17th "	2 Lt. Kent joined unit attached from 2nd Fd Coy R.E.	
" 18th "	Unit attached to 19th Inf. Bde. who were relieving tps South of LABASSEE. BETHUNE ROAD at CAMBRIN	
" 19 & 20th "	Construction of Dug Outs. General Work & one	

Signed [signature]
Major,
Commanding,
1st Field Company,
East Anglian Divl. Royal Engineers.

1247 W 3299 200,000 (E) 8/14 J.B.C. & A. Forms/C. 2118/11.

WAR DIARY or INTELLIGENCE SUMMARY

Army Form C. 2118.

September 1915

(Erase heading not required.)

Instructions regarding War Diaries and Intelligence Summaries are contained in F. S. Regs, Part II. and the Staff Manual respectively. Title pages will be prepared in manuscript.

Hour, Date, Place	Summary of Events and Information	Remarks and references to Appendices
Sept. 21 to 24 GORRE	Bombardment of German positions commenced Oct 21 & continued to Sep 24th	
24	Two Sections of Coy proceeded to the trenches held by 19th Bde to be in readiness in event of an advance & consolidating the positions gained. Two Sections were in reserve at GORRE with two Sections of Gentry Bath, purpose of repairing the main roads in the event of an advance.	
25	Rested. Attacked German trenches. (GIVENCHY to BULLY GRENAY.) Sections went in trenches repairing damage & keeping lines of communication open.	
25	2 Other Ranks Wounded	
26	do	
26 & 30	Continuation of work in Trenches	

Murphy Capt
Commanding,
1st Field Company,
East Anglian Div. Royal Engineers.

12/7399

2nd Blouin

1st P. Co.
East Anglian R.E.

Dec 1915

Vol VI

Army Form C. 2118.

WAR DIARY
or
INTELLIGENCE SUMMARY
(Erase heading not required.)

October 1915

Instructions regarding War Diaries and Intelligence Summaries are contained in F. S. Regs., Part II. and the Staff Manual respectively. Title pages will be prepared in manuscript.

Hour, Date, Place	Summary of Events and Information	Remarks and references to Appendices
Oct 1st to Oct 2nd ANNEQUIN	Organising & construction of Working Party with wire digging communication trenches from our Original Front line to the Captured German trenches in the area East of Vermelles. One Other Rank Wounded.	
Oct 3.		
Oct 3rd & BEUVRY 10 " 10.	Boys with Division in Corps Reserve.	
Oct. 3.	Draft of one other Rank for Searchlight Section attached from L.E.F.T.	
Oct 3 & 10 BEUVRY	Repairs of Billets & installation of Electric Light to Billets.	
Oct. 6.	Draft of one other Rank R.A.M.C. attached.	
Oct 11th & Oct 21st ANNEQUIN	General Work in Trenches with 5th Inf. Bde. Construction of Dug Outs. Construction of new Wired Redoubt out in front of HOHENZOLLERN REDOUBT part of which was held by Guards Division.	

[signature]
Capt/Major
Commanding, 1st Field Company,
East Anglian Divl. Royal Engineers.

WAR DIARY
or
INTELLIGENCE SUMMARY
(Erase heading not required.)

Army Form C. 2118.

October 1915.

Hour, Date, Place	Summary of Events and Information	Remarks and references to Appendices
Oct 15 ANNEQUIN	Draft of 2 Other Ranks.	
Oct 15 — do —	2 Other Ranks Wounded.	
Oct 16 — do —	— do —	
Oct 22 — do —	Coy proceeds at to Billets at LE PREOL.	
Oct 23 Nº 63 f LE PREOL	Construction of new Third Line from the Railway (South of a tunnel parallel to the Main (LABASSEE ROAD) to the LABASSEE CANAL. The general line of the trench ran just East of the FACTORY, MAISON ROUGE, BRAIDELL POINT, where it joined up with the old YELLOW LINE. Construction of new trenches "doge à go" M.G. Emplacements, wire entanglements, dug outs, latrines &c.	

Mirielle Captain
Major,
Commanding
1st Field Company.
East Anglian Divl. Royal Engineers.

WAR DIARY
or
INTELLIGENCE SUMMARY

Army Form C. 2118.

November 1915

Hour, Date, Place	Summary of Events and Information	Remarks and references to Appendices
Nov. 1st to Nov. 30.15 LE PREOL	Construction of a new Third Line, Support Line, from the ANNEQUIN AUCHY RAILWAY to the LA BASSEE CANAL. The General line of the trenches ran just East of the FACTORY MAISON ROUGE BRADDELL POINT. where it joined up with the OLD WILLOW LINE, running just East of HARLEY STREET & then joining the PONT FIXE Defences. Construction of new trenches, Dug. legs. No.8 Emplacements, wire entanglements, dug. outs. Latrines &c & repair of existing trenches which were adopted as part of the line. This work was continued during the whole of the month & was under C.E. 1st Corps	
Nov. 3rd to Nov. 11.15 LE PREOL	Repair work was done on the front line, spoken of trenches which had become in a very bad state owing to heavy rains	

Clough Batt
Major
Commanding,
1st Field Company,
East Anglian Divl. Royal Engineers.

WAR DIARY
or
INTELLIGENCE SUMMARY
(Erase heading not required.)

Army Form C. 2118.

December 1915

Hour, Date, Place	Summary of Events and Information	Remarks and references to Appendices
Dec 1st to Dec 15 1915. LE PREOL.	Construction of new third line, support line, from the ANNEQUIN ROAD, Railway to the LABASSEE CANAL. The general line of the trenches ran just East of the FACTORY, MAISON ROUGE BRADDELL POINT where it joined up with the OLD WILLOW LINE running just East of HARLEY STREET & then joining the FORT FINS Defences. Construction of new trestles, door legs, M.G. emplacements, wire entanglements, dug outs, latrines &c. A year of existing trenches which were adopted as part of the line. This work was continuous during the whole of the time from Dec 1 to Dec 16.	
Dec 16/15 to Dec 26/15 LE PREOL	Repair work on Front Line in GIVENCHY Section about 600 yds N. of LA BASSEE CANAL. The work consisted of the revetting of the parapet & parados of the trench with wooden frames, the placing of trench floor boards.	
Dec 6th LE PREOL	8 Other Ranks Joined Unit (Reinforcements)	
" 10th	1st Lt. C.H. Humphrey's Rejoined Unit (— " —)	
" 23rd	1 Other Rank Killed (at CANDRIN)	
" 27th	The Unit went in Reserve with 2nd Division, and marched from LE PREOL at 9 A.M. via BETHUNE CHOCQUES & LILLERS to billets at LA MOQUELLERIE	

Marin (?) Captain
Commanding,
1st Field Company,
1st Canadian Divl. Royal Engineers

WAR DIARY or INTELLIGENCE SUMMARY

Army Form C. 2118.

December

Hour, Date, Place	Summary of Events and Information	Remarks and references to Appendices
3 P.M. Dec 24/15 LA MIQUELLERIE	Unit arrived at LA MIQUELLERIE at 3 P.M.	
" 28 to 31 do	Unit was engaged in Divisional training during which time all equipment, transport, stores &c were overhauled. Transport carts repainted. Instruction in Infantry Drill, Smoke Helmet Drill & various engineering subjects.	

Mayu Capt for
Major.
Commanding.
1st Field Company,
East Anglian Divl. Royal Engineers.

2ND DIVISION
DIVL ENGINEERS

1-1ST EAST ANGLIAN FIELD COY. R.E.

JAN - DEC 1916

2nd Divisional Engineers

1/1st EAST ANGLIAN FIELD COMPANY R. E.

JANUARY 1916.

Army Form C. 2118.

WAR DIARY
or
INTELLIGENCE SUMMARY
(Erase heading not required.)

JANUARY 1916

Instructions regarding War Diaries and Intelligence Summaries are contained in F. S. Regs., Part II. and the Staff Manual respectively. Title pages will be prepared in manuscript.

Hour, Date, Place	Summary of Events and Information	Remarks and references to Appendices
Jan. 14th LA MIQUELLERIE	Unit was engaged in Divisional Training, during which time all equipment, transport, stores &c. were overhauled. Transport and mounted Instructors in Infantry Drill, Smoke Helmet Drill & various engineering subjects.	
Jan. 15th "	Two Officers & four N.C.O. proceeded to LE TOURET to take over work from 70th & 84th Co.y R.E. 12th Division.	
" 16th "	14 Other Ranks proceeded to LE TOURET to take over work on M.G. Emplacements.	
" 17th "	Unit marched from LA MIQUELLERIE at 9 A.M. to LE TOURET via BUSNES, ROBECQ, Mt BERNENCHON, BETHUNE.	
" 17 LE TOURET	Unit arrived at LE TOURET 2.45 P.M.	
" 18 to 31 "	Unit was detailed for work in Sector C. (FESTUBERT) of the Divisional Front which had been taken over from 12th Division. One Section attached to Brigade for general work in the front & support trenches.	

[signature] Capt & Major.

Commanding, 1st Field Company, East Anglian Divl. Royal Engineers.

Army Form C. 2118.

WAR DIARY
or
INTELLIGENCE SUMMARY

(Erase heading not required.)

JANUARY 1916.

Instructions regarding War Diaries and Intelligence Summaries are contained in F. S. Regs, Part II. and the Staff Manual respectively. Title pages will be prepared in manuscript.

Hour, Date, Place	Summary of Events and Information	Remarks and references to Appendices
Jan 1st to 31st LE TOURET	One section detailed for work on M.G. Emplacements in front of support line trenches. M.G. Emplacements were constructed, some open others covered with concrete roofs. One section detailed for work on No. 9. Emplacement in half bottom of the VILLAGE LINE contained in SECTOR C. These M.G. emplacements are all concrete or brick structures with roofs of reinforced concrete supported by iron girders. Each emplacement had two roofs with an air space of about 6" between them. One section was employed on the construction of the various wooden frames needed for M.G. Emplacements, dug outs &c. Trench floors, revetting hurdles &c. The work was continuous as far as the Unit was concerned, but the required working parties were drawn from the Brigade then holding the line.	

Allanuf Capt of
Major
Commanding,
1st Field Company.
East Anglian Divl Royal Engineers.

2nd Divisional Engineers

1/1st EAST ANGLIAN FIELD COMPANY R. E.

FEBRUARY 1916.

Army Form C. 2118.

WAR DIARY
or
INTELLIGENCE SUMMARY
(Erase heading not required.)

1st Section 1/1st 92. 7 C R E

FEBRUARY 1916

Instructions regarding War Diaries and Intelligence Summaries are contained in F. S. Regs., Part II. and the Staff Manual respectively. Title pages will be prepared in manuscript.

Hour, Date, Place	Summary of Events and Information	Remarks and references to Appendices
Feb. 1st to 17th LE TOURET	Work was continued in Section C (FESTUBERT) of the 2nd Division Front. Work was carried on, M.G. Emplacements in front and support line trenches & part of the Village Line in Sector (C). One Section was detailed for work under the G.O.C. of the Brigade holding the line and for construction of frames required for M.G. Emplacements, Dug outs, &c. 20 Other Ranks Reinforcements joined unit.	
Feb 15th		
Feb. 17th LE TOURET	The Company left LE TOURET at 9 A.M. and marched via BETHUNE, CHOQUES, BUSNES to LA MIQUELLERIE.	
Feb 17th LA MIQUELLERIE	The Unit arrived at LA MIQUELLERIE at 2.45 P.M. & went into Billets here.	
Feb 18 to 24th LA MIQUELLERIE	The Company was resting for the period during which time, Bayonet & Infantry Drill, Mounted Section Drill, Smoke Helmet Drill &c was carried on work. Also the Company was engaged in Squad Making for use in Front Line investments in his Book was given to the Sapping Platoons of the 5th & 7th Bde.	

Signed [illegible]

Army Form C. 2118.

WAR DIARY
or
INTELLIGENCE SUMMARY
(Erase heading not required.)

FEBRUARY 1916.

Hour, Date, Place	Summary of Events and Information	Remarks and references to Appendices
21 2/16 LA MIQUELLERIE	5 Other Ranks. Reinforcements. Joined Unit.	
24 2/16 —do—	2nd Lt. L. R. HARWOOD. Joined Unit. Reinforcement.	
25 2/16 —do—	The Unit left LA MIQUELLERIE at 9 A.M. and proceeded to GONNEHEM and billeted there for the night of the 25/26.	
26 2/16 GONNEHEM	The Company left GONNEHEM at 2 P.M. and proceeded to (FOSSE 10) PETIT SAINS via BETHUNE & NOEUX LES MINES. The Company arrived at FOSSE 10 at 6 P.M.	
27 2/16 FOSSE 10	Four Sections proceeded to BULLY GRENAY and went in billets there, leaving the Horse Transport at FOSSE 10.	
29 2/16 BULLY GRENAY	O.C. Company & two Sections proceeded to billets in the Cellars of CITÉ CALONNE, just in rear of the Front Line. Company was then billeted as follows O.C. Unit and two Sections at CITÉ CALONNE Two Sections at BULLY GRENAY. H.Q. Section Horse Transport at FOSSE 10.	

Morgan Capt
f. Major
Commanding, 1st Field Company,
East Anglian Divl. Royal Engineers.

Army Form C. 2118.

WAR DIARY
or
INTELLIGENCE SUMMARY   FEBRUARY 1916
(Erase heading not required.)

Instructions regarding War Diaries and Intelligence Summaries are contained in F. S. Regs., Part II. and the Staff Manual respectively. Title pages will be prepared in manuscript.

Hour, Date, Place	Summary of Events and Information	Remarks and references to Appendices
Feb. 27. to 29. BULLY GRENAY & CALONNE	Work was carried on in the Front & Reserve system of trenches in the CALONNE SECTOR (held by 6th Inf Bde) the Front held by 2nd Divn. The frontage now held by the 2nd Divn had previously up to Feb 25th been held by the 1st Indian Troops (Details of the work are given in Watch Diary)	

Commanding, 1st Field Company, 1st Anzac Divl. Royal Engineers.

2nd Divisional Engineers

1/1st EAST ANGLIAN FIELD COMPANY R. E.

MARCH 1916.

Army Form C. 2118.

WAR DIARY
or
INTELLIGENCE SUMMARY
(Erase heading not required.)

MARCH 1916

Instructions regarding War Diaries and Intelligence Summaries are contained in F. S. Regs., Part II. and the Staff Manual respectively. Title pages will be prepared in manuscript.

Hour, Date, Place	Summary of Events and Information	Remarks and references to Appendices
March 1st – 31st CALONNE BULLY GRENAY	The work commenced in the latter end of February in the front and reserve system of trenches in the CALONNE SECTOR (held by the 6th Infantry Brigade) of the front held by the 2nd Division. The work of putting the mining village known as CITÉ CALONNE into a state of defence as a large defended locality was commenced. The work was very varied and consisted of the construction of concrete M.G. emplacements on the support line & the main system of trenches and also in strong points, the construction of brick observation posts for artillery observation and observation posts for the Infantry holding the line, the construction of tunnels already commenced by the French for the passage of troops to the front line, the construction of Reserve Line running through the tunnels of CALONNE – the tunnels being fortified with overhead	[signature] Commanding 1st Field Company East Anglian Div. Royal Engineers

Army Form C. 2118.

MARCH 1916

WAR DIARY
or
INTELLIGENCE SUMMARY
(Erase heading not required.)

Hour, Date, Place	Summary of Events and Information	Remarks and references to Appendices
	cont:d - the construction of strong posts with cement M.G emplacements, the construction of timber overhead cover for lateral communication trenches.	
	The revetting and fire stepping of certain trenches in the support line was carried out, and also in the second line of trenches known as the LIGNE BATOLLE.	
	The main communication trenches to the front line were deepened and new boards put down.	
March 11th		
March 17th	Two other ranks reinforcements joined unit.	
	2nd Division relieved by 23rd Division, the 68th Infantry Brigade holding the CALONNE SECTOR. The unit did not go into reserve with the 2nd Division but stayed on the	
March 25th	CALONNE SECTOR.	
	14 other ranks reinforcements joined unit.	
March 31st	Two other ranks wounded.	

Commanding,
1st Field Company,
East Anglian Divl. Royal Engineers.

Major,
Capt.

x   2nd Divisional Engineers

1/1st EAST ANGLIAN FIELD COMPANY R. E.

APRIL 1916.

WAR DIARY
or
INTELLIGENCE SUMMARY

(Erase heading not required.) APRIL 1916

Army Form C. 2118.

Hour, Date, Place	Summary of Events and Information	Remarks and references to Appendices
April 1st – 30th. CALONNE BULLY GRENAY.	The work of putting CITÉ CALONNE into a state of defence was continued. The work as before consisted of the construction of concrete M.G. emplacements on the support line of the main system of trenches, and also a strong point, the construction of observation posts for artillery observation and observation posts for the infantry holding the line, the construction of tunnels already commenced by the French for the passage of troops to the front line, the construction for Rieure line running through the houses of CALONNE – the tunnels being interfered with overhead cover – the construction of strong points with overhead cover – the construction of timber concrete M.G. emplacements, the construction of timber overhead cover for lateral communication trenches. The revetting and fire stepping of trenches in the support line was continued also in the LIGNE	

Commanding,
1st Field Company,
East Anglian Divl. Royal Engineers.

Army Form C. 2118A

WAR DIARY
or
INTELLIGENCE SUMMARY
(Erase heading not required.) APRIL 1916

Instructions regarding War Diaries and Intelligence Summaries are contained in F. S. Regs., Part II. and the Staff Manual respectively. Title pages will be prepared in manuscript.

Hour, Date, Place	Summary of Events and Information	Remarks and references to Appendices
	BATAILLE:	
April 18th	The main communication trench to the front line were deepened and floor boards put down. The 23rd Division were relieved by the 2nd Division, the 6th Infantry Brigade returning to the CALONNE SECTOR.	
April 25th	One other rank wounded.	
April 27th	One other rank reinforcement joined unit.	
April 28th	A draft consisting of 10 other ranks of the London Electrical Engineers (T) (attached to the unit for work # with searchlights) left the unit for the Base	

Wade
Capt
for ?????
Commanding
1st Field Company,
East Anglian Divl. Royal Engineers.

2nd Divisional Engineers

1/1st EAST ANGLIAN FIELD COMPANY R. E.

M A Y   1916.

Army Form C. 2118.

You 1st Jy 14 -8
May 1916
1/1 E A Fd Cy RE

WAR DIARY
or
INTELLIGENCE SUMMARY
(Erase heading not required.)

Instructions regarding War Diaries and Intelligence Summaries are contained in F. S. Regs., Part II. and the Staff Manual respectively. Title pages will be prepared in manuscript.

Hour, Date, Place	Summary of Events and Information	Remarks and references to Appendices
May 1st to May 17th CALONNE. BULLY GRENAY	The work of putting Cité Calonne into a state of defence and of improvement to the communications Reserve & Support lines as described the April Diary was continued (Reinforcement) formed unit.	
May 2nd to May 11th CALONNE. BULLY GRENAY.	May 6. Two sections were detached for work in the Angres Sector which was being held by the 6th Inf Bde. The work consisted of improvement of front & support lines and also on a Reserve line known as LIGNE BATOLLE. Construction of M.G. Emplacements and Dug Outs in the Support Lines and the LIGNE BATOLLE. These two sections rejoined the Company and continued work in Calonne Sector on May 15.	
May 18th Cité JEANNE D'ARC	During the day the Company concentrated at FOSSE 10. and at 7.30 pm moved into Rest Billets at Cité Jeanne D'Arc. BARLIN. The Calonne Sector being taken over by FD 2	
May 19th to May 21st Cité JEANNE D'ARC	While in the Rest Area construction in wiring & trench work was given to the Labouring Sections of the 6th Inf Bde also experiments were carried out with a method of Wiring Drill suggested by IV th Corps.	

Mirralis Capt RE
O.C.
1st East Anglian Fd Coy.
R.E. (T)

Army Form C. 2118.

WAR DIARY
or
INTELLIGENCE SUMMARY
(Erase heading not required.)

Instructions regarding War Diaries and Intelligence Summaries are contained in F. S. Regs., Part II. and the Staff Manual respectively. Title pages will be prepared in manuscript.

May 1916

Hour, Date, Place	Summary of Events and Information	Remarks and references to Appendices
May 22nd CITÉ JEANNE D'ARC.	Orders were received to be prepared to move at short notice.	
May 25th GRAND SERVIN	Orders to move were received & the Company moved off at 4 PM & marched to GRAND SERVIN & here went into billets for the night.	
May 26th to May 31st GOUY SERVINS	The Company left GRAND SERVIN at Noon and marched to GOUY SERVINS where billets were taken over from the 447th Divn. The 2nd Divn had taken over the sector of the Line (SOUCHEZ – VIMY.) previously held by the 47th Divn and the Company was employed on the Reserve Line & Communication. The Reserve Line known as LIONS BATOLHE ended was in a very bad condition was deepened & revetted. Firestepped & traverses constructed. & what portion running from the SOUCHEZ – CARENCY ROAD to BOYAU 123 several deep dug outs were also commenced. Deep dug outs were also commenced at the junction of BOYAU 123 & HOSPITAL ROAD in HOSPITAL ROAD and at HOSPITAL CORNER. Work was commenced on the deepening & trench boarding of BAVIERE ROAD & BOYAU 123.	A Wraith Maj. O.C. 1st Cardinghan Fd Coy R.E. (T)

1247 W 3299 200,000 (E) 8/14 J.B.C. & A. Forms/C. 2118/11.

2nd Divisional Engineers

1/1st EAST ANGLIAN FIELD COMPANY R. E.

JUNE 1916.

WAR DIARY or INTELLIGENCE SUMMARY

Army Form C. 2118.

JUNE. 1916

Hour, Date, Place	Summary of Events and Information	Remarks and references to Appendices
June 1st to June 30th 1916 GOUY SERVINS	The works described in the May Diary were continued. They included the firestepping, revetting & deepening of the LIGNE BATOLLE. The construction of Machine Gun Emplacements, the deepening, improvement & revetment & boarding of the communication trenches known as BAVIERE ROAD, REDOUBT ROAD and BOYAU 125. A new trench BEDFORD ROAD was sited and dug in order to provide communication avoiding CARENCY VILLAGE. Many existing dugouts were improved and new ones constructed. The Company had in hand upwards of 100 dugouts in the sector of the Divisional Area. An O.P. for the Field Survey Coy was made near the BATOLLE LINE. CABARET ROAD was improved & trench boards renewed. The Dressing Station in HOSPITAL ROAD was timbered and about 6 ft of head cover provided. Repairs to the well and pump at Hospital Corner were carried out and storage tanks were erected. A petrol engine & circular saw were installed in the Carpenter's Shop at the Divisional Dump, GOUY SERVINS.	

June 6. 2 Other Ranks (Reinforcements) joined Unit.
" 9. 2 " " " " "
" 20. 2 " " " " "
" 29. 3 " " " " "

Ovall Capt.
O.C.
1st East Anglian Field Coy
R.E. (T)

2nd Divisional Engineers

1/1st EAST ANGLIAN FIELD COMPANY R. E.

JULY 1916.

WAR DIARY
or
INTELLIGENCE SUMMARY
(Erase heading not required.)

1/1st E A 2nd Coy   Army Form C. 2118.
July 1916

Vol 15 7/16

Hour, Date, Place	Summary of Events and Information	Remarks and references to Appendices
July 1st GODT SERVINS	Work in the Reserve Brigade Area of the SOUCHEZ-VIMY Sector was continued as described in the June Diary.	
July 6th	Reinforcements – 2 Other Ranks joined Unit	
July 10th	" " – 1 " " " "	
July 15th	" " – 8 " " " "	
GODT SERVINS – BRUAY	The Company left GODT SERVINS at 2p.m. and marched to BRUAY via GRAND SERVINS, LES 4 VENTS, GRUCHINLEGAL and LA COMTE. Company Drill & Smoke Helmet Drill were carried out. All transport and technical stores overhauled.	
July 16.17.18th BRUAY		
July – BRUAY – GROSSART	The Company left BRUAY at 11a.m. and marched to GROSSART via LATHIEULOYE and BEVRY, arriving there at 2p.m.	
July 19th & 20th GROSSART	The Company left GROSSART at 2p.m. and entrained at BEVRY.	
July 21st VILLE SOUS CORBIE	The Unit detrained at 3a.m. at LONGEAU (S.W. of AMIENS) and marched to VILLE SOUS CORBIE via GUSY, CORBIE and MERICOURT, arriving there at 9-30 a.m. and went into billets.	
	Reinforcements – 2/Lt T.H.F. MOON } Joined Unit	
July 21st Do	2/Lt W.R. SHAW }	
July 22-23 VILLE SOUS CORBIE	One Section was sent to the CITADEL F.21.b. (reference map FRANCE sheet 62c 1/40,000) to erect huts at 2nd Divn H.Q. and one Section was employed in the Construction of the tramework of the huts.	
July 23rd – SANDPIT	The Coy left VILLE SOUS CORBIE at 10a.m. and marched to the SANDPIT at F.24.d.9 (close to LONGUEVAL)	
July 24th SANDPIT	The Company remained at the SANDPIT. One Section attached at the CITADEL.	
July 25th – CARNOY-HAPPY VALLEY	The Transport of the Company was sent to the Happy Valley (C.3.d.2.3) and the Dismounted Sections moved into Dug outs.	
July 25th CARNOY	The Company Coo transport moved into Dug outs at CARNOY, under instructions from C.R.E. A Strong point with 3 M.G. emplacements to hold 1 Platoon was set out at about S.17.c.5.7 about 300 yards S. of LONGUEVAL Church. The setting this Redoubt required concentration and given to obtaining a good field of fire towards WATERLOT FARM. A reconnaissance was made of the strip of field between BERNAFAY WOOD and LONGUEVAL for the purpose of siting a communication trench between these two.	
July 26th CARNOY	Work was not started on the strong point or communication trench owing to preparations being made for the attack on DELVILLE WOOD the following morning. Two Sections were detailed for work in conjunction with the attack on	

A Shaw Capt
p/o 2/Lt O.C. 1st E A Coy R.E.

WAR DIARY or INTELLIGENCE SUMMARY

Army Form C. 2118.

July 1916.

Hour, Date, Place	Summary of Events and Information	Remarks and references to Appendices
July 26th CARNOY (Cont'd)	DELVILLE WOOD on the morning of July 27th and were to be in position on the south side at dawn and to report to the O.C.'s of Consolidating Companies in support of BERNAFAY WOOD and the FOURTH (C?) (Royal Berks (?)). One Section was detailed to proceed in support of the FOURTH Bn. Royal Berks at CARNOY at 10pm and proceeded via MONTAUBAN to LONGUEVAL – just N of MONTAUBAN a very heavy barrage of Gas Shells was encountered – with the result that the strength of the Section was reduced to 1 Officer and 12 Other Ranks. This barrage was continuous for 3½ hours and the enemy shelling down to the wood (LONGUEVAL ALLEY) was very severe. During the evening of the 27th, other than the Section 2 Officers and the Section had to pass through violence (LONGUEVAL ALLEY) was very heavy on account of a great severe enemy bombardment.	
July 27th CARNOY	The Section reported to the O.C. 1st R. Berks about 5.17d.4.7 about 3 a.m. and proceeded with him along ANGLE TRENCH to the S.E. edge of DELVILLE WOOD where it found the Left Consolidating Company of the 1st R Berks were about to work. The situation at dawn on the S.v S.E. edge of DELVILLE WOOD appeared to be as follows :- The North of ANGLE TRENCH was not connected across the LONGUEVAL - GINCHY road and it was necessary to cross the latter in order to get into DELVILLE WOOD. - CRUCKS. He went a fairly deep trench from about 5.18.b.3.1. to about 5.18.b.7.2. This trench was held by parties of men of the 1st R. R's who were to form the S.E. edge of the attacking wave of the 15th Bde and was also accommodating a considerable number of men of the 1st R. R's who were to form one S.E. to be a combined wave at about 5.18.b.2. Angle trench from 5.18.b.7.2 to about 5.18.b.6.4 the trench was held by about 30 men of the 1st R. R's who were ordered to fall back by the attacking waves previously mentioned. At 5.18.b. but a trench about those ran in a pulling direction. This trench ... at about [15?] days at the closest became eg?? a [abandoned?] about ... any warning. The Coy 1st R. Berks went forward and commenced digging a series of fire ??? about 5.18.c.9.7 to 5.18.5.9.	

(signatures)

WAR DIARY or INTELLIGENCE SUMMARY

Army Form C. 2118.

July 1916.

Hour, Date, Place	Summary of Events and Information	Remarks and references to Appendices

July 27th Carnoy (cont) The line being then consolidated by the Bombs was attacked about 50 yards further to the Eastern edge of the wood and at 5.30 a light blue rocket was sent up on the air, and at about the same time another German flare was noted. The forty [?] 9.6 Co. did get up a good fire, but many bombs fell and S.18.d.8.1. and S.18.d.9.6. They did up a little fire was too not presently observed in part of the way. It was therefore observed that the sappers could be still employed viz:

(1) The construction of 2 M.G. Emplacements at S.18.d.9.6, one with an arc from N.W. to E. The other with an arc from E. to S.W.

(2) The clearing, improvement & construction of the line from S.18.c.8.4. to S.18.d.9.6.(2) in order to provide a communication trench up to the new front line and (3) to provide standing fire in a S.E. direction.

(3) The construction of a strong point including the M.G. Emplacements at S.18.d.9.6.

The Company commenced the work at 7 P.M. Bks. no 1 R.E's and 2nd Lieut Evans was in charge and of this could quickly supply parties for the carrying out of these works. There were about fifty men with the Co. only of these was one Cpl. officer and these the 15 R. Berks had not sufficient men to carry out their own parties & two pieces of Co. operations and applied to G.O.C. 15 E.P. R.Co. R.E. acting for 50 extra men. The officer looked continuously for many hours out in advance of the M.G. Emplacements. They wanted a considerable portion of new trench, however avoiding the enemy & friendly to attempting a counter attack on the Eastern edge of the wood. That the sappers are called upon to do added bombing. After a considerable amount of rifle fire & fighting, the others were repulsed Capt H.6.E. of the infantry did not consider the position very secure and according, acting under the orders, & letters of the Line and Cliff's & the 3rd H. Hampshire returned the night. Casualties - 1 Other Rank wounded.

[signatures]
C.E. [?]
R. Coote, Captain
1st East Anglian F.C. Coy R.E. (T)

July 27th Carnoy.

WAR DIARY or INTELLIGENCE SUMMARY

Army Form C. 2118.

July 1916.

Hour, Date, Place	Summary of Events and Information	Remarks and references to Appendices

July 23rd Carnoy — At dawn 16.1 Section employed carrying petrol tins to the advanced water tanks after the attack. Others were engaged on the work of a new rifle section relaying 16.1 Section in Delville Wood – No 2 before the fresh and strong enemy counter attacks. After manning the fire step on the main defence line 1 Section continued on the trench and watering services at about 2.30 p.m. when the Section returned to Billets at Carnoy. Owing to there being only 1 Officer & 3 other ranks remaining the whole unit was ordered to Carnoy that nite as a working party and GOC 5th Field Coy R.E. and Gen. — At 11 PM the Officer and GOC 5th Field Coy proceeded to Delville Wood with a section of the 5th Field Coy R.E. and Coy Consolidation. 1 to 2 A.D.C.L. 1. to obtain work and the stores of Coy Consolidation — Owing to heavy shell fire the Coy party could not get through and about 1 am were ordered back. The G.O.C. 5th Field Coy then left the Section Officer with Capt. Smallwood Coy to R. Park to left Carnoy at 11.30 p.m. and proceeded to Longueval where up until Capt. Park continuing Capt. L.C. Beke.

July 26th Carnoy — Reported to O.C. Company about 11 a.m. Left the Section under Lieut. Cooper for Company ly of the 1st R. Berks with the Section of Section attached. He proceeded to Coy at 8.10 a.m. with a plan of a new line to Longueval being on the infantry Coy moving to Longueval being commenced carrying the stores to Longueval. They were eventually engaged and a line was drawn up and as the Infantry thought the wood was reached nevertheless who commenced —

July 27th Carnoy — The officers were put on digging in the track each in his sector — They were sniped at continually on the advance but with the sniper sniped of they carried out their work. Remainder of the Sth Division (Norcot's Rest) at about 6.17.20.

Albert Park O.S.
5th East Anglian Fd. Coy. R.E. (T)

WAR DIARY or INTELLIGENCE SUMMARY

Army Form C. 2113.

July 1916

Hour, Date, Place	Summary of Events and Information	Remarks and references to Appendices
July 27th CARNOY (contd)	After the strafe had been, they suffered severely & had to provide shelter for riflemen. Orders about 5.10. 5.30 sub to be ready to proceed and carry flag out to be purposed a great diversion for the string belts which were completely out and two M.G. emplacements were demolished in the DELVILLE WOOD sector about 7 P.M. corps acting under orders & trying to get a view of the 72nd R. Berks Capron on the strategical line of support. But reports were raised by the 3 divisions to the fore victor.	
July 28th CARNOY	O.C. Y platoon were given on the Princes Street but it was only "D" the Company firing of life still and were given ordered to stay in the area & prepare troops. Ordered state that the enemy only getting two and only two machine guns at 5.15. & 8.8 and at 5.10. 9.9. - These were completed and the enemy was later composed and for whipped - the distance was estimated about 1½ km. -	
July 28th CARNOY July 27th CARNOY	Casualties - 2 other Ranks killed. do 4 " " wounded. One Section of "H" platoon and Cpl Roy D.C.L.I. (George) commenced front digging to dig a portion of the Future sucker from BERNAFAY WOOD to LONGUEVAL got any work was commenced. -	
July 29th CARNOY July 30th CARNOY	To work was done. Casualties - 1 O.R. wounded. The No. 1, No. 2 & 3rd Companies crews were up afraid to carry on while digging cont. of the Company & the Communication trench between BERNAFAY WOOD and LONGUEVAL. We were also done to the parties were unable to reach their objective.	

Attack C/JR
1st East Anglian R.E.

O.C. S.W. Coy 66 R.E. (G).

Army Form C. 2118.

WAR DIARY
or
INTELLIGENCE SUMMARY

(Erase heading not required.)

July 1916.

Instructions regarding War Diaries and Intelligence Summaries are contained in F. S. Regs., Part II. and the Staff Manual respectively. Title pages will be prepared in manuscript.

Hour, Date, Place	Summary of Events and Information	Remarks and references to Appendices
July 30th CARNOY (Cont?)	owing to heavy hostile artillery fire and gas shell barrage. – Two Platoons shared with one Company 10. H.D.C. R.F. and an Infantry Bty of 206 then proceded to wire the Communication trench from BERNAFAY WOOD to LONGUEVAL but then were again employed owing to heavy shell fire. Casualties. – { MAJOR F. WILSON - D.S.O. (SHELL SHOCK) { Lieut. C.H. HUMPHREYS (GASSED) { Other Ranks – Wounded	Tracing attached shewing approximate old British trench & new work constructed during the period from July 27th to August 8th 1916.
July 31 at CARNOY		

A. Wall Captⁿ.
2nd/2nd O.C.
1st East Anglia Field Coy R.E. (T.)

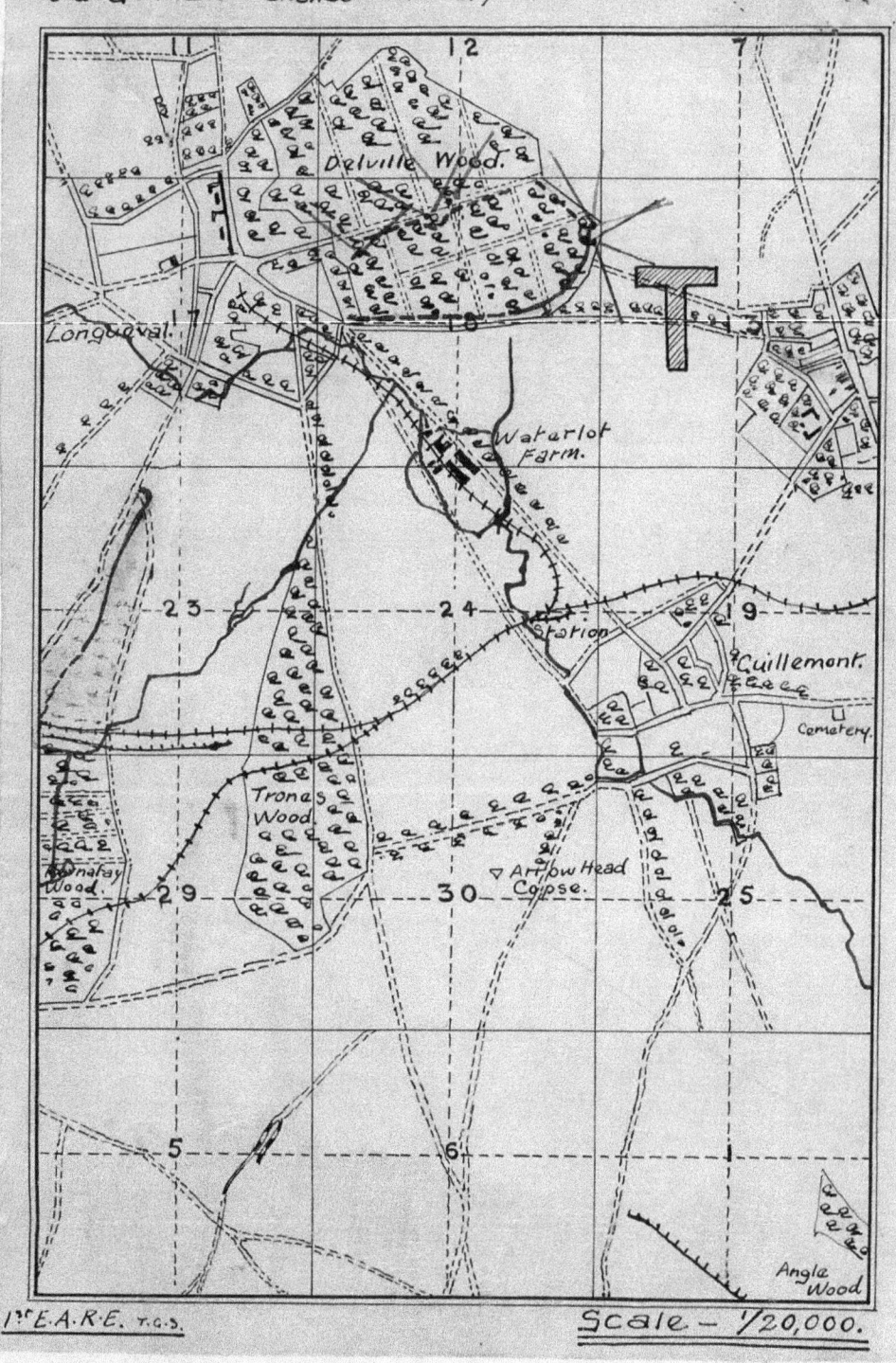

2nd Divisional Engineers

1/1st EAST ANGLIAN FIELD COMPANY R. E.

AUGUST 1916

WAR DIARY or **INTELLIGENCE SUMMARY**
(Erase heading not required.)

Army Form C. 2118

AUGUST 1916

Hour, Date, Place	Summary of Events and Information	Remarks and references to Appendices
AUGUST 1ST CARNOY	Two Section Sappers, 1 Coy D.C.L.I. and 60 men from the 6th Inf. Bde worked on the new Communication Trench between BERNAFAY WOOD & LONGUEVAL. The trench was started near the offshoot about S.23.a.7.8. about 50 yards from the road and ran in a S.W. direction. About 300 yds were dug to an average depth of 3'6".	
AUGUST 2ND CARNOY	Work was again continued on above trench with two Sections Sappers and an Infantry party of 200 Men. The excavation of the previous night was improved and a new portion was commenced in a Southerly direction to join up with the trench dug by the 5th Field Coy R.E. who were working from BERNAFAY WOOD Northwards.	
AUGUST 3RD CARNOY	Orders were received to dig two trenches one in front of WATERLOT FARM from about S.24.b.4.7. to about S.18.d.4.4. and a second from DELVILLE WOOD in a S.W. direction from about S.12.b.50 to S.18.d.4.6. For the first mentioned trench a party of 200 Men was provided, and for the Northern Trench running from DELVILLE WOOD. S. the party consisted of 1 Section Sappers, 1 Coy D.C.L.I. & 200 Men of the 2nd South Staffs, no work was commenced owing to very heavy shell fire.	

[signature] Capt
O.C.
1st East Anglian 2d Coy R.E.
(T.)

Army Form C. 2118.

WAR DIARY or INTELLIGENCE SUMMARY

(Erase heading not required.)

AUGUST 1916

Hour, Date, Place	Summary of Events and Information	Remarks and references to Appendices
August 4th CARNOY	The two trenches which were not commenced on the night of the 3rd were constructed on the night of the 4th. The Northern portion did not connect with DELVILLE WOOD but ran from about S.18.d.5.8 to S.18.d.4.4. When this trench was left it had an average depth of 8ft and an average width of 2'6". The Southern portion was dug East of WATERLOT FARM from about S.24.b.4.6 to S.18.d.1.2. This also had an average depth of 3'6" and an average width of 3ft. The work was carried out by two sections of Sappers & Two boy Pioneers.	
August 5th CARNOY	The two assembly trenches dug on the night of the 4th were joined up making a continuous connection from about S.18.d.5.8 to our existing Front Line at S.24.b.4.6. The party consisted of 1 section Sappers & 1 Coy 10th D.L.I. Casualties. 7 Other Ranks Wounded.	
August 6th CARNOY	A Communication Trench was required to be dug from the New Assembly Trenches dug on the night of the 4th S.24.5, back to our Front Line at about S.18.a.8.2. This was commenced on the night of the 6th. The whole of it was not completed but was dug for a length of 200 yds from S.18.d.1.2. towards our front line.	

C.H. Mitchell Capt. R.E. O.C. 1st East Anglian Fd. Coy R.E.
(7)

WAR DIARY
INTELLIGENCE SUMMARY

Army Form C. 2118.

August 1916

Hour, Date, Place	Summary of Events and Information	Remarks and references to Appendices
August 7th CARNOY	and this left a gap of about 60 yds to be completed. The work was carried out by 1 Section Sappers and an Infantry Party of 160 Men, supplied by the 99th Infy Bde. Casualties 3 Other Ranks Wounded	
August 7th CARNOY	The Company left CARNOY and bivouacked at F.23.d.2.9. No work was carried out.	
August 8th F.23.d.2.9.	Instructions were received to work on Cover Reserve Lines known as "C" & "D" and Communications to the Rear. Reconnaissance was carried out in the afternoon and an Report was sent to C.R.E. 2nd Div. But no work was carried out as the orders were cancelled as the Divn was going out of the line.	
August 9th HAPPY VALLEY	The Company left F.23.d.2.9. at 11.0 A.M. and marched to HAPPY VALLEY arriving there L.5.d.2.3. at 12 noon and bivouacked.	
August 11th HAPPY VALLEY	Reinforcements 8 Other Ranks arrived. The whole of the Transport of the Unit was ordered to proceed with 2nd Divl Train at 12.10 P.M. to IDAOORS.	

M. White Capt. M.
O.C.
1st East Anglian Fd Coy R.E.
(T)

Army Form C. 2118

WAR DIARY
or
INTELLIGENCE SUMMARY

(Erase heading not required.)

August. 1916.

Hour, Date, Place	Summary of Events and Information	Remarks and references to Appendices
August 12th HAPPY VALLEY.	The Company Bus Transport paraded at 2.45 P.M. and marched to Billets in MEAULTE arriving there at 5. P.M.	
August 13th MEAULTE.	The Company Bus Transport paraded at 2.0 P.M. and marched to MERICOURT where it entrained with other units of the 6th Inft Bde.	
August 14th LA CHAUSSEE	The Company Bus Transport reached SALEUX by train arriving there at 3.15 A.M, it then marched to LA CHAUSSEE where it joined the transport which had preceded it by road. The Company went into billets at LA CHAUSSEE at 9 A.M.	
August 16th LA CHAUSSEE	The Company paraded at 2.30 p.m. and marched to billets at VIGNACOURT.	
August 17th VIGNACOURT.	The Company paraded at 12.30 p.m. and marched to billets at BEAUMETZ.	
August 18th BEAUMETZ	The Company paraded at 9.0 A.M. and marched to billets at SARTON arriving there at 6.0 P.M. (via BERNAVILLE, CANDAS, BEAUVAL, BEAUQUESNE, NARIEX)	

[signature] Capt M.
O.C.
1st East Anglian Fd Coy R.E. F.

Army Form C. 2118

WAR DIARY or INTELLIGENCE SUMMARY

(Erase heading not required.)

Instructions regarding War Diaries and Intelligence Summaries are contained in F. S. Regs., Part II. and the Staff Manual respectively. Title pages will be prepared in manuscript.

AUGUST. 1916.

Hour, Date, Place	Summary of Events and Information	Remarks and references to Appendices
August 20th SARTON.	The Company paraded at 8.0 A.M. and marched via AUTHIE and BUS-LES-ARTOIS to COURCELLES AU BOIS, arriving there at 12.0 NOON. The Company took over billets vacated by a Field Coy of the Guards Division.	
August 20th to 31st COURCELLES AU BOIS.	The 2nd Durm took over the Line HEBUTERNE - BEAUMONT HAMEL. The Company was employed on work in 6th Infy Brigade Area. This included the building of Dug Outs M.G. Emplacements, Heavy Trench Mortar Emplacements, Repairs to pumping engine and water supply, Supervising the repair work to Trenches and controlling the issue of Stores from the R.E Dump COURCELLES.	
August 20th COURCELLES AU BOIS	Reinforcements 8 other ranks arrived	
August 31st —do—	— " — 2/Lt. O.H. KEELING arrived	

Alfred? Capt.
O.C.
1st East Anglian Fd Coy R.E. (T)

2nd Di vis ional Engineers

1/1st EAST ANGLIAN FIELD COMPANY R. E.

September 1916.

WAR DIARY
or
INTELLIGENCE SUMMARY

Army Form C. 2118.

1/1 E A 2A Coy September 1916

Hour, Date, Place	Summary of Events and Information	Remarks and references to Appendices
Sept. 1st to Sept 30th COURCELLES AU BOIS	Work was continued in the SERRE Section of the Line held by the 2nd Division. This consisted of the construction of M.G. Emplacements, Deep Dug Outs, Heavy & Medium Trench Mortar Emplacements, Repair & control of Water Supply, Repair & control of Trench Tramway. General work in trenches in this Area, construction of Strong points in Reserve Line, Observation Posts &c. Construction of Trench boards, dug out frames, notice boards, frames for Trench Mortar Emplacements, revetting screens & control of issue of all R.E. Stores at COURCELLES Dump.	
Sept. 1st — do —	4 O.Rs. Reinforcements Joined Unit.	
" 11th — do —	1 O.R. Wounded	
" 13th — do —	6 O.Rs Reinforcements Joined Unit	
" 19th — do —	2 O.Rs do	
" 21st — do —	7/Lt. C.E. FRANKLIN do	
" 29th — do —	1 O.R. Wounded.	

Alluck Capt.
Commanding, 1st Field Company.
East ??? Divl. Royal Engineers

2nd Divisional Engineers

1/1st EAST ANGLIAN FIELD COMPANY R. E.

OCTOBER 1916.

1/1 E A Coy R E
October 1916.

WAR DIARY
or
INTELLIGENCE SUMMARY
(Erase heading not required.)

Army Form C. 2118.

Instructions regarding War Diaries and Intelligence Summaries are contained in F. S. Regs., Part II. and the Staff Manual respectively. Title pages will be prepared in manuscript.

Hour, Date, Place	Summary of Events and Information	Remarks and references to Appendices
Oct. 1st to 31st. COURCELLES-AU-BOIS.	Work was continued in SERRE SECTOR as for September.	
Oct. 3rd. COURCELLES-AU-BOIS } ENGLEBELMER	Coy. moved to ENGLEBELMER. Work was as before.	
Oct. 4th ENGLEBELMER } MAILLY-MAILLET	Coy. moved to MAILLY-MAILLET. Work was as before.	
Oct. 10th MAILLY-MAILLET } PUCHEVILLERS	Coy. went on rest to PUCHEVILLERS and handed over work to 1st East Riding Ft. Coy R.E. and Cheshire Ft. Coy R.E.	
Oct. 11th PUCHVILLERS.	3 O.R's. Reinforcements joined Unit.	
Oct. 17th PUCHEVILLERS } PIP-SRUC 51st	Coy. returned to camp on BEAUSSART-MAILLY RD. PIP Shut 54 D. scale 1/40,000, and took over northern portion of REDAN sector.	
Oct. 18th to 31st PIP-Shut 57?.	Work up to end of month consisted of improving & making new dug-outs, improvement & upkeep of communication trenches, water supply, observation posts and general work in the field.	
Oct. 26th —do— Oct. 30th —do—	1 O.R. Wounded 1 O.R. Reinforcement - Joined Unit.	

Matthews
2/Lt
Officer
Commanding,
1st Field Company,
East Anglian Divl. Royal Engineers.

2nd Divisional Engineers

1/1st EAST ANGLIAN FIELD COMPANY R.E.

NOVEMBER 1916.

WAR DIARY or INTELLIGENCE SUMMARY

Army Form C. 2118.

1 E A Ja Coy R E

NOVEMBER 1916

Hour, Date, Place	Summary of Events and Information	Remarks and references to Appendices
Nov 1st BEAUSSART-MAILLY ROAD. Nov 11th P.11.d. Sheet 57.D.	Work was carried on in the REDAN SECTION on improvements of Dug Outs for Brigade H.Q. Batt H.Q. and general accommodation for troops holding the line. Improvement of keeps & communication trenches. Construction of Water Dumps in the forward area and general work on Water Supply.	
Nov 3rd — do —	6. O.R. Reinforcements joined unit.	
Nov 12th — do —	Two Sections moved into Dug Outs in GREEN STREET to be ready for work in consolidation of trenches captured on K.18 west when an advance had been ordered on this sector in combination with the general advance N. & S. of the ANCRE. Two Sections were sent in the assembly trenches near 2nd Dvn H.Q. (B.2 Central Av.). No avail orders from C.R.E. & instructions were received to construct a strong point at a point at K.36.c.6.5. 1 Section R.E. with 1 Platoon of Pioneers (10.E.D.6.o.L.6) were sent to H.Q. Essex Regt. at EGG STREET to obtain a guide to the position. After consultation with O.C. 13th ESSEX Regt. it was decided that the work could not be done and a trench running from the Junction of EGG STREET. K.34.d.6.7. in a S.E. direction towards the GERMAN FRONT LINE was commenced to form a defensive flank to the North. This work was started at dusk but owing to the limited number of men available only about 100 yards was dug out to an average depth of 3ft.	
Nov. 13th — do —		

CMoad Capt
Commanding, 1st Field Company,
East Anglian Divl. Royal Engineers.

WAR DIARY
or
INTELLIGENCE SUMMARY
(Erase heading not required.)

Army Form C. 2118.

NOVEMBER 1916

Hour, Date, Place	Summary of Events and Information	Remarks and references to Appendices
Nov. 13th BEAUSSART-MAILLY RD F.n.d. Sheet 57.D	II Lt H.F. MOON. Wounded. (With unit). 1. O.R. Wounded. (Died of Wounds) 1. O.R. Shell Shock.	
— do —		
Nov. 14 — do —	The trench commenced on the night of 13/14. was continued and connection was made with the GERMAN FRONT LINE at a point about K.36.C.26.40. When the party 'bivvied' work at dawn the depth of the trench varied from 6'6" at the Western End to about 2'0" at the Eastern End, where it connected with the GERMAN LINE. The men employed on the work were 1 Section R.E. & 1 Coy Pioneers (10th D.C.L.I.)	
Nov. 15th — do —	2. O.R.'s Killed. 2 O.R.'s Wounded. 1 O.R. Shell Shock. Instructions were received to dig a new B'vie and communication trench for the Junction of MINOR TRENCH with the Front Line (K34.d.9026) to the North Western Corner of the QUADRILATERAL (K35.a.15.20). Owing to the late arrival of the boy of Pioneers and to the exhaustion of the men and heavy shell fire the trench was not dug, but after the men had been rested my Officer continued work on the communication trench dug the previous evening, and this was deepened to an average depth of 6'6" for the greater part of its length. 1 Section R.E. and 1 Coy Pioneers (10th D.C.L.I.) were employed on this work.	

Commanding,
1st Field Company,
East Anglian Divl. Royal Engineers.

Army Form C. 2118.

WAR DIARY
or
INTELLIGENCE SUMMARY
(Erase heading not required.)

NOVEMBER 1916

Hour, Date, Place	Summary of Events and Information	Remarks and references to Appendices
Nov. 16th BEAUSSART-MAILLY F.11.d. Sheet 57D.	Orders were received to dig the Communication Trench from (K.24.d.90.25.) to (K.25.a.15.20.) which had not been completed the previous night. 1. Section R.E. and 1/2 Coy Pioneers (10 D.B.L.I.) were sent to dig this trench. The trench was completed to a depth of 4'.6" and two T Leads were constructed one on either side of the SERRE ROAD. On old GERMAN SAP running West from the QUADRILATERAL was cleared of obstacles and new Joints to part of the trench. Work was also continued on the trench running from EGG STREET to the GERMAN FRONT LINE. Six T leads were constructed off the trench to admit of fire in North & North Easterly directions. 2 Platoons of Pioneers (10 D.B.L.I.) were employed on the work. No attack allowing work constructed during these operations.	
Nov. 17-18 — do —	1. O.R. Reinforcement joined Unit. The Coy Rested & awaiting movement orders.	
Nov. 19th — do —	The Coy moved off at 1.15 P.M. and marched to LONGUEVILLETTE & billeted for the night.	
Nov. 20th LONGUEVILLETTE	The Coy Remained in Billets, resting	
Nov. 21st — do —	The Coy Marched off at 9.25 A.M. to CANDAS & went into Billets	
Nov. 22 CANDAS	The Coy remained in Billets resting. (1 Lt J.H. KING. Reinforcement joined Unit) Lt/Capt	
Nov. 23 — do —	The Coy Marched off at 10 A.M. to LONGUVILLERS & went into Billets.	

Commanding,
1st Field Company,
East Anglian Divl. Royal Engineers

Army Form C. 2118.

WAR DIARY
or
INTELLIGENCE SUMMARY

(Erase heading not required.)

NOVEMBER 1916

Instructions regarding War Diaries and Intelligence Summaries are contained in F.S. Regs., Part II. and the Staff Manual respectively. Title pages will be prepared in manuscript.

Hour, Date, Place	Summary of Events and Information	Remarks and references to Appendices
Nov. 24th LONGVILLERS to	The march was continued. The Coy marched off at 9.30 A.M.	
Nov. 25. CORNEHOTTE	6 CORNEHOTTE & went into Billets	
Nov. 26 CAOURS.	The Coy marched at 9.30 A.M. to CAOURS. went in Billets	
Nov. 27 — do —	The Coy remained in Billets resting	
Nov. 28 CONTEVILLE	The Coy marched at 10 A.M. to CONTEVILLE went into Billets	
Nov. 29 — do —	The Coy remained in Billets resting	
Nov. 30 — do —	11. O.R's Reinforcements joined unit. Orders were received for H.Q. R.E. 2nd Div to proceed to AVELUY via FROUVILLE & BEAUVAL. The Coy marched off at 9.30 A.M. to FROUVILLE went into Billets for the night. (less 2 Officers & 13 O.R's who were attached to H.Q. 2nd Div.) Capt. KEELING was detailed for construction of ranges in the rest area & Lt. A.M. MATTHEWS was detailed as instructor in Field Works to the 2nd Div Labor	

Commanding
1st Field Company,
East Anglian Divl. Royal Engineers.

[signature] Major

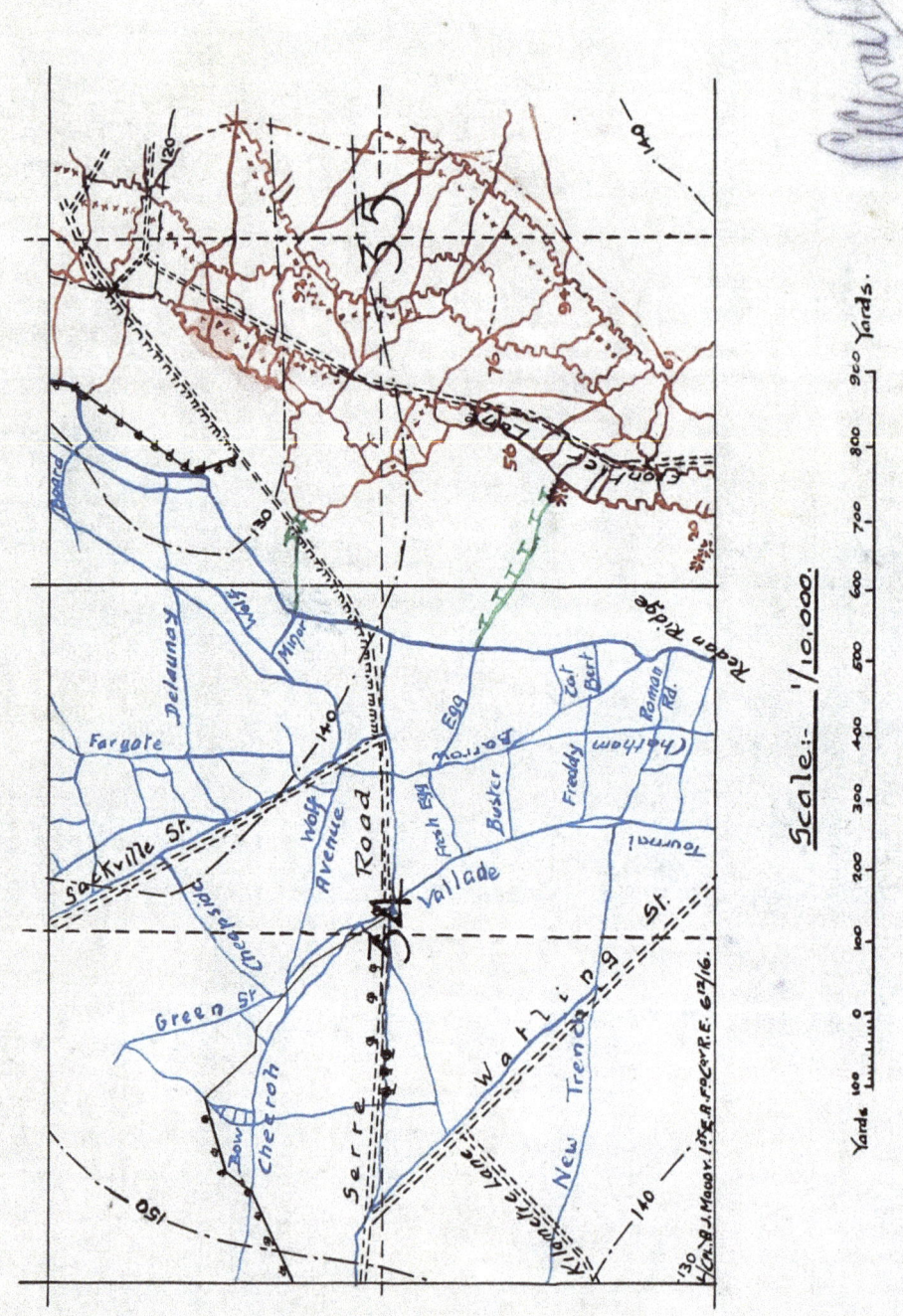

Commanding,
1st Field Company,
East Anglian Divl. Royal Engineers.

2nd Divisional Engineers

1/1st EAST ANGLIAN FIELD COMPANY R. E.

DECEMBER 1916.

WAR DIARY or INTELLIGENCE SUMMARY

Army Form C. 2118.

East Anglian E. RE

DECEMBER 1916.

Hour, Date, Place		Summary of Events and Information	Remarks and references to Appendices
Dec. 1st	PROUVILLE	The march continued - The Company left PROUVILLE at 10 A.M. for BERNAVAL and went into Billets.	
" 2nd	BERNAVAL	The dismounted portion of the Company proceeded on Motor Buses to BOUSINCOURT from there, marched to AVELUY, where they were quartered in Dug outs (Map ref. W.11.d.9.2. Sheet 57.D.5.E.). The mounted portion proceeded by road and arrived late the same night.	
Dec. 3rd	AVELUY	Work was started on the YELLOW LINE on Machine Gun emplacements (Map ref. between R.21.c.95 R.21.d.9.5. Sheet 57.D.S.E.) & also on repairing tramways up to this point - Dug-outs were also commenced in this area - This work continued during the period the Coy. was in this sector.	
Dec. 11th	do	1.O.R. Reinforcement joined Unit.	
" 16th	do	2.O.R's do do	
" 17th	do	Capt. G. C. Walker left Unit to proceed on leave to England. 2/Capt. E. H. Keeling took over command of the Company	
Dec. 20th	do	3. O.R's Reinforcements joined Unit.	
Dec. 21st	PUCHVILLERS	The mounted section left for PUCHVILLERS at 9.30 A.M. & there went into billets.	
" 21st	{AVELUY, BERNATRE	Proceeded to BERNATRE at 9 A.M. and went into billets. The dismounted portion of the Company left AVELUY at 4-30 A.M. & proceeded to ALBERT, where they entrained at 8 P.M. & proceeded to CONTEVILLE, arriving there at 6 P.M. - This portion then marched to BERNATRE & went into billets.	
Dec. 22nd	{BEAUMETZ, BERNATRE	The mounted portion of Company left BERNATRE at 9 A.M. & proceeded to BEAUMETZ, where they arrived & went into billets. The remainder of Coy. left BERNATRE at BEAUMETZ at 9.30 am.	

Hustings
Lieut. R.E.
A/O.C.
Commanding, 1st Field Company,
East Anglian Divl. Royal Engineers.

WAR DIARY or INTELLIGENCE SUMMARY

(Erase heading not required.)

Army Form C. 2118.

DECEMBER 1916.

Hour, Date, Place	Summary of Events and Information	Remarks and references to Appendices
DEC. 23rd BERNÂTRE	The Company went into training, which included Infantry + Bombing Drill, Bayoneting, Map reading, Field Geometry + setting out trenches &c — training was impeded owing to too ½ of the Sections having to leave the Unit.	
Dec. 24th do	1 Sergt. + 20 ORs of No.1 Section proceeded to ARGENVILLERS to construct NISSEN HUTS.	
" 27th do	Remainder of No.1. joined their Section at ARGENVILLERS.	
" 28th do	1. N.C.O + 16 men of No.3 Section proceeded to GAPENNES for the purpose of erecting NISSEN HUTS. Capt. C.H. Keeling left Unit to proceed to England on leave + Lt. L.R. HARWOOD took over Command of the Company.	
Dec. 29th do	1. O.R. Reinforcement Joined Unit.	
Dec. 31st do	1 Sergt + 9. O.R's of No.3 Section joined their Section at GAPENNES. Lieut. A.M. Matthews rejoined Unit from Leave + took over command from Lt. L.R. Harwood.	

Matthews
Lieut. R E
A/6 C

Commd. 1st [?] [?]
East Anglian Divl. Royal Engineers.

2ND DIVISION
DIVL. ENGINEERS

483RD FIELD COMPANY R.E.

JAN-DEC 1917

2nd Divisional Engineers

483rd FIELD COMPANY R. E. :: JANUARY 1917.

Army Form C. 2118.

WAR DIARY
or
INTELLIGENCE SUMMARY
(Erase heading not required.)

January 1917.

Hour, Date, Place	Summary of Events and Information	Remarks and references to Appendices
Jan.y 1st BERNATRE	2/Lt HARWOOD took up duties as Officer i/c Hutting at ARGENVILLERS & GAPENNES with Nos 1 & 3 Sections. Hutting was continued until Jan.y 8th. The remaining Sections continued training.	
Jan.y 9th BERNATRE / BERNAVILLE	Coy. left BERNATRE 10-15am & marched to BERNAVILLE arriving at 1-30 p.m.	
Jan.y 10th BERNAVILLE	Capt. O.H. KEELING rejoined Unit from leave & took over Command.	
Jan.y 11th BERNAVILLE / RUBEMPRE	Coy. left BERNAVILLE at 8 a.m. and marched to RUBEMPRE arriving at 2 p.m.	
Jan.y 12th RUBEMPRE / SENLIS	Coy. left RUBEMPRE at 10-30 a.m. and marched to SENLIS arriving at 4 p.m. — 2/Lt R.H. PEARSALL was detailed as Old Divl R.E. Dump & Left Coy. to assume these duties.	
Jan.y 13th SENLIS / WOLSELEY HUTS	Coy. left SENLIS 9 a.m. and marched to WOLSELEY HUTS arriving 12-30 p.m. Took over work from 32nd Highland Field Coy. R.E. Staff Dist. Consisted of work of rear Field Coy. of Divl R.E. Supplying labour for Dire Tramline R.E. Dumps — Repairs to Huttments — Cutting pitprops — Making Crubwood mats in AVELUY WOOD. 2/Lt HARWOOD was detailed Divl Hutting Officer & left Coy. to assume these duties.	
Jan.y 15th WOLSELEY HUTS. W/68.	25. O.Rs. each from 2/5. STAFFS. 1/5th ESSEX and 19 other & 25. O.Rs. each from 13th KINGS & 17th MIDDLESEX att'd to Coy. as "Sappers Mates"	Huckthorn D.R.C.
Jan.y 20th WOLSELEY HUTS. W/68. WOLFE HUTS X9c	Coy. took over WOLFE HUTS (M.R9.1.X9.c.) Security Mounted Section at WOLSELEY HUTS. (W/3.6.)	for Hucklethorne (East Anglian) Royal Engineers M.B. 7/2/17
Jan.y 21st WOLFE HUTS X9c	Took over work of 226th Field Coy. R.E. at H Coy. R.E. Hecate Coy. from 226th Bde. Work Consisted of under orders from G.O.C. 6th Inf.y Employment of Front Line Pats —	

1247 W 3299 200,000 (E) 8/11 J.B.C. & A. Forms/C. 2118/11.

WAR DIARY or INTELLIGENCE SUMMARY

Army Form C. 2118.

483 yo Coy R.E.

January 1917.

Hour, Date, Place	Summary of Events and Information	Remarks and references to Appendices
Cont^d		
Jany 21st WOLFE HUTS, X.9.C.	Extension of Dugouts H.Q. Dugout - Repair and construction of Inglewood & Inglewood Huts. Also Billets. Labour supplied to Divisional Shooting Officer and Divisional R.E. Dump.	
Jany 28th do	1. O.R. joined Unit.	
Jany 30th do	Took over work of 170 Intermediate Fd. Coy. Jan 226th Fd. Coy. R.E. - This consisted of supply of Filled Labour as above. — Construction of D.O.'s in YELLOW LINE and at CREIGHTON'S POST. — Repairs to Billets to the order of the Town Major, OUVIERS AREA — Laying of Trench Boards in communication Trenches — Building of cavalry Barricade across DYKE VALLEY.	
Jany 31st do	do	

Shattock Lt RE

7/2/17 for Commanding
483rd Field Company
(East Anglian) Royal Engineers

2nd Divisional Engineers

483rd FIELD COMPANY R. E. :: FEBRUARY A 1917.

WAR DIARY
or
INTELLIGENCE SUMMARY

(Erase heading not required.)

Army Form C. 2118.

483 Jn Coy R.E.

FEBRUARY 1917.

Vol 22

Hour, Date, Place	Summary of Events and Information	Remarks and references to Appendices
FEB. 1ST WOLFE HUTS. X.9.c.	Work in Intermediate Area continued as in last report.	
FEB. 6TH WOLFE HUTS. X.9.c. WOLSELEY HUTS. W.8.d.	The Company moved to WOLSELEY HUTS and took over work of rear Sub Coy. (226th) at mid-night. The work consisted of supplying skilled labour to Div: Stuffing Gliders, making brushwood mats & cutting timber in AVELUY WOOD, preparing Bangalore Torpedoes for use of 6th Inf. Bde, erecting Camouflage screen at COURCELLETTE and the establishment of Wire Dumps near Front Line for the attack on DESIRE SUPPORT TRENCH on Feb. 17th.	
FEB. 16TH WOLSELEY HUTS W.8.d. WOLFE HUTS. X.9.c.	Sections No. 1, 2, 3 & 4 of this Unit together with attached Sappers/Maters of 226th Fd. Coy. at WOLFE HUTS where preparations were made for the carrying out of work allotted this Coy. This work consisted of two sections to construct posts for the consolidation of ground to be captured by the 6th Inf. Bde. The attd Sappers/Maters L.I. were under orders of the O.C. and 1/2 Company 10th D.C. Their work was to excavate the existing in front of ground to be captured by Brigade.	Quarters WPCE for O.C. 483rd (Canl) Fg.In.Coy R.E.

Army Form C. 2118.

WAR DIARY
or
INTELLIGENCE SUMMARY
(Erase heading not required.)

FEBRUARY 1917

Hour, Date, Place	Summary of Events and Information	Remarks and references to Appendices
FEBY 16TH WOLFE HUTS Nge. Coy 2.	The other two sections were att. to the 5th Yks Coy R.E. for the consolidation of ground to be captured by the 99th Inf. Bde between EAST and WEST BEAUMONT ROADS.	
FEBY 17TH do	Owing to the failure of the SUPPORT TRENCH by the 6th Camp'n Bde neither the two sections att. to this Bde were called for — Under orders from advanced G.H. Left. Bde H.Q the attached sappers Matlo shd ½ Coy. 10th D.C.L.I. left billets at 11 p.m. + proceeded to work, which consisted of repairing the wire of our own front Pline, which had been cut to permit the attack made in the morning. With reference to the 2 sections att. to 5th Sigl. Coy. R.E., as only the first objective was reached by the 99th Left. Bde, only No 4 section under 2/Lt. J.H. KING was sent up to perform its allotted work — Previous to this, a daylight reconnaissance of the positions of the strong points to be constructed had been made by 2/Lt. J.H. KING.	Statement Late for O.C. 4834 (Cpl Elgl.) Ld Coy R.E.

WAR DIARY or INTELLIGENCE SUMMARY

Army Form C. 2118.

FEBRUARY 1917.

Hour, Date, Place	Summary of Events and Information	Remarks and references to Appendices
FEB.Y 17TH WOLFE HUTS. cont.d	advantage of the mist. This Section, together with a/det Sappers' Mates and one platoon 10TH D.C.L.I. started work about 4-30 P.M. and completed strong point No. 1. and also did a considerable amount of work on Strong point No. 6. 2/Lt. G.H. KING and 1 O.R. were slightly wounded, both remaining at duty.	
FEB.Y 18TH — do —	The remainder of the Unit/Coy Transport, moved into WOLFE HUTS. Coy took over work of forward area under orders of G.O.C 67th Inf.y Bde - this consisted of continuation of work on Strong Points Nos 6 & 7), the enlargement of Bde H.Q at R29 central, the building of bunks in W. MIRAUMONT Rd dug-outs, and the laying of Brushwood mats from old Butterfly Lane to new front line.	
FEB.Y 19TH — do —	2/Lt. C.E. FRANKLIN + 1. O.R. Wounded.	
FEB.Y 20TH — do —	2/Lt. C.E. FRANKLIN Died of Wounds. Buried in AVELUY Cemetery. (Military)	J.Matthews Lt.R.E. for O.C. 483rd (Caernarfonshire) Field Coy, R.E.

WAR DIARY or INTELLIGENCE SUMMARY

Army Form C. 2118.

FEBRUARY 1917

Hour, Date, Place	Summary of Events and Information	Remarks and references to Appendices
FEB 25TH WOLFE HUTS - X9c. TO FEB 28TH	Took over work of Intermediate Area from 226th F.d. Coy. R.E. The work consisted of the Continuation of YELLOW LINE Dug-outs, however, only for a few days owing to evacuation of the enemy front MIRAUMONT the installation of water supply system from the SUCRERIE well, the building of several Mines etc at N MIRAUMONT ROAD Dug-outs to Kilometre 2 for use of Divl H.Q., the Construction of N°6 Dug-out, YELLOW LINE for R.F.A. Bde H.Q., fitting of Gas curtains in Dug-outs at COURCELETTE, the erection of Camouflage screens, Construction of an office at CENTRE WAY DUMP, maintenance and repair of duck-board track to CENTRE WAY and the Construction of a Bombstore at N°5. Dug-out YELLOW LINE.	Illustrations LATE for O.C. (Signed) .E. O.C. 403rd (East Anglian) Fd Coy, R.E.

2nd Divisional Engineers

483rd FIELD COMPANY R. E.

MARCH 1917.

WAR DIARY
or
INTELLIGENCE SUMMARY.

(Erase heading not required.)

Army Form C. 2118.

483 Fd Coy R.E.
MARCH 1917.

VM 25

Place	Date	Hour	Summary of Events and Information	Remarks and references to Appendices
WOLFE HUTS X.9.c.	March 1st–11th		Work in intermediate area continued as in last report. 1 Officer (2nd Lt. D.W. LANCASTER) & 25 O.R's of 2nd Batt. S. STAFFS & 26 O.R's of 17th MIDDLESEX were attached to this Company as Sappers Mates.	
do	Mar. 12th		Owing to evacuation of ACHIET – LOUPART LINE by enemy, Company was placed at disposal of G.O.C. 6th Inf. Bde. Reinforcements joined Unit.	
do	Mar. 13th		Orders were received at 6.45 a.m. that Coy was to consolidate strong points behind new front line to be taken up by 6th Inf. Bde. on IRLES–GREVILLERS Road. The Infantry advance being successful, the Company, with att'd Sappers Mates constructed and wired 5 strong points, viz, at G.28.c.5.5. G.28.d.1.1. G.28.d.8.1. G.29.a.1.5. G.29.c.9.0. the wire taking about 2 hours, from 12.30 p.m. to 8.30 p.m. – Casualties 3 O.R's Wounded – (2 O.R's have since died of wounds)	
do DYKE VALLEY M.14.d.1.1.	Mar. 14th		Company (less transport) moved and built a camp in DYKE VALLEY about M.14.d.1.1. 2nd Lt. J.M. KING evacuated sick. 2nd Lt. H.F. MOON evacuated sick.	
do	Mar. 15th		Company continued work as Field Coy. under orders of Forward Brigade (6th Inf. Bde.) Work consisted of the construction of Duckwalk Tracks from AQUEDUCT FORD M.8.d.8.7. to near LOUPART WOOD. G.33.b.5.5., the improvement of old German Dug-outs & the improvement of the camp. 2nd Lt. L.R. HARWOOD rejoined Company from duty as Divisional Shooting Officer.	
do W. SECT. do SAPIGNIES.	Mar. 18th		2nd Lt. L.R. HARWOOD & No. 1 Section (with attached Sappers Mates) were detailed to proceed as R.E. of advance guard under command of Lt. Col. S.E. MORRIS, D.S.O. (1st KINGS) – They left camp about 9 a.m. & proceeded, with pack transport for tools, to SAPIGNIES, where they constructed a strong point at H.2.d.9.6. – Transport of Company moved off to DYKE VALLEY from WOLSELEY HUTS.	

C.M. Keeling Capt R.E.
483rd (East Anglian) Fd. Coy. R.E.

Army Form C. 2118.

WAR DIARY
or
INTELLIGENCE SUMMARY.
(Erase heading not required.)

MARCH. 1917.

Instructions regarding War Diaries and Intelligence Summaries are contained in F.S. Regs. Part II. and the Staff Manual respectively. Title pages will be prepared in manuscript.

Place	Date	Hour	Summary of Events and Information	Remarks and references to Appendices
DYKE VALLEY (M14.d.1.1.) SAPIGNIES. Nº1.Sect.{SAPIGNIES. MORY.	Mar.19th		Tool cart & Limber was sent to Nº1. Section at SAPIGNIES via BAPAUME.– Company (less one section detailed as advance-guard) received orders at 10 A.M. from 6th Inf.¹ Bde. to move to SAPIGNIES, as R.E. of main guard (formed by 6th Inf.¹ Bde) of 2nd Division advance. Company arrived (via BAPAUME) at SAPIGNIES about 3-30 p.m., cleared roads around two mine craters, one at H.2.C.2.6 and the other at H.2.c.8.8., removed wire obstacles across SAPIGNIES - MORY road at H.2.d.3.7. and made reconnaissances of roads in forward area.– Nº1.Section, (The R.E. of vanguard) moved from SAPIGNIES to MORY.	
			Owing to the relief of 2nd DIVN by 18th DIVN, the Company (less Nº1 Section (with vanguard) received orders about 5-30 P.M. to return to camp at DYKE VALLEY. (M.14.d.1.1.)	
DYKE VALLEY Mar.20th (M.14.d.1.1.) Nº1.Sect.{MORY.- DYKE VALLEY.			Owing to BAPAUME - LE SARS road being in an extremely bad condition and blocked by traffic, the East transport of the Company did not return to camp until 5-30 a.m. 2nd Lt. L.R.HARWOOD and Nº1.Section with att.ᵈ Sappers Males (R.E. of vanguard) rejoined Unit about noon. Sappers Males were returned to their Batt:–	
DYKE VALLEY (M.14.d.1.1.) WOLFE HUTS X 9 c.	March 21st		Company moved to WOLFE HUTS (X9c), the transport returning to WOLSELEY HUTS	
WOLFE HUTS X9c WARLOY-BAILLON			2nd Lt. R.H. PEARSALL rejoined Company from duty as O.C. 2nd DIVN R.E. DUMP. Company moved to WARLOY-BAILLON, forming part of 6th Inf.¹ Bde. group.	
do	24th		I.O.R. Reinforcement Joined Unit.	
do	25th		H.O.R.S. do do do	
LA VICOGNE	26th		Company moved to LA VICOGNE forming part of 6th Inf.¹ Bde. group.	

J.H. Kiely Capt.
463rd (East Anglian) A. Coy. R.E. O.C.

Army Form C. 2118.

WAR DIARY
or
INTELLIGENCE SUMMARY.
(Erase heading not required.)

MARCH 1917.

Instructions regarding War Diaries and Intelligence Summaries are contained in F. S. Regs., Part II. and the Staff Manual respectively. Title pages will be prepared in manuscript.

Place	Date	Hour	Summary of Events and Information	Remarks and references to Appendices
R. VICOGNE. NEUVILLETTE.	March 27th		Company moved to NEUVILLETTE, forming part of 6th Inf't Bde. group.	
NEUVILLETTE SIBIVILLE (LA MONT-JOIE FARM)	28th		— do — do — SIBIVILLE (LA MONT-JOIE FARM) — do — do —	
SIBIVILLE (LA MONT-JOIE FARM) ANTIN.	30th		— do — do — ANTIN	

C.H. Kuhn Capt R.E.
O.C.
463rd (East Anglian) Fd. Coy. R.E.

2nd Divisional Engineers

483rd FIELD COMPANY R. E.

APRIL 1917.

WAR DIARY
or
INTELLIGENCE SUMMARY.

Army Form C. 2118.

483 2nd Army L. of C. Tn

APRIL 1917

Place	Date	Hour	Summary of Events and Information	Remarks and references to Appendices
ANTIN.	April 1st		Training was commenced, the work chiefly consisting of Coy Drill. All Foot Carts were overhauled, & the waggons were painted. This continued to the 5th inst.	
—do—	5th		Capt. O.M. KEELING was sent to hospital sick. LIEUT. R.M. MATTHEWS being on special leave to England, 2nd LT. R.H. PEARSALL took over command of the Company.	
—do—	6th		2/LT. G.H. DUNDON and 2/LT. W.E. OLIVER were attached from 5 Kt field Coy. R.E. owing to the shortage of Officers.	
ANTIN - OURTON	7th		Company left ANTIN at 3 P.M. for OURTON, arriving at 5 P.M. forming part of 6th Corps Rds. Troops.	
OURTON.	8th		2/LT. W.A. SHAW was sent to hospital sick.	
—do—	9th		MAJOR G.C. WALKER rejoined Unit & took over command.	
—do— ECOIVRES. "X" HUTS Map Ref F.A. sheet 51.E	10th		Company left OURTON. 10.45 a.m. arriving at "X" Huts at 6.30 p.m. - Mounted section were billeted in ACQ.	
—do— MARŒUIL	11th		MAJOR G.C. WALKER was again sent to Hospital sick, 2/LT. PEARSALL taking over command. Coy. left "X" Huts at 5 p.m. No 3 Section went to ANZIN, and took over sawmill from 51st Division - Nos 1, 2 & 4 Sections and O.C. were billeted in dug outs at ECURIE - about A.27.b.84. (51.B.) H.Q. & mounted section were billeted in MARŒUIL.	

R.H. MATTHEWS Lieut M/for
MAJOR R.E.
483rd (6. A.) 2nd Army L. of C. Coy.

Army Form C. 2118.

WAR DIARY
or
INTELLIGENCE SUMMARY.
(Erase heading not required.)

APRIL 1917

Place	Date	Hour	Summary of Events and Information	Remarks and references to Appendices
MAROEUIL	April 12th		Owing to the cramped & bad accommodation in ECURIE, No 2 Section were sent to billet in ANZIN.	
do	14th to 19th		The Company took over back area work of the Division, this work chiefly consisted of erection of huts for Div H.Q. & O.R. Infy. Battalion. ROCLINCOURT & the construction of approaches to billets.	
do	16th		This work was continued to the 19th inst. 2/Lt. J.H. KING rejoined Unit from Hospital.	
ANZIN	16th		H.Q. & Mounted Section moved to ANZIN.	
do	17th		LIEUT. R.M. MATTHEWS took over command of Company. A Corps R.E. Dump was sighted & wired in.	
do	19th		Work of the forward area taken over & fresh area work handed over to that Company. Coy. R.E. and the back area were converted to the laying out of a "Jumping off" trench 300 yards from the OPPY LINE, the length being about 1200 yards. 3 Sections came under orders of G.O.C. 6th Infy. Bde. 1 Section under orders of C.R.E. 51st Div. of the latter Section was repair of roads from MAISON-DE-LA-COTE to BAILLEUL - construction of trench road tracks.	
do	20th to 21st		Three Strong Posts were made on WILLERVAL-BAILLEUL line at about B.15.d.5.0., B.9.d.5.1. and B.9.d.4.9.(51st B). Each Post was capable of taking 20 rifles and 2 M.G.s. A garrison took over each Post where instructed how to go on improving the P.C. C/Pt Section bivouaced West of Railway Embankment about B.21.a.7.6. and worked on dug-outs in the embankment - improving accommodation & traversing entrances which faced East of the Embankment.	

R.M. Matthews Lieut H/Capt

463.0 (C.O.) No 2 Coy R.E. Condy

MAJOR R.E.

WAR DIARY
or
INTELLIGENCE SUMMARY.

Army Form C. 2118.

APRIL 1917.

Place	Date	Hour	Summary of Events and Information	Remarks and references to Appendices
ANZIN (cont)	20th to 21st		Railway Embankment - This work was continued to the 27th inclusive. Nos 3 Section were billeted in A.18.d.3.6. made billets for 2 more sections out of timber laying about & tarpaulins. Floor tarpaulins again found to be most valuable, their weight being the only thing against them. S.C.R's were averaging 5.6 commenced wiring of strong posts commenced - owing to whole working parties & the fact that every German wire had to be fetched from BAILLEUL. Billets at Ecurie Camp were improved - 4 Carpenters were sent to Camp Commandant of 2nd Division.	
—do—	22nd			
—do—	23rd		A reconnaissance was made to decide the position of a new defensive line to be known as the "RAILWAY TRENCH", about 150 yards east of the Railway Line - this line was taped out at night. The work. Gun bays & traverses from about B.15.c.9.0. to B.2.6.c.9.4. As usual, there was much difficulty in obtaining & facing tape & the tape eventually obtained was in very short lengths.	
—do—	24th		The digging of the "RAILWAY TRENCH was commenced, one Battn (Reg. W. Lab.) being supplied as working-party. Three Companies did digging with an interval between each Company, the other Company did wiring 40 yards in front.	

W. Williams Lieut R.E. for
483rd (E.A.) MAJOR R.E. Cmdg
483rd Fd Coy R.E.

Army Form C. 2118.

WAR DIARY
or
INTELLIGENCE SUMMARY.
(Erase heading not required.)

APRIL 1917

Place	Date	Hour	Summary of Events and Information	Remarks and references to Appendices
ANZIN (cont)	24th		of the intervals between the 3 Companies digging. No.1 Section moved to billets at A.18.b.3.6.	
do	25th		The wiring of the "RAILWAY TRENCH" was continued, only two Coys. of Infantry were supplied as a working party, nearly ½ whole of the party had to be employed in carrying wire from BAILLEUL dump. All 4 Sections came under orders of G.O.C. 6th Inf. Bde. No working party could be obtained to continue the "RAILWAY TRENCH".	
do	26th		A reconnaissance was made as to the state of the Support Line running through B.17 Central (3/13) and a full report sent to the G.O.C. 6th Inf. Bde. who reported was asked for in spite of the fact that Infantry Officers of the same Bde. held been holding the support line for several days. G.O.C. 6th Inf. Bde. was relieved by G.O.C. 99th Inf. Bde. & the Working Sections came under the orders of the latter. G.O.C. Section moved back to B.18.d. as the holding of the Railway Embankment became too extensive. A tape was laid from the front line trench.	

J. Whatters
Lieut. R.E. Comdg.

4834 (E.A. ...)
MAJOR R.E. Comdg.

WAR DIARY or INTELLIGENCE SUMMARY

Army Form C. 2118.

APRIL 1917

Place	Date	Hour	Summary of Events and Information	Remarks and references to Appendices
ANZIN (Cont.)	26th		Southwards to new Divl. Boundary to act as a jumping off line.	
do	27th		H.Q. & Mounted Section moved to Camp at ECURIE. A "jumping-off" line was taced out 100 yards behind the front line on the whole of the Brigade front. Nos. 1 & 3 Sections were detailed to make strong posts at about (a) C.13.d.4.0, (b) C.13.d.4.1, (c) C.13.b.3.8 and (d) C.7.c.8.3. after the attack to be made at 4-25am next day, if circumstances permitted. O.C. Company moved to Brigade H.Q. to be in touch with the G.O.C. during operations.	
ECURIE			2/Lt. G. STEEL joined Unit – Reinforcement.	
do	28th			
do		12.35 a.m.	Nos. 1 & 3 Sections moved into Dug-outs in the Railway Embankment allotted to them by Bde.	
		1.30 a.m.	2/Lt. HARWOOD (No. 1 Section) & 2/Lt. OLIVER (No. 3 Section) were ordered by G.O.C. Brigade to go forward, without their sections, to Batt. H.Q. in B.2d.3.4. (Support line) in order to be in closer touch with forthcoming operations & hence be able to judge better when a reconnaissance could be made for selecting strong points.	
		8.am	No. 2 Section moved to A.18.d.	

Hubert Evans
Lieut Rt. Jo.
Cmdg. 403rd (E.A.) A/Majr T.E.

A.5834. Wt. W4973/M687. 750,000. 8/16 D. D. & L. Ltd. Forms/C.2118/13.

Army Form C. 2118.

WAR DIARY
or
INTELLIGENCE SUMMARY
(Erase heading not required.)

Instructions regarding War Diaries and Intelligence Summaries are contained in F. S. Regs., Part II. and the Staff Manual respectively. Title pages will be prepared in manuscript.

APRIL 1917

PLACE.	Date.	Hour.	Summary of Events and Information	Remarks and references to Appendices
ECURIE.	April 28th contd.	8.45 a.m.	that they had orders from O.C. of Batt. H.Q. to make Strong Points West of road running from B.18.d.9.0. N.E. to OPPY at about B.18.d.2.3. and C.13a.2.0. and that they were going to take their Sections up to the ridge - the G.O.C. 6th Left Bde decided that the situation was not clear enough to send these sections up & the order was cancelled -	
do	do	8.15 p.m.	Nos 1 & 3 Sections were ordered to be ready for a counter-attack as enemy patrols were reported to be in B.23c and B.23d. The sections held a position at the Railway line -	
do	do	8.25 p.m.	99 R.I. Bde relieved 6 Left Bde. The 4 Sections then came under orders of the former.	
do	29th		MAJOR W.C. COOPER joined Unit, Resupment, took over Command of Company. Several positions for Strong Points were suggested by G.O.C. 99th Bde but owing to felt very uncertain situation, the sections were not sent out to work. -	
do	30th	1.30 a.m.	Bde HQ. dug-outs became badly gassed by German Gas-Shells. Blankets wet temporarily nailed across the entrance. Prymer stoves & Brayers were used to clear dug-outs of the Gas, effectively -	Hallattours Lieut. N.E. for MAJOR R.E. Cmdg. 483rd (E) Field Coy R.E.

WAR DIARY
or
INTELLIGENCE SUMMARY

(Erase heading not required.)

Army Form C. 2118.

APRIL 1917

PLACE.	Date.	Hour.	Summary of Events and Information	Remarks and references to Appendices
ECURIE.	30th cont.	9.a.m.	Roper, Geo. Coustan, James were fitted to the 4 entrances of Bde H.Q. and Gladiates with solution offered to them.	
do	do	10.30 a.m.	G.O.C. 99th Inf.Bde. ordered a communication trench to be taped out from about B.18.c.9.4 to about B.18.a.3.6. – Envelopes were to be made so as to form a defensive flank in case of an attack from N.E. – This work was carried out at dusk.	
do	do	8.p.m.	Relieved G.O.C. 92nd Inf. Bde. (31st Division) G.O.C. 99th Inf. Bde. the following then came under orders of the former.	

Andrews
Lieut. V.E. for
Major R.E.
Commanding
483rd (East Anglia) Fld. Coy. R.E.

483RD
(EAST ANGLIAN)
FIELD COMPANY, R.E.
No. O.R.
Date. 6.5.17.

2nd Divisional Engineers

483rd FIELD COMPANY R. E. :: M A Y 1917.

WAR DIARY or INTELLIGENCE SUMMARY

Army Form C. 2118.

483 Fd Coy R.E.
MAY 1917

Place	Date	Hour	Summary of Events and Information	Remarks and references to Appendices
ECURIE	MAY 1st		The Company was relieved by 5th Fd Coy R.E. of work in the forward area – All returned to ECURIE CAMP.	
do	"2nd"		Work of back area was taken over from 5th Fd Coy R.E. This consisted of maintenance of duckboard track, mule track & artillery track. The work was continued to the 4th inst. The billets of the Company were much improved, a drainage system was made & latrines moved in for summer use. Shelling at H.Q. R.E. continued. 4. O.R's. (Reinforcements) joined Unit.	
do	"4th"		Major W.E. Cooper took over C.R.E. 2nd Divn at 10am Lieut. A.H. Matthews took over command of Coy. Erection of 2 Nissen Huts commenced. one hut of timber & felt.	
do	"5th"		Officers made a reconnaissance of work to be carried out under orders of XIIIth Corps. (The 2nd Divn having gone out of the line on rest).	
do	6th to 24th		Work for XIIIth Corps commenced – This consisted of Cross-Country track ANZIN-ROCLINCOURT, ANZIN-BAILLEUL and track running parallel to ARRAS-LENS road. – Supervision of infantry working parties repairing the ARRAS-BAILLEUL road & ECURIE-ROCLINCOURT road. – Constructing lean-to shelters in ROCLINCOURT in the billeting of troops – Elbow of water troughs with corduroy standings at GUNNER'S POST & ECURIE STATION. Erection of two Nissen Huts & a hut of timber & felt for C.R.E. 2nd Divn.	483 Fd Coy R.E. (First Army) FIELD COMPANY, R.E. Date 5/6/17
do	7th		Company (Adv. from 5 Mls/11/15) left the Unit & regt. her over L-- J.H.Matthews Lieut. O.C.	

WAR DIARY or INTELLIGENCE SUMMARY

Army Form C. 2118.

MAY. 1917.

Place	Date	Hour	Summary of Events and Information	Remarks and references to Appendices
ECURIE	May 8	—	Major W.E. Cooper took over command of Coy.	
do	" 11th	—	3. O.R's (Reinforcements) joined Unit.	
do	" 13th	—	2/Lt J. Wilton joined Unit (Reinforcement)	
do	" 15th	—	2/Lt G. Vey do	
			Major W.E. Cooper took over C.M.E. 2nd Divn. Lieut. A.M. Matthews took over command of Company.	
do	" 25th	—	Work on Kand Jn XIII Corps was taken over by the 59th Lo Coy. R.E. & the work of the 59th Lo Coy left off into taken over by this Unit. This work was that of the Back area that of the Division in the line, consisted of repairs to & deepening of an old german well at A.17.d.6.5.65. (Sht.51.c.N.W) - getting of a HEWCE chain pump to same - Completion of causeway road through ammunition dump at A.17.a.3.7. (Sht.51.B). Supplying to R.E. of sleepers to supervise the construction by sappers & tracing light railway ammunition dumps - clearing & grading light railway from A.M.a.1.3 (Sht.51.B) to Commandants stores also shared & reconstructing trucks for the Light railway - Improving drainage at Divl. Baths, POCUNCOURT.	
do	" 26th 31st		The work handed over by the 59th Lo Coy was continued. In addition a reconnaissance was made of the Back area of the Division to improve existing maps. The Buck road back from...	

W.E.C.
O.C.

483rd (EAST ANGLIAN)
FIELD COMPANY. R.E.
No. 54/1
Date

Army Form C. 2118.

WAR DIARY
or
INTELLIGENCE SUMMARY.
(Erase heading not required.)

MAY. 1917.

Instructions regarding War Diaries and Intelligence Summaries are contained in F. S. Regs., Part II. and the Staff Manual respectively. Title pages will be prepared in manuscript.

Place	Date	Hour	Summary of Events and Information	Remarks and references to Appendices
ECURIE.	26th 31st cont'd		MAISON-DE-LE-COTE to B.19.c.8.7. (Sheet 51B N.W.) was taken up & a track laid from this point to OOSE ALLEY at B.19.8.3.5 thence to TOMMY ALLEY at B.19.b.3.9. 1300 yards of duck-boards were laid from this point in TOMMY ALLEY to the French Eastwards.	
do	22nd		11. O.R.s. (Reinforcements) joined Unit.	
do	23rd		2/Lt. W. E. OLIVER (2nd Lon Staffs R.E.) left this Unit to join his own Company.	
do	24th		1. O.R. wounded to Hospital.	
do	do		1. O.R. (Reinforcement) joined Unit.	
do	26th		During the early morning (about 4a.m.) hostile aircraft dropped 4 bombs on Company Lines. — 5 O.R.s. were wounded but only two 1 however, was admitted to Hospital. One of these bombs fell right in the midst of the Horse Lines & in a result, 33 horses were either killed outright or had to be shot, 5 evacuated to the M.V.S. & 9 slightly wounded animals remained under treatment in Camp. Making the total number of Horse casualties 47.	
do	31st		Major. W. C. Cooper took over command of Company. Section Officers made a reconnaissance of the work of the 5th Ply: Co. R.E., which was the front-line system of the right Bde — viz 99th Inf.Bde.	J M Matthew Lt G.E.

483RD (EAST ANGLIAN) FIELD COMPANY, G.E.
No. 5.19
Date.

2nd Divisional Engineers

483rd FIELD COMPANY R. E. :::   JUNE   1917.

WAR DIARY or INTELLIGENCE SUMMARY

Army Form C. 2118.

483rd Field Coy R.E.

JUNE 1917

(Erase heading not required.)

Place	Date	Hour	Summary of Events and Information	Remarks and references to Appendices
ECURIE.	MAY 31.		H.Q. proceeded to Advanced billets A.15d.8.6. Coy transport which remained at Matthieu at Ecurie.	
	JUNE 1.		Work of forward area was taken over from 5th Y & L Coy R.E. All sectors were relieved by 5th Y/L Coy R.E. of work in back area. The work consisted of improvement of accommodation in Right Batt HQ. Breaking one new stairway entrance to dug-out at Batt: HQ. (B10d.4.5). Making dug-outs at Stokes Mortar Emplacements (B.12 c.95.) (B.12 c.7.8.) Improvement to change in M.G. TRENCH & KENT ROAD by deepening & dumping. Marking out pathway from A.15c.9.5 ~ 7.5 (+ roads) - South of dug out Right Batt: HQ.	
ADVANCED BILLETS.			Work as handed over by 5th Y & L R.E. continued except last item. L addition. Some short traffic - erected round Batt: HQ. (B10d.6.7) completed. Improvement & changing of 2 Grand forward system. Deepening & Dumping - also Trench Tramway.	
—do—	2.		Work continued on B June 1st. At Batt. HQ. (B10d.4.5) recommence made in dug out for Artillery advanced observation Artillery Liaison Officer.	
—do—	3.		Work continued. — In addition, dug out recommendation started (at Batt HQ.) for A.L. Officer.	
—do—	4.		Work continued as for June 1st. In addition shelters were laid in Trench at Right Batt: HQ.	
—do—	5.		Work continued as for June 4th. Gas curtain material used for getting up to dug out there.	
—do—	6.		Work continued as for June 4th. In addition improvising Dump was carried in KING ST. - Dump. — Y at Right Bde. HQ. - gas curtains in dug out stairways begun. — also bunks - accord.	
—do—	7.		Work continued as for June 5th. In addition: Dug outs filled up - dug outs at Advanced billets - a deepening area made by Cpl Wilson & No 5, 7 & 8 dug outs. RED LINE phosphor tube. was used a "dud lift". Capt Kennedy, F.A. French Unit (Concrete) (Removable way at Batt. H.Q. was completed)	V/Dilution July 2 Page 48 Folder 52

WAR DIARY or INTELLIGENCE SUMMARY

Army Form C. 2118.

Month: **JUNE 1917**

Place	Date	Hour	Summary of Events and Information	Remarks and references to Appendices
ADVANCED BILLETS	7th Cont'd		In addition, Gas curtain - dug-outs, Sunken Road (B15c x d) being fitted up.	
do	8th		Work as for 7th Cont'd - In addition repair camouflage screen on TOMMY ALLEY. Coffs war Advanced Billet. Half allowance took over command at ADVANCED BILLET.	
do	9th		Work as for 8th Cont'd. Reconnaissance of Nos Roo. 100 of Rgt 15 Bde H.Q. made by O/C Wilson with regard to strength.	
do	10th		Work as for 9th Cont'd. In addition. Preparations for 'V' framed tramway at junction of 2 roads, ARLEUX LOOP & KING ST., was completed. Material delivered at Bde HQ ready to start on strengthening of moss room roof (The job was not done by Rd 65), but looked over to succeed by B.67.	
do	11th		Work as for 10th Continued. In addition Tracey cut new support trench from B.18.c.6.0.9.5. to B.12.c.3.5.15. This was done in conjunction with 10 KD.C.L.I. This was completed.	
do	12th		Work as for June 11th Cont'd. Major Cooper assumed command of Advanced Billet. O/C Honor Stoh - Lt. Coy on Right the following events - 1 pl Coys Indian Wagon - 2 pl Coys Tool. Cart - 3/4 mile Cross Country Race - 2nd prize won by D. HAFFENDEN. 4th Section Coy carrying 3 cwt in Gas Curtain completed - Dug-out - SUNKEN ROAD. (B.15.c.d) allot at Batt". HQ. (B.10.d.4.5)	
do	13th			
BILLET ANZIN.	14th		The Coy was relieved by 527th Lt. Coy R.E. of work in Gwyl area. H.Q. 1 Section (No 2) proceeded to ANZIN - Nos 1 & 3 Sections to 28.a.8.5 near ECURIE & No 4 Sect. to BAILLEUL ROAD G.12.a.6.8. each respectively transport - 1/HQ, 3/(R.E.) 2 in MR.Cs 4/ by A6 Columns 2 in MR.Cs 3 Hos 2/(R.E.)	

WAR DIARY
or
INTELLIGENCE SUMMARY.
(Erase heading not required.)

Army Form C. 2118.

JUNE 1917

Place	Date	Hour	Summary of Events and Information	Remarks and references to Appendices
BILLET ANZIN.	June 14th		N.B. Work of each area was taken over from #91st (Home Counties) Coy R.E. The corridor of deepen/widen required to be widened out of RED LINE - Work TIRED ALLEY & TOMMY ALLEY - While allotted out of RED LINE - Work on TIRED ALLEY was started. Joint. Repairs to ARRAS-BAILLEUL Rd. from B.20.d.7.1 to B.21.c.6.7.	
do	15th		Supervision of Infantry party work on TIRSO ALLEY. deepen/widen of our position June 14th 1 section RE. party Tired Alley Infantry - by clearing from revetted partn width. Tired Alley party occupied from RED LINE to ARLEUX LOOP - upper ARRAS - BAILLEUL Rd from B20.d to B.21.c.6.7 trenches. T.W.P.- same. Erect C.I. culvert at G.6.d.2.12. Reconnaissance made of road from MAISON-de-la Côte to B22.a.7.4. Jubles.	
do	16th		Work as for June 15th cont. work on ARRAS-BAILLEUL ROAD up to B.21.c.7.7.	
do	17th		Work as for June 16th cont. do do to B.21.c.6.8.8. Work on erecting C.I. culvert almost finished. additional - making curb almp/railway at R.E. dump G.6.d.2.2. Supervision continued metal for dump along West Slopes Roads for road.	
do	18th		Repairs to ARRAS-BAILLEUL Road cont. to B.21.c.7.7 to B.21.c.8.8. Other work on as for June 17th except that work of F. W. Piers carried on at TOMMY Alley & E. of REDLINE - Deepening/widening ye as for June 15th TIRED ALLEY owing / completed.	

H.W. Bentley

WAR DIARY or INTELLIGENCE SUMMARY

Army Form C. 2118.

JUNE 1917

Place	Date	Hour	Summary of Events and Information	Remarks and references to Appendices
BILLET ANZIN	18th		The Coy. was relieved of back area work as follows:- the 248th Coy. took over E½ of RED LINE - the 20th A.T. Coy. infront of BAILLEUL ROAD & the 251st A.T. Coy. for Railway work at ANZIN -	
do	19th		All sections proceeded to ANZIN & joined H.Q. their preparations were made to move next day.	
BEUVRY BILLET F.20.b.5.2	20th		The Coy. moved to ANZIN & proceeded to BEUVRY via BETHUNE & reported to 66th Div. 11th & 12th Coys. in billets in followers. 2 Os. believed 11th Coy took over the billets at F.21.a.5.2 & NOYELLES. Also the work from 432 Coy R.E. The work consisted of M.T.M. Emplacements & Back Sd. - Signal Lab, Box La BASSEE ROAD - at A.19.d.5.1. Cleaning Rly Alley, West End & front line Wing Trench - Comm out from Rd. Alley to Surrey Alley. Laying & cult 7 ft 4" water pipe from FOUNTAIN KEEP - Improvements of FOUNTAIN KEEP Defence Scheme - main water supply.	
do	21st		I.O.R. Rangers who joined last night. Artillery O.P. at BACK ST. Work taken over from 432 Coy R.C.S. as described - 251 was relieved by Major Coopers Section officer along with 432 Coy O.C. Lts Officer spot	
do	22nd		Col. P.K. Betty, D.S.O. R.E. at H.Q. turned over along with Major Cooper & Major Grave of 432 Coy R.E visited others at all Major Gould No 1 Sect proceeded to all billets at NOYELLES with Serjeant. Work began as follows:- No 1 Sect. (day) improvement of South Keep Defence Scheme.	

Army Form C. 2118.

WAR DIARY
or
INTELLIGENCE SUMMARY.
(Erase heading not required.)

JUNE 1917

Place	Date	Hour	Summary of Events and Information	Remarks and references to Appendices
BEUVRY BILLET 21.a.5.2.	22nd		No 2 Sect. (night) Carried out "waterproof" for FOUNTAIN. KEEP WATER SUPPLY - No 3 (day) M.T. N.F. Emplacement BACK ST. SIGNAL TESTING BOX - L'ABBSEE ROAD. Clear up ALLEY Jn trench. Bds. - No 4 Sect. (night) Artillery O.P. BACK ST. Tidy Cuffin RLY. ALLEY & QUARRY ALLEY.	
do	23rd		Work on Jn. Com 22nd Cont'd. add'l splinter proof roof to Anti-air Off Batt. H.A.	
do	24th		Work on Jn Com 23rd Cont'd Add'l Roof on Left Batt HA. Completed. Improvement of BRAYS KEEP Defence Scheme.	
do	25th		Work on Jn Com 24th Cont'd. Work at CHATEAU-des-PRES near BEUVRY 2/Lt. T. WILSON destroyed a German AERIAL BOMB which had fallen unexploded.	
do	26th		Work on Carbine Sect's defences cont'd	
do	30th		Ditto	

Ditto

[signature] Major
O.C. 433rd (East Anglian)
Field Coy. R.E.

433rd
(EAST ANGLIAN)
FIELD COMPANY, R.E.

No. A.K.
Date 5/7/17

2nd Divisional Engineers

483rd FIELD COMPANY R. E. ::: JULY 1917.

WAR DIARY
or
INTELLIGENCE SUMMARY.

(Erase heading not required.)

Army Form C. 2118.

483rd (EAST ANGLIAN) FIELD COMPANY, R.E.

JULY - 1917

Place	Date	Hour	Summary of Events and Information	Remarks and references to Appendices
BEUVRY BILLETS F.21.a.5.2.	JULY 1ST		Work on Cambrin Sector continued. - This consisted of :- Water supply, R.A periscopic O.P, French from LEFT BATN. H.Q to QUARRY ALLEY, gas curtains and defensive gates for tunnel entrances, up keep and revetting communication trenches, constructing French mortar emplacement in MAISON ROUGE ALLEY supervising & maintenance of tramway system, fixing gas curtains to dug outs, repairs to enlistments in SUPPORT LINE, camouflaging LA BASSEE ROAD.	
do	JULY 2ND		Lieut H.C.M. Matthews proceeded to England on leave. One other rank joined (reinforcement ?)	
do	" 3RD		Work on SAVILLE ROW Tunnel discontinued. Water supply to RESERVE LINE and MUNSTER PARADE, 1,600 gallon tank erected on stand 6 feet high, 4 pipe line completed, taps and stop cocks fitted in various places.	
do	" 4TH		Major W.C. Cooper proceeded to 1st Army Rest Camp. Lieut Harwood took over command of Company.	
do	" 5TH		One other rank (reinforcement) joined.	
do	" 7TH		All entrances to SAVILLE TUNNEL fitted with double gas curtains, also gates under construction.	
do	" 8TH		All entrances to QUARRY TUNNEL fitted with double gas curtains, and gates under construction. Four other ranks (reinforcements) joined One other rank to Hospital - sick.	

Mu Harwood
Capt. R.E.
a/ O.C.
483rd (E.A.) F'ld Coy R.E.

Army Form C. 2118.

WAR DIARY
or
INTELLIGENCE SUMMARY.
(Erase heading not required.)

JULY - 1917

Place	Date	Hour	Summary of Events and Information	Remarks and references to Appendices
BEUVRY BILLETS	JULY 10TH		LEFT BOYAU FRANK 15C clearing & relaying FRENCH boards completed.	
F.21.c.5.2.	" 12TH		Four other ranks (reinforcements) joined.	
do:			New railway siding and loop at CAMBRIN-DUMP started. Three other ranks (reinforcements) joined.	
			Capt. Matthews rejoined from leave and took over Comd of Company.	
do:	" 13TH		Three other ranks joined. (one of these evacuated to hospital)	
do:	" 14TH		Commenced surveying all work in CAMBRIN SECTOR.	
			One other rank joined on the 13TH died from gas poisoning. The other rank joined on the 13TH evacuated to hospital.	
			Four other ranks - 71ST LABOUR BATTN attached.	
do:	" 15TH		Drainage system in CAMBRIN SECTOR reconnoitred	
			One other rank joined on the 13TH evacuated to hospital.	
			" Lieut Harward proceeded to LA BOURSE to take over duties of H.Q. R.E. Corps troops.	
do:	" 16TH		One other rank accompanied " Lieut Harward. Instruction and demonstration in use of Bangalore Torpedoes given at	
			2ND DIVISIONAL SCHOOL by " Lieut King.	
do:	" 17TH		One other rank (reinforcement) joined.	
			Commenced work on clearing LEWIS ALLEY to SIMS·KEEP.	
			Duckboarding GORDON·ALLEY from RAILWAY to RESERVE·LINE, and drainage.	
			Major Cooper returned from Rest Camp, and took over command of Coy.	
			Two H.G. emplacements sited on "CHAMPAGNE" principal to be made from	
do:	" 18TH		MUNSTER·TUNNEL and a gallery from there to H.G. emplacement, to be in front of Reserve line wire.	

[Stamp: 403RD (EAST ANGLIAN) FIELD COMPANY, R.E. No......... Date.........]

483 [signature] C.H. [signature] a/o.C.

Army Form C. 2118.

WAR DIARY
or
INTELLIGENCE SUMMARY.
(Erase heading not required.)

JULY 1917

Instructions regarding War Diaries and Intelligence Summaries are contained in F. S. Regs., Part II. and the Staff Manual respectively. Title pages will be prepared in manuscript.

Place	Date	Hour	Summary of Events and Information	Remarks and references to Appendices
BEUVRY BILLETS	JULY 23rd		Three officers from Battns of 99th Infantry Brigade were attached to the Coy. to receive lessons between Infantry and R.E.'s	
F 21.a.5.2	" 28th		Officers of Berkshire Regiment and 23rd R.F. attached, returned to their Battalions and were relieved by two other officers.	
— do —	" 30th		The officer attached from 22nd R.F. returned to his Battalion. The work in hand on this date was as follows:—	
— do —	" 31st		Improving defence of TUNNEL ENTRANCES. Up keep of map shewing all communication trenches. Making map shewing all dug-outs in the CAMBRIN SECTOR also their accommodation and condition etc. Supervision of the making of Light Trench Mortar Emplacement. Completion of WATER SUPPLY to Left and Right Battalion. Construction of No. 6. H.G. emplacement off MUNSTER TUNNEL. Making plan of KEEPS and posting them in the keeps. Supervising the cleaning out of the drainage system West of VILLAGE LINE. Making a periscope R.A.O.P. between FRONT and RESERVE lines; this consisted of a dug-out through the roof of which a hole was bored and trunk of a tree above this roof was also bored so as to allow the periscope being fixed inside it. Making a dug-out for a Medium and Heavy emplacement in MAISON ROUGE ALLEY. Making a new tramway siding at CAMBRIN CHURCH and maintenance of tramway system.	403rd (EAST ANGLIAN) FIELD COMPANY, R.E.

J.H. Matthew
Capt. R.E.
O/C

WAR DIARY or INTELLIGENCE SUMMARY

Army Form C. 2118.

JULY 1917

Place	Date	Hour	Summary of Events and Information	Remarks and references to Appendices
BEUVRY BILLET F.21.a.5.2	July 31st		Repairing Coy. Stables for the Winter and improving billets. Infantry crew country tracks had previously been made up to the front line in case the enemy should retire. Officers of this Coy. made a reconnaissance of same and the repair of these tracks including bridges was in hand on this date. Beaune R.E. forward dumps were also made for this purpose. There was a marked shortage of sappers for work during the month owing to inoculation and leave for the men, averaging 2 per day – these men had served 18 months in France since their last leave. A. R. E. musketry competition was arranged for the next month and training for this was carried out in the evenings, the range being available twice a week. In spite of a strenuous month's work, the change of conditions for working after the SOMME and OPPY had the effect of a "rest cure" rather than the reverse. The horses were looking well and an epidemic of mange which broke out in the area at the beginning of the month was practically knocked out of the heat. A "Corps" Conservation gave lectures in the area, and was of great assistance. The cooking of food for the men was brought to a more marked pitch though the installation of daily dixy sheets – the bread ration was never so good before and the quality better than that obtainable in England.	

400rd (EAST ANGLIAN) FIELD COMPANY, R.E.

W.A. Mallaud
Capt 4 R.E.
O/c 483 (E.A.) F.E. Coy. R.E.

2nd Divisional Engineers

483rd FIELD COMPANY R. E. ::: AUGUST 1917.

SECRET.

483rd (E.A.) Field Coy. R.E.   Vol 28

War Diary

August 1917.

Mcmatthews
Capt. R.E.
M.O.C.
483rd E.A. Coy. R.E.

433RD
(EAST ANGLIAN)
FIELD COMPANY, R.E.
No. QR
Date 5 Aug.

Army Form C. 2118.

WAR DIARY
or
INTELLIGENCE SUMMARY. — AUGUST 1917.
(Erase heading not required.)

Place	Date	Hour	Summary of Events and Information	Remarks and references to Appendices
BEUVRY. F.21.A.5.2.	Aug 1st		Work in hand at the end of July was continued — I.O.R. List to Staff.	
"	"	5 pm	Major W.C. Cooper proceeded on leave to England — Capt. G.M. Matthews took over command of the Company. The following work had been done since the beginning of the month:—	
			SAVILLE TUNNEL. 1 Sets Kerry completed.	
			NEW CUT TUNNEL. 2 Gates Kerry not complete with floatings. Entrance to NORTHAMPTON TRENCH cleared & timbered.	
			QUARRY TUNNEL. Entrances cumped & cleared. Slinging of 3 gates in hand.	
			LEFT BOYAU. Clearing completed.	
			KERRY ROW. Revetting & strengthening where collapsed owing to rain.	
			SAVILLE ROW. Clearing commenced Eastwards from tunnel entrance to KAISERIN TRENCH.	
			QUARRY ALLEY. Repairing & revetting.	
			GORDON ALLEY. Repairing revetting to Railway.	
			MUNSTER PARADE. Duckboarded from RAILWAY ALLEY to OLD BOOTS, including 2 standings and stops in front of Water tanks.	
			MAISON ROUGE ALLEY. Stonemacadal.	
			RAILWAY ALLEY. Clearing & revetting commenced.	
			HUMANITY TRENCH. Cleared & duckboarded to LEWIS ALLEY.	
			LEWIS ALLEY. Cleared from OLD BOOTS TRENCH to BACK STREET.	
			ROUTES. N° 2,3,4 picketted, wired & railway. 5,6,7. Reconnoitred. — Bridges built & repaired. Sign-boards fixed. Trench-boards laid over sumps at about A.26.a.3.4 on ROUTE 7.	
			N° 6. M.G. EMPL.T — MUNSTER TUNNEL. Dug-out excavated & timbered. — Fire steps found.	
			DUG-OUT for GROUP. CABLE BACKS (A.28.c.31.18). being strengthened. 2 frames fitted.	

G.M. Matthews
Capt. O.C.

P.T.O.

WAR DIARY or INTELLIGENCE SUMMARY

Army Form C. 2118.

AUGUST 1917 (Cont'd)

Place	Date	Hour	Summary of Events and Information	Remarks and references to Appendices
BEUVRY. F.21.a.5.2.	Aug 5th		DUG-OUT at R.27.a. 95.20. Entrance completed. Chamber commenced.	
			L.T.M.B. Empt. R.28.c. Two dapper were sent to T.M.B. Officer for filling of frontain.	
			FOUNTAIN KEEP. Gas curtains fitted in Dug-outs.	
			R.A. PERISCOPIC O.P. at R.27.b.2.2. Completed & handed over to R.A.	
			TRAMWAY. Siding at CAMBRIN completed. Maintenance of tramway system. G. Breaks repaired & rolling stock kept in order.	
			TRAMWAY at about R.26.a. 5.5. raised above existing water level 20 lengths re-placed & being ballasted.	
			WATER SUPPLY: Connection of 4" pipe to main tank altered.	
			TANKS - MINSTER PARADE. Seepage pits dug - pipes & ball cocks fitted, etc.	
			TANK. RESERVE LINE. Slump-pits dug - trench-boards laid - pipe & ball cock fitted to one tank. Emplacement excavated for second tank.	
			TANK - CENTRAL KEEP. Excavating & levelling for tanks - shuttering sides of trench.	
			OLDWELL - QUARRY ALLEY. Digging sump - pits & laying trench - boards - 2 tanks erected & connected up. Funnels made for filling petrol - cans.	
			WATER POINT at R.26.a. 5.5. Damaged pumps replaced.	
			PUMP in BEUVRY SQUARE. Dismantled for examination.	
			PUMPS at ANNEQUIN B.19.d.6.2. F.30.a.2.6. Two french pumps marked as existing	
			FRONT TO VILLAGE LINE. Nos 12B & No 27 being repaired. Surveying of Dug-outs & S.9 front shelters etc. Commenced. Shewing number of entrance, accommodation rate of repair etc. on map.	
			99th BDE. H.Q. Roof 75% of roof repaired.	

J. M. Attwell
Capt. R.E.
O.C.

P.T.O.

Army Form C. 2118.

WAR DIARY
or
INTELLIGENCE SUMMARY.
(Erase heading not required.)

AUGUST 1917. (Cont)

Place	Date	Hour	Summary of Events and Information	Remarks and references to Appendices
BEUVRY. F.21.a.5.2	Aug 5th		BILLETS. Various repairs done to Buildings & stairs improved.	
— do —	" 9th		COY. HORSELINES. Railway made good, repairs to Harness-Room roof & land.	
			I.O.R. Sick to Hospital.	
— do —	" 13th		The following work had been done since the 5th inst :-	
			NEW CUT TUNNEL - Hanging of 2 defensive gates completed.	
			QUARRY TUNNEL. Hanging of 3 defensive gates completed.	
			No. 13 Post. Repairing entrances to Nos 2 & 10 Posts completed. Dot No 7 Post & 1 at	
			TUNNELS - QUARRY, NEW CUT & SAVILLE TUNNELS - The curtain's repaired where damaged	
			GORDON ALLEY. Clearing & revetting in places, housemaiding and old revettments strengthened from West entrance to BARTS ALLEY - Also Butts Bridge crossing this Tunnel were shutted up.	
			QUARRY ALLEY. Clearing, revetting & housemaiding had been done & was shutted in Road from West entrance to RESERVE LINE - Also Butts Bridge crossing this tunnel were shutted up.	
			LEFT BOYAU. Repairing & revetting - 200 yds Completed.	
			BARTS ALLEY. Clearing, revetting & repairing & revetting revettments, housemaiding 100 yds. Completed.	
			MAISON ROUGE ALLEY. housemaiding & revetting. First 300 yds of track where needed.	
			TRILBY ALLEY. from OLD BOOTS to West entrance. revetted in places & cleared where blown in. Fallen in the bridge over this tunnel near Bell's H.Q. was re-constructed.	
			TRILBY ALLEY from OLD BOOTS to FRONT LINE. Cleared, revetted & repaired where blown in by "Minnies" - 40 yds. Completed - the whole tunnel was 2 day blown up - cleared up -	

[signature]
Capt. R.E.
7.O.C.

P.T.O.

WAR DIARY
or
INTELLIGENCE SUMMARY

Army Form C. 2118.

AUGUST 1917 (Contd)

Place	Date	Hour	Summary of Events and Information	Remarks and references to Appendices
BEUVRY F.21.a.5.2.	Aug 13		ROUTE No 2. Guide fence repaired. Filling in shell hole. repairs to bridge in Rear.	
			ROUTES: 120yds french boards laid along Route 7 at A.26.c.6.7. Bridge prepared for Route 6 over OLD BOOTS TRENCH (Ramps & Covers). Bridge over RAILWAY ALLEY completed on ROUTE 6. Bridge over OLD BOOTS for ROUTE 7 repaired after being damaged by shell fire.	
			CAMOUFLAGE O.P. - See removed from HUMANITY TRENCH & dumped at CAMBRIN.	
			No 5. M.G. EMP / MUNSTER TUNNEL. Entrance to Chamber completed. Chamber commenced. 3' excavated.	
			No 6. M.G. EMP / MUNSTER TUNNEL. Chamber completed. Gallery & Emplacement earth 3 feet of surface - east position of emplacement found correct. Repairing emplacement. Shuttering & revetting sides.	
			M.T.M. EMPT. G.4.c. 85.45. Chamber excavated to 7 feet. 3 frames fixed.	
			M.T.M. DUG-OUT at A.27.a. 95.20. New tunneling erected - Entrance repaired - completed	
			SIGNAL DUG-OUT - BRK ST. A.28.c. 31.18. Survey of dug-outs in CAMBRIN SECTOR completed, Las	
			FRONT TO VILLAGE LINE. Trench revetted at tank, duckboards laid	
			WATER SUPPLY: CENTRAL KEEP G.3.d.3. & dump - pits dug -	
			RESERVE LINE G.4.c. 3.6. Fixed tank in position with frames Erected trench / dug camp-fort, laid trench boards, dug up - brick & Laid 2" pipe from No 1 tank to No 2 Tank - filled kalt cocks rec- ROBACK ALLEY G.3.b.4.21. Deepening widening revetting trench at tank - laying duck boards - Moving Cover for 400 gal tanks completed.	

Richard Ullmann
Capt R.E.
O.C.

710

WAR DIARY
or
INTELLIGENCE SUMMARY

(Erase heading not required.)

Army Form C. 2118.

AUGUST 1917 (Contd)

Hour, Date, Place	Summary of Events and Information	Remarks and references to Appendices

August 13th. BEUVRY (F.21a.5.2)

WATER SUPPLY Cont.d

PUMPS: CAMBRIN. A.26.a.5.5. Pump repaired. Preventor Employed on fuel.
CAMBRIN. B.19.d.8.2. Being repaired.
ANNEQUIN. B.19.d.1.2. & F.30.a.2.6. N°s 28 & 27 repairs completed.

SUPPORT BATT H.Q. Rings repaired.

TRAMWAY. Light Rail provided up to night of 11th Line + 1 bridge repaired, also tracks repaired.
ANNEQUIN. F.30.c.7.4. A small bridge over stream at this point was erected for Infantry passage.

RESERVE LINE. G.10.8.7.9. Repairs to top of Cookhouse.

Bde. H.Q. Roof completed.
NOTICE BOARDS. removed from main Ln-BASSEE ROAD
Cy. BULLETS + Horse Lines repaired - road made round covered standing - Harness Room re- roofed.
A new Company Cook house was commenced &a.

Army Stores for 260 men.
1.O.R. Offrs Unit Iron. Roofs.
MAJOR. W. C. COOPER R.E. took over Command of the Coy.

The following work had been done since the 13th inst:-

QUARRY ALLEY. Cleaning, revetting & remaking West of RESERVE LINE - Special repairs where Retail had & RESERVE LINE. Duck Bridges over trench at Junctions Revetted

Mullen Capt
90.C.

P.T.O.

August 14th	do
" 16th	do
" 21st	do

WAR DIARY
or
INTELLIGENCE SUMMARY

Army Form C. 2118.

AUGUST 1917. (Cont'd)

Hour, Date, Place	Summary of Events and Information	Remarks and references to Appendices
August 22nd BEUVRY (F.21.a.5.2.)	GORDEN ALLEY. Clearing & revetting & connecting to Junction south. BORTS ALLEY – 3 bridges strengthened & revetted. CANDERN A.9.d.62. Domestic pump repaired – not giving a good supply. H.7.N.B. EMP. G.4.C. 85.45. Repairs to interior of emplacement completed. ROUTE 2, 3 & 4. Maintenance of fences, bridges on hand & self R.O. filled in rear posts. RESERVE LINE. G.4.a.1.1. Loads & bridge improved to give men more road room. DUG-OUTS IN P.SUB-SECTOR. Surveying, measuring & tabulating dug-outs completed. LEFT BOYAU. Clearing & revetting & reconnecting – about 200 yds done. BORTS ALLEY. Clearing & revetting between CENTRAL KEEP & RESERVE LINE & reconnecting – about 330 yds done. COOK-HOUSE G.10.a.6.8. Making new roof – delayed owing to lack of corrugated iron – connecting up second tank & RESERVE LINE. WATER SUPPLY. Making dumps & fitting pumps – orders at Batt. HQ. CENTRAL KEEP AND MUNSTER PARADE. Fitting tank. Overs – Cementing pipe at main tank. Leaving notice boards. RAILWAY ALLEY. Clearing & revetting where blown in. Mainly Joint Batt. AHO. – also clearing & revetting between old Batt. AHO – OLD BOOTS. Entrance to FACTORY TRENCH. Reconnecting. MUNSTER PARADE. Reconnecting. ROUTE 6. Revetting abutments of bridge over RAILWAY ALLEY AT G.3.a.8.3. DUNDEE WALK. Repairs to water tank started. M.G.E.E. New cold dump & emplacement nearly dug. Bomb-pit dug.	P.T.O. J. McMillan Capt. NZE % O.C.

WAR DIARY or INTELLIGENCE SUMMARY

Army Form C. 2118.

AUGUST 1917. (Cont'd.)

Hour, Date, Place	Summary of Events and Information	Remarks and references to Appendices
Aug. 22nd BEUVRY. (F.21a.5.2.)	M.G.E.5. 6th Lane G' Chamber filled. nearly ready. plat stair. M.T.M. Emp't. A.27a. 95.20. Chamber completed & Sponge frames fixed. ROUTE 1. Laying Joomies & shale fitt over swamp. Parang hand boards & putting in Special long pickets. Repairs to Bridge over OLD BOOTS. LEWIS ALLEY. Cleaning & boarding from OLD BOOTS to Front Line completed. MAISON ROUSE ALLEY. Cleaning f.t.6. Specially at rear and clearing a few bad bits. Front of OLD BOOTS forwards M.T.M. Emp't. A.27a. 95.20. Strengthening to L. Batt: H.Q. ROUTE 6. Making Ridge over trench. HUMANITY TRENCH. Silt cleared for about 100 yards. Coy. H.Q. Repairs to Billet 10% 80% finished. During Fatal 20% Odema. Improvements made to drainage - Cookhouse - Coal outside Table & C.Q.M.S. stores. Repairs to thomas hun - tarring roof. Making shelter benches, refuse covers & shelter traps &c. The officers of this Unit took over officers of 465 Coy. R.E. round the work with a view to handing over next day. Major W.C. Cooper took over C.R.E. 2nd Div. from Lt. Col. Betty, who proceeded on a month's leave. Capt. A.M. Matthews took over Command of Coy. 99 H & "U" Bde. were relieved by the 46th Division & 1st Cent 2nd little work of the Coy was handed over to the 465 & 2nd Coy R.E.	
23rd — do		
24th — do		

PTO

Arthur Stewart
Capt. R.E.
2/6 C.

WAR DIARY or INTELLIGENCE SUMMARY

Army Form C. 2118.

AUGUST 1917 (Cont)

Place	Date	Hour	Summary of Events and Information	Remarks and references to Appendices
LE TOURET.	Aug 25th		The Company including all Offrs Mate. (less 1 Section) moved to billets at LE TOURET, leaving BEUVRY at 11 a.m. & arriving at LE TOURET at 11 p.m. The men were billeted in Moor Huts 2 a great improvement after the huts inhabited when the Coy. were at this billet before. The whole of the Camp was in a dirty & dilapidated state & the whole Company was immediately put on clearing the camp.	
do	26th		2/Lieut. STEEL proceeded with his Section to OBLINGHEM (Map ref Sheet 36A S.E. N.20 d.1.3) to build a range for the use of the Division at 2nd Infantry School attached to their Batt'n. The 3 Sections 500 Chinese Natives & 150 labour men att.d were employed on clearing & repairing billets. A quantity of whitewash was found very necessary - standing. A road of decaux in-pl.k was commenced round the floor of the standing. The construction & erection of standing was taken up for 2 Coy's & a Forage store, Harness room & Hay shelter, repaired. A large quantity of timber & corrugated iron was salved from old embanked shelter which were pulled down.	
do	29th		O.C. & 2IC Officers of the Coy. went round the Left sector of GIVENCHY SECTOR with Officers of 5th F.C.R.E. with a view to taking over the work next day.	
do			I.O.R. left to days.	
do	30th		The Company took over the Left Sector of GIVENCHY SECTOR (L.F. & R. Sub) from No. 2 Coy 4th L. Cohort concealed as follows:- Construction of Concrete M.G. Emp.t. S.27 a. 05. 02. of Shelter for a Coy. H.Q. in BARNTON TCE. A 3 a. 50. 65. Epsom to Willans French S.21 d. Epsom to Camouflage screens.	

Huhsahand
Cap.t A.C.

P.T.O.

WAR DIARY or INTELLIGENCE SUMMARY

Army Form C. 2118.

AUGUST 1917. (Cont.)

Place	Date	Hour	Summary of Events and Information	Remarks and references to Appendices
LE TOURET.	Aug 30th (Cont.)		Clearing BOAR BURN S.26.c. Sandbagging of Water tanks in the line. Construction G.O.P. in FESTUBERT S.25.d.6.9. Two Sections with Sappers & Mates were employed on this work, one by day - the other by night. The remaining Section continued the work on Rifle Standings & Billets & completed the Cook house & dining hall commenced at BEUVRY. Constructional work for the Range at OBLINGHEM was also commenced. I.O.R. & 5 Non Coms Offrs.	
do	" 31st.		Work as continued as for the days previous. Throughout the month the Coy. noted the Rifle Range twice a week & the majority of the Unit showed a marked improvement - The upkeep of Fort - Standing in the Bee Area was experienced by the Company. I.O.K. Lieut. & 6 Offrs.	

The following Secret Maps attd:-
CAMBRIN SECTOR. SCALE. 1/5,000.
GIVENCHY SECTOR (LEFT) - " 1/5,000.

Dunbar Laws
Capt. Off.
O.C.
483rd (E.A.) Fld. Coy. R.E.

483RD (EAST ANGLIAN) FIELD COMPANY, R.E.
No. P.R.
Date. 5/9/17.

o/s

6/s

X

2nd Divisional Engineers

483rd (East Anglian) FIELD COMPANY R. E.

SEPTEMBER 1917.

WAR DIARY or INTELLIGENCE SUMMARY

Army Form C. 2118.

483 2nd Coy R.E.

SEPTEMBER 1917.

Vol 29

Place	Date	Hour	Summary of Events and Information	Remarks and references to Appendices
LE TOURET	SEPT. 1st		Work in hand at the end of August was continued.	
"	3rd		2/Lieut Fey proceeded with his Section to billets in LANNERVIN & commenced work on the Improvement of the Construction of Concrete Gun Emplacements in the Rue area. The two remaining Sections worked on the O.P. Billets, Horse Standings, also the Constructional work for the range & section of Mess Coy. Cookhouse & dining hall at BEUVRY.	
"	4th		Work was continued as for day previous in the morning – Musketry instruction was given in the afternoon to 1 and 4 Sections. Continued the programme to the 9th inst inclusive. A musketry Competition was held between Nos 2 Sections to decide which should represent the Coy on the Divl R.E. Competition. No. 3 Section continued work on Gun emplacements in Rue area & O.P.s 2 Lieut Fey continued work on Rifle Range at OBLINGHEN – which was completed on the 9th inst.	
"	9th		I.O.R. reported Water from Stops. Officers made a reconnaissance of Left Sector, GIVENCHY with a view to taking over the work from the 5th Field Coy R.E. next day as 2nd Coy R.E. was taken over from 5th Field Coy 162. work in Left Sector, GIVENCHY Section repairs to Camouflage Screens.	
"	10th		This consisted of :– S.21d. SHETLAND ROAD – Widening, Levelling, Clearing. S.25d. S.26 a c. CAILLOUX CANAL. Completing construction. S.25b. 6.1. O.P. PESTUBERT. S.20 d. 3.3. O.P. RUE-DE-CAILLOUX (Bluey) Repairing damage caused by shell fire. S.26 a. 3.9. O.P. COVER TRENCH. Strengthening Loophole in Front Line. A.3 a. 6.6. BRENTON TEE. Coy. H.Q. Completing Hut that Was. No Sappers were sent to 5th Fd. Coy for Work at Divl R.E. Workshops – No. 2 Section returned from OBLINGHEN. I.O.R. Sick to Hospital.	

463-
[signature] Capt
O.C. 483 Coy R.E.
P.T.O.

Army Form C. 2118.

WAR DIARY
or
INTELLIGENCE SUMMARY

SEPTEMBER 1917

(Erase heading not required.)

Instructions regarding War Diaries and Intelligence Summaries are contained in F.S. Regs., Part II. and the Staff Manual respectively. Title Pages will be prepared in manuscript.

Place	Date	Hour	Summary of Events and Information	Remarks and references to Appendices
LE TOURET	Sept 11th		Nos 1 + 2 Sections continued the Coy. work at this date was a follows:— No.1 + 2 Sections in Sept Sector, GIVENCHY. No.3 Section on Gun Emplacements in Div. Sector. No. 4 Section – 14 men at Div. H.E. Workshops, the remainder working on Coy. Horse Standing, Gas Cookhouse & Dining Shed at BEUVRY. It appears impossibility. Construction of Horse Standings in Div. Area. 2/Lieut F.A. KENNEDY was recalled to England for duty.	See Appx Letter No. of Engineers 4/3th (M.S.12) 4pl. 30/7.9/M3; N°A/27578/2330 c.m 5H
—	13th		2nd Lieuts — were detailed in that time — I.O.R. — Regimnl Unit from Hospital.	
— —	15th 16th		I.O.R. Lieut D. HOPE 2/Lieut G.W. RUDDLE James Unit (Reinforcement)	
—	17th		I.O.R. Lieut Unit (Reinforcement)	
—	19th		I.O.R. Sick to Hosp	
			Work continued. The 19th met mid-work in the Left Sector – GIVENCHY Officers of 5th Field Coy. N.E. made a reconnaissance of the work in order to take over the next day. The only work to be carried over was the repair of SHETLAND ROAD. Casing of Pillbox Corps and erection of Camouflage Screen in the Sector, all the other work started on the 11th inst having been completed.	
BEUVRY	20th		5th Field Coy. N.E. took over work in GIVENCHY Left Sector 1403 (G.S.) 5th Corps, N.E. moved to old Billets in BEUVRY (F21.a.5.2) Starting at 10 am Warning at 11.35 am. – No. 4 Section took over billets from No. 3 Section in ANNEQUIN. – The latter Section returning to BEUVRY.	
BEUVRY F21.a.5.2.	21st		5th Field Coy. N.E. the work on Gun Emplacements in Ligny Group was handed over to the 5th Field Coy. N.E. The Coy. paraded for Horse's Gas Helmet Drill, & afterwards cleaned up billets. The Coy. & An ‘arch aromas' came. Officer made a reconnaissance of the Cambrin Sector in order to take over the work from the 465th Fld Coy. N.E. Next day.	
—	22nd		Coy took over work in Cambrin Sector from 465th Fld Coy. R.E. which consisted as follows:—	4834 (En) Coy. R.E. P.T.O

J. Whitemann
Capt.

WAR DIARY or INTELLIGENCE SUMMARY

Army Form C. 2118.

(Erase heading not required.)

SEPTEMBER 1917.

Place	Date	Hour	Summary of Events and Information	Remarks and references to Appendices
BEUVRY. F.21a.5.2.	Sept 22nd 1917		G.4a.6.10. to G.4a.1.5. RAILWAY ALLEY. Repairing trench fr. revetting, & carrying 'A' frames etc. from Dump to Bomb store. also stonemailing.	
			G.3a.6.2. to G.4a.2.3. QUARRY ALLEY. Stonemailing etc.	
			G.4a.4.3. QUARRY TUNNEL. Repairing 3 Gas-proof doors.	
			A.27a.8.1.X. A.27d.1.7. OLD BOOTS TRENCH. Repairing trench, general revetting. also widening & deepening.	
			A.27a.9.8. A.27a.8.1. MAISON ROUGE ALLEY. Stonemailing.	
			A.27c.4.3. HUMANITY TRENCH & LEWIS ALLEY. Repairing floor of Dug-outs.	
			RAILWAY ALLEY.	
	26th		No 4 Section & No 2 Section moved to hills at 465.R.26/Old ANNEQUIN (F.23d.4.5.) after the day's work - 52 Sappers Wales (1st N.R.C.) joined Unit.	
			Major W.C. Cooper returned from M.O.R.E. & took over Command of the Coy.	
			Two Infantry Officers were attd to the Company from 22nd R. Fus. & 23rd R. Fus. respectively.	
	30th		The work in hand at the end of the month was as follows:-	
			OLD BOOTS TRENCH. G.4a. 05.50. Improving from RAILWAY ALLEY northwards.	
			M.G. EMPLACEMENT. A.27d.5.2. Breaking out of surface. floors dug out, making Bomb-pit & erecting gas curtains.	
			ROUTE. 7. A.26a.3.5. Laying facines across swamp at this point.	
			FRONT LINE. A.27b.v.d.	
			OLD BOOTS. A.27a.c.d. Repairing, renewing gas curtains.	
			SIDINGS. 1.v.2. A.27a.	
			SHELTERS. A.26d.6.5. Work on entrance.	
			VILLAGE LINE. A.26b.75.40. Erection of Belt getting shelter for M.G.	

3)

P.T.O.

Army Form C. 2118.

WAR DIARY
or
INTELLIGENCE SUMMARY

(Erase heading not required.)

SEPTEMBER 1917

Place	Date	Hour	Summary of Events and Information	Remarks and references to Appendices
BEUVRY F.21.a.5.2	Sept. 30TH		OLD BOOTS TRENCH. A.27.a.5.1 X A.27.d.1.7 RAILWAY ALLEY. TUNNELS. C.T's. BDE. H.Q. RECREATION ROOM BEUVRY. Work under C.R.E. DIV. DRAFT SCHOOL. 9TH BATTY. R.F.A. (VESPERS) F.24.d.4.8. Improving revetting with "A" frames. Improving revetting near front end. Fixing Anti-Gas doors. Revetment of all C.T.S. & RESERVE LINE and OLD BOOTS TRENCH. Repairs & glazing - making new etc. Constructing Sleeping room, Bunks, two new Windows & various repairs. Fixing joists & Gallery. Creating & construction of new shamrock pit in land. Musketry Training was continued throughout the month. The rifle range was used twice a week - The Lines are in very good condition & look as if they will face the coming winter well - The system of "Central Messing" has proved most successful - The Cooking for the Company was centralized & a dining hall made for the men. Note:- For locating maps reference re given herewith, reference should be made to War Diary for August 1917. Arthur Owens Capt. R.E. O/C 483rd (E.A.) Coy R.E. 483/(E.A.) Coy R.E.	

483RD
(EAST ANGLIAN)
FIELD COMPANY, R.E.

Copy

2nd Division No.
G.S. 1197/Gen/87.

C.R.E. 2nd Division.

I have been shown a report on the handing over of the CAMBRIN Section by the 483rd Field Coy. R.E. to the 465th Field Coy. R.E. in which the C.R.E. 46th Division says how satisfactory the handing over was.

I am very glad to have seen this good report, & I shall be glad if you will convey to the 483rd Field Coy. R.E. my thanks for the very excellent work they have carried out in that Section.

Signed. G.E. Pereira
Major-General,
Commanding 2nd Division.

6th September, 1917.

(Office Copy of)

Handing over Report.

483rd (E.A.) Fd. Coy. R.E. to 465th F.Coy. R.E.

> 483RD
> (EAST ANGLIAN)
> FIELD COMPANY, R.E.
> No. OK
> Date 24/8/17

CAMBRIN SECTOR.

Copy

Handing-over Report by
483rd (E.A) Fd Coy. R.E. to 465th Fd Coy. R.E.

Cambrin Sector.

1. DESCRIPTION & BOUNDARIES.
The Sector is divided into two Sub-Sectors known respectively as CAMBRIN RIGHT and CAMBRIN LEFT.

CAMBRIN RIGHT. The boundaries of these are as follows:- SOUTHERN Boundary - CLIFFORD ST. along GORDON ALLEY as far as G.10.b.0.8.6.8. & thence along communication trench to G.10.a.7.7.4.7. The whole Exclusive. NORTHERN Boundary. Junction of RAILWAY ALLEY & front line at G.4.a.6.8.9.7. RAILWAY ALLEY to Left Battⁿ H.Q. Railway Line to BRAYS KEEP - The whole Exclusive.

CAMBRIN LEFT. SOUTHERN Boundary as shewn for NORTHERN Boundary of CAMBRIN RIGHT but Inclusive. - NORTHERN Boundary Boyau 15 to its junction with BACK STREET - thence to junction of KINGSWAY & BURBURE ALLEY. BURBURE ALLEY then South of CAMBRIN to CARTER'S KEEP - all Exclusive.

2. LINES OF DEFENCE.
The present Lines of Defence are as follows:-

FRONT LINE or "A" LINE. is held by a series of Posts & kept open as far as possible for communication & patrolling.

RESERVE or "B" LINE. is main line of Defence, about 300 to 500 yards behind the Front line Posts. Named from Right to Left - RESERVE TRENCH - OLD BOOTS TRENCH.

VILLAGE LINE. This consists in the Right Sub-Sector of one main trench known as LANCASHIRE TRENCH continued into the Left Sub-Sector where it develops into parallel lines of trenches.

3. COMMUNICATIONS. FRONT to RESERVE LINE. Certain tunnels supplement & for the most part supercede existing communication trenches from "B" Line to "A" Line - These Tunnels are as follows, named from Right to Left.

R. SUB-SECTOR. SAVILLE ROW - NEWCUT & QUARRY -

L. SUB-SECTOR. MUNSTER.

P.T.O

3. COMMUNICATIONS.
Cont'd.

Of the Communication Trenches in Right Sub-Sector, LEFT BOYAU, BARTS & SAVILLE ROW are passable, but in a spooky state of repair.

Of the Left Sub Section RAILWAY ALLEY & LEWIS ALLEY are ~~very~~ good to the front line posts.

DUNDEE WALK is passable - MUNSTER PARADE is now blocked up.

From RESERVE LINE westwards. most of the communication trenches are good.

RIGHT SUB-SECTION - BARTS ALLEY from RESERVE LINE to railway is good. From this point Westwards, BARTS ALLEY has not been kept up & GORDON ALLEY is used, which is in very good repair. GORDON ALLEY, East of Railway Line has not been kept in repair.

LEFT BOYAU and QUARRY ALLEY are in good condition from RESERVE LINE to Western entrance.

LEFT SUB-SECTION. RAILWAY ALLEY, MAISON ROUGE ALLEY and MUNSTER PARADE are in good condition from RESERVE LINE to Western entrance. LEWIS ALLEY has not been kept up.

4. LATERAL TRENCHES.

VIGO and NORTHAMPTON TRENCH in Right Sub-Sector are passable - Otherwise the trenches between Front & RESERVE LINE are practically derelict.

RESERVE or "B" Line, although clear, is badly in want of repair & requires skilled labour on it.

RAILWAY RESERVE is good between LEFT BOYAU & QUARRY ALLEY - CANNON STREET is in a fair condition.

HUMANITY TRENCH is in a good state of repair. This work was done with a view to reclaiming LEWIS ALLEY from its junction with HUMANITY TRENCH to RESERVE LINE

There are two connections between RAILWAY ALLEY and QUARRY ALLEY, one by Right Batt-H.Q and the other by Left Batt-H.Q. These cuttings are in good condition.

Very little work has been done on the VILLAGE LINE and it is not in a good state of repair, especially in the Right Sector.

P.T.O

5. R.E. Dumps.   There are two R.E. Advanced dumps - one at CAMBRIN (A.26.c.1.1.) for Left Battⁿ Area & one at CLARKE'S KEEP (G.8.a.9.8) for Right Battⁿ area. In each of these dumps there is a Reserve Dump in case of an enemy retirement.
   List of Stores at each Dump - attached.

6. Routes. (1 to 7) See Route Map.   Nº 1 is in good condition up to QUARRY ALLEY - From there eastwards it is in bad condition - Nº 2 & 4 are in good condition as far as Railway line - From there, they are badly pitted with shell holes - The whole of Nº 3 is in good condition.
   The bridges of Nos. 1, 2 & 4 are in good condition up to RESERVE LINE, with the exception of bridge on Nº 1 Route between RAILWAY and QUARRY ALLEY - The bridges of Nº 3 Route require attention. Nºˢ 5 & 6 are in good condition to RESERVE LINE - A bridge is stored at CAMBRIN DUMP in readiness for Nº 6 to cross RESERVE LINE - it is not advisable to place this bridge until required. Route Nº 7 is flooded at its crossing over the stream at A.26.a.5.5. - A road has been commenced at this point to enable traffic (cookers) to get to the quarry at the entrance of RAILWAY ALLEY. This Route is otherwise in good condition up to RESERVE LINE.

7. Drains.   The main drain of the CAMBRIN SECTOR is the stream running from FOUNTAIN KEEP (G.2.c.) North to CAMBRIN at A.20.c. Infantry parties from the RESERVE Battⁿ have cleared this stream from FOUNTAIN KEEP to the railway line at A.26.c - about 50% completed.   A system of drains in G.2.c running Westwards to the main drain have also been cleared. This work has been under the supervision of R.E.
   Working party 4 hours daily, 1 Officer 20 men.

8. Water Supply. (See report to 99th Infy Bde attd).

P.T.O.

9. WORK IN HAND. The following are the Works in hand:—

(a) Repair & upkeep of

BARTS ALLEY — From railway line in G.9a. to RESERVE LINE.
GORDON ALLEY — From Western entrance to railway line in G.9a.
LEFT BOYAU — From Western entrance to RESERVE LINE.
QUARRY ALLEY. " "
RAILWAY ALLEY. FRONT LINE.
MUNSTER PARADE. RESERVE LINE.
LEWIS ALLEY — OLD BOOTS to Front Line.
MAISON ROUGE ALLEY from Western Entrance to RESERVE LINE.

(b) Clearing of LEWIS ALLEY from HUMANITY TRENCH to OLD BOOTS.

(c) Repair & upkeep of ROUTES 1 to 7 inclusive. Repair of Route 1 from QUARRY ALLEY to RAILWAY ALLEY. Construction of road over flooded portion of Route 7 at A.26.a.5.5. 20x of road is completed & 40x of fascines laid.

(d) Construction of No. 5. M.G. Emplacement off MUNSTER TUNNEL — The dug-out for the crew is completed except the revetting of the walls — 5 steps of the gallery to the M.G. Emplacement have been fixed — Sandbags are emptied by party supplied by M.G. Coy. in MUNSTER PARADE forward of OLD BOOTS.

(e) Construction of dug-out for M.T.M. Empt. off MAISON ROUGE at A.29.a.95.20. — The chamber only requires distance pieces & revetting — The shaft is damaged by shell fire & requires repairing. About 8' of earth has yet to be excavated to connect up the shaft with the chamber.
A party of 4 men to empty sandbags &c. was supplied by T.M. Batt.y.

(f) Camouflaging of roads in ANNEQUIN on the North side of BETHUNE – LA-BASSEE road.

10. PROPOSED WORK. All the Communication trenches require a Berm before the winter sets in — This is of course a very big job & night work. M.G. No. 8. near junction of WILSON'S TUNNEL and OLD BOOTS (just North of your Div.l boundary) is to be made. Site not yet definitely selected — Though it is in the Bde area on your left it will be constructed by you as it covers your front. — Revetment of unrevetted communication trenches in worst & most important parts —
The back part of RAILWAY ALLEY is important.

P.T.O.

10. PROPOSED WORK CONT^D.

SAVILLE ROW in front of entrance to Tunnel particularly to be improved.

BARTS. ALLEY in front of RESERVE LINE to be improved, particularly close behind NORTHAMPTON TRENCH.

VIGO STREET to be improved.

LEFT BOYAU in front of RESERVE LINE to be improved.

RESERVE LINE - OLD BOOTS - general reconstruction.

The defensive gates at the Eastern entrances of the tunnels require attention.

Dug-outs to be numbered & good, but dirty, ones to be cleaned.

L.T.M's - Several deep emplacements have been suggested.

WATER SUPPLY. Proposed pipe from about G.3.d.2.4 to Cookhouse near junction of BERWICK TRENCH and DUNDEE WALK. Tank at G.3.d.3.8. should be scraped & painted inside & tank at G.3.d.6.1. is leaking & should be repaired.

Copy of Report to 99th Inf. Bde.

Fountain Keep Water Supply.

1. This supply is pumped from Fountain Keep to a 1,600 gallon tank near Right Battn H.Qrs — G.3.d.3.5. There are two gravity pipes from this tank — one to MUNSTER PARADE and one to RESERVE TRENCH. Water can be obtained at following points:—

   (a) Main tank. G.3.d.3.5 — tap.

   (b) R. Battn H. Qrs. G.3.c.4.0 — tap

   (c) Dry well off Quarry Alley. Two 150 gallon tanks with taps at G.3.c.3.1.
   These tanks are supplied by a tap which must be turned off by the troops. They should be filled during pumping hours — about 9 a.m to 10-30 a.m.

   (d) Two 400 gallon tanks with taps and supply regulated by ball valve at junction of OLD. BOOTS. TRENCH and MUNSTER. PARADE. — A. 27 d 3.1.

   (e) A 200 gallon tank with tap at CENTRAL. KEEP — G.3 d.6.1.

   (f) A 400 gallon tank with taps & ball valve at RESERVE. LINE — G. 4 c 2.7. Another similar is being fixed in RESERVE. LINE 50 yards South of this & will be ready in a day or two.

2. There is a tell-tale on main tank to shew how much water there is in it. If enough water is not pumped, reference should be made by the Battn in the line in the first instance to the 2 men of 350th E & M Coy: R.E. who are i/c of pumps and line at FOUNTAIN KEEP. If satisfaction is not obtained, reference should be made to the Field Coy: R.E. of the CAMBRIN. SECTOR. to whom also any other defects should be referred.

3. Troops should not attempt to interfere with the ball-valves themselves.

4. It is hoped that taps will be properly turned off when not in use.

5. The water may be rusty for a bit, but this will disappear in time.

6. Notice boards are fixed giving instructions as to the proper control of these tanks etc.

(Signed) C. Cooper.
Major. R.E
483rd (EA) Field Coy. R.E.

General Condition of Trenches.

LATERAL TRENCHES.

FRONT LINE. — A series of posts in a fair state of repair, partially connected up by a trench.

NORTHAMPTON TR: & VIGO TRENCH. — Passable but in a bad condition.

RESERVE LINE. — Clear & duckboarded, but if not soon attended to with skilled labour, will collapse.

RAILWAY RESERVE LINE. — Good from Quarry Alley to Left Boyau, remainder of this trench is in a bad condition.

CANNON STREET. — Good.

HUMANITY TRENCH. — Good.

VILLAGE LINE. — Fair.

1, 2, & 3. SIDINGS. — Fair.

COMMUNICATIONS.

BARTS ALLEY — From railway line in G.Q.a to Reserve Line — good. Remainder of trench — fair.

GORDON ALLEY — From Western entrance to railway line in G.Q.a — good. Remainder of trench not kept in repair.

LEFT BOYAU — From Western entrance to Reserve Line good. Remainder to Front Line — fairly good.

QUARRY ALLEY. — From Western entrance to Quarry — good. Remainder — derelict.

RAILWAY ALLEY — From Western entrance to front line — good.

MUNSTER PARADE. — From Western entrance to Reserve Line — good. Remainder now blocked up.

LEWIS ALLEY. — From Old Boots to Front line — good. Remainder to Western entrance — passable.

MAISON ROUGE ALLEY. — From Western entrance to Reserve Line — good. Remainder to Front Line cannot be used.

LIST OF DOCUMENTS.

* 1. Handing over Report.
2. R.E. Stores lists at Cambrin & Clarks Keep Dumps.
* 3. List of Maps and Plans etc.
4. 99th Infantry Brigade letter No. B.M(S) 1049. "Instructions in the event of an enemy retirement."
5. 99th Infantry Brigade Defence Scheme, with appendices:- A, B, C, D, E, F, G, H and J, also amendment No: 1 and addendum Nos 2 & 3 to this Defence Scheme and B.M(S) 1110.
6. Anti-tank measures - 66th Divisional R.E.s No. S.C.9/14
7. Communication trenches. - Special progress report - 432nd Field Coy. R.E. - No. S.C.3.
8. Boundaries - 66th Divisional R.E - No: O.P. 1/3.
9. List of communication trenches - 66th Div: R.E.
10. Report on M.G.Es - 66th Div: R.E.
11. Report on Keeps.
12. 99th Infantry Bde. B.M.(S) 1051 and B.M.(S) 1098. Reference Nos. 5, 6 and 8 emplacements.
13. Tunnels - 99th Inf: Bde. B.M.(S) 1038 and tracing B.M(S) 1038.

* Office Copy kept Abe

Received above Documents.

Willis
Major R.E
O.C. 465 Field Coy R.E.

23.8.17

LIST OF PLANS DRAWINGS & DETAILS of the CAMBRIN SECTOR HANDED OVER to the 465th FIELD Co: R.E.

August 24th 1917.

12	TRENCH MAP	36^c N.W.3	(LOOS)		
7	" "	36^c N.W.			
2	" "	36^c N.W.1	(LA BASSEE)		
1	MAP	36^c N.E.2	(BEUVRY)		
2	"	36^c N.E.4	(NŒUX-LES-MINES)		
1	TRENCH MAP	CAMBRIN SECTOR	1:10,000		

~~1~~	~~CAMBRIN SECTOR~~	~~D.L.A.~~	~~GENERAL MAP~~	~~1:5,000~~	~~PRINT~~
1	" "	D.I.	" " & Water Supply.	1:5,000	LINEN TRACING
5	" "	" "	" "	1:10,000	PRINTS
1	" "	" "	TRENCH "	1:5,000 (in 2 parts)	PRINT
1	" "	" "	" "	1:5,000 " "	LINEN TRACING
1	" "	" "	DEFENCE "	1:10,000	PRINT (BLUE)
1	" "	" "	WATER SUPPLY	1:10,000	LINEN TRACING
1	"	" "	ROUTE "	1:10,000	PRINT.
1	"	" "	ROUTES 1 to 5 revised with notes.	1:10,000	LINEN TRACING
1	"	" "	M.G.E. & T.M.	1:5,000	LINEN TRACING.
1	"	" "	CAMBRIN N. to LOOS S.	1:20,000	PRINT.
2	"	" "	NEW CUT TUNNEL	1:800.	LINEN TRACING.
2	"	" "	SAVILLE "	1:800.	" "
2	"	" "	QUARRY "	1:800.	" "
1	"	" "	ENLARGED MAP SQUARE A 28c.	1:500.	PRINT.
1	"	" "	" " " A.14c.	1:2500.	"
2	"	" "	MAPS MARKED A & B SQUARES RESPECTIVELY.	1:500	"
1	"	" "	Crater Map.	1:16000	Tracing
1		MAP OF CANAL BETHUNE to LA BASSEE		1:10,000	LINEN TRACING

1	CAMBRIN SECTOR		BOYS KEEP	1:500	LINEN TRACING
1	" "		LEWIS	1:500	

1	CAMBRIN SECTOR	BULLY KEEP.	1:500.	LINEN TRACING.
1	" "	INGLIS "	1:500	" "
1	" "	CLARKES "	1:1000	" "
1	" "	FOUNTAIN "	1:500.	" "
1	" "	RAILWAY (RIGHT) "	1:500	" "
1	" "	" (LEFT) "	1:500	" "
1	" "	CHURCH (WEST) "	1:500	" "
1	" "	" (MORE) "	1:360.	" "
1	" "	CENTRAL KEEP	1:500	" "
1	" "	ARTHURS.	1:500	" "
1	AEROPLANE PHOTOGRAPH	2 A 909.		
1	" "	2 AB 56		
1	" "	2 AB 106		
1	" "	2 AB 52		
1	" "	2 AB 48		
1	" "	2 AB 47		
1	" "	2 AB 347		
1	" "	2 AB 40		
1	" "	2 AB 105		
1	" "	2 AB 851		
1	" "	25 JB 100		
1	" "	25 JB 112		
1	" "	4 C 101		
1	" "	3 C 27		
1	" "	3 C 66		
1	" "	3 C 115		

PLAN of NEW STOREHOUSE & MESS ROOMS. (under construction)

1	AEROPLANE PHOTOGRAPH	No 14.	
1	" "	No 16.	
1	" "	No 22	
1	" "	No 25	

1	Aeroplane Photograph No 39.
1	" " No 45.
1	Plan shewing position of Nos 5 & 6 M.G. Empl.

Skilles
Major RE
OC. 465 Field Coy RE

24/8/17

2nd Divisional Engineers

483rd FIELD COMPANY R. E. ::: OCTOBER 1917.

Army Form C. 2118.

WAR DIARY
or
INTELLIGENCE SUMMARY
(Erase heading not required.)

OCTOBER, 1917.
483 2nd Coy.

Place	Date	Hour	Summary of Events and Information	Remarks and references to Appendices
BEUVRY	Oct. 1st		Work was continued as for the last month. On the night 1st/2nd, the Coy billeting area in BEUVRY was affected by Gas shell falling in the neighbourhood of ANNEQUIN – "GAS ALARM" was given and all ranks wore helmets for about 1 hour. The billets were practically free from Gas in spite of it being fairly thick outside.	
	3rd		A "Warning Order" was received saying that the 2nd Division would be relieved by the 25th Division & relief to be completed by 6 a.m. on the 5th inst. Eye witness states when it landed over on 5th inst – not yet met.	
	4th		Work continued, but contents were packed in anyone ready for moving. Kneading oven notes were prepared. The Coys' Mess & attached Offrs' Mess packed up. 2 Officers returned to their Battn. (LIKERS) & advance party of 1 Officer & 5 O.Rs. went to FANQUEVENHEM (near a billeting party of the Coy to go into next day. An advance orderly was received at 7 o.p.m. saying no billets were obtainable at BUSNETTES and no further order than received from C.R.E. to say the Coy would proceed to billets at BUSNETTES in G.T. mise –	
	5th	10.0 p.m.	Order by C.R.E. were received, confirming 'phone message of night before. The billeting party at FANQUEVENHEM were taken by lorry (to BUSNETTES) to arrange billets for the Company.	
		8.0 a.m.	O.C. 105th Ft Coy R.E. arrived to take over billets work of this Coy.	
		12 noon	The Coy moved billets from BEUVRY at 1.15 p.m. – Major Cooper with 1 Officer & 2 O.R's remained billeted to hand over the work –	
BUSNETTES		4.30 p.m.	The Coy. arrived at BUSNETTES – Billets were poor compared with billets in the line handed over.	
	6th		Work in Line handed over. Kit inspection – weather very wet. Church Parade – Louis Gas. Drill.	
	7th to 31st		The Coy went into training which included Physical Drill, Infantry Sawing, Musketry, Entering, Map reading, Setting out trenches, Demolitions etc.	

George Ireland 2/Lt.
for O.C. 483 Ft Coy R.E.

Army Form C. 2118.

WAR DIARY
or
INTELLIGENCE SUMMARY
(Erase heading not required.)

OCTOBER 1917.

Place	Date	Hour	Summary of Events and Information	Remarks and references to Appendices
BUSNETTES	Oct. 10th		2/Capt. A.M. MATTHEWS proceeded to England on Leave (1 month - 11.9.17 to 10.11.17). Lieut. G. VEY taking over 2nd i/c Command of Coy.	
"	12th		Copy of 1st Army No. A 239 received saying that the Army Commander was pleased with the administrative arrangements of 2nd Div. while in XI Corps Area. 2/Lieut. G. STEEL proceeded to LABEUVRIÈRE to be medically examined by A.D.M.S. 1.O.R. Sick to Hosp. 2.O.R.	
"	14th			
"	15th		Letter received (XI Corps K.H.S. 1194/21) in which G.O.C. XI Corps spoke of the good work of the Field Companies while in his Corps Area. 1.O.R. Sick to Hosp.	
"	16th		2/Lieut. G. STEEL proceeded to No. 4 R.E. Base Depot, ROUEN (Medical Grounds) in accordance with 2nd Div. Q. 387/255 dd 13-10-17. Afterwards classified P.B. by medical board at Base. Inspection of Coy. at work by G.O.C. 2nd Divn. 1.O.R. rejoined Unit from Hosp.	
"	18th	11.30 a.m	One Section at work with Chinese Labour repairing Rifle Range at OBLINGHEM.	
"	21st 22nd 23rd		Divl. Machine gun Competition for the best R.E. Section in the 2nd Division held at RAIMBERT - The Pryse Cup given in this Competition was won by No. 1 Section of this Unit.	
"	22nd	10.30 a.m	2/Lieut. M.A. GRAHAM joined the Coy. from the Base. 1.O.R. rejoined Unit from Hospital. 1 Officer of the 1st K.R.R.C. att. to Coy.	
"	23rd			
"	2nd 21st 22nd 24th 30th		Work done in tidying up GONNEHEM CEMETERY (French) at request of Town Major. 1.O.R. Sick to Hospital.	
"	31st		The Mounted Section (including 1 Officer) together with horses & transport moved to GONNEHEM (N.18.d.9) where the horses were stabled in covered standings. This move was necessary on account of the bad state of the Horse-Lines at BUSNETTES. Lieut. J.H. KING evacuated sick to Hospital.	

Henley Lieut. M.So. O.C.
483/E.O.F. Coy R.E.

2nd Divisional Engineers

483rd FIELD COMPANY R. E. ::: NOVEMBER 1917.

Army Form C. 2118.

WAR DIARY
or
INTELLIGENCE SUMMARY

(Erase heading not required.)

483rd (E.A.) Field Coy. Royal Engineers.

NOVEMBER 1917.

Instructions regarding War Diaries and Intelligence Summaries are contained in F.S. Regs., Part II. and the Staff Manual respectively. Title Pages will be prepared in manuscript.

Place	Date	Hour	Summary of Events and Information	Remarks and references to Appendices
BUSNETTES	Nov 1st	8.30 a.m.	Coy continued training.	
"	2nd		Warning order received saying that the 99th Bde. could move on Nov. 5th to Mt. BERLIENCHON and on Nov. 6th to MERVILLE - NEUF-BERQUIN area	
"	3rd	4.15 p.m.	Warning order received saying that Coy. would move by bus on Nov. 4.	
"	4th	8.0 a.m.	Order received for Company to move to POPERINGHE.	
"	4th	10.0 a.m.	Mounted Section & Transport left GONNEHEM for MORBEQUE.	
POPERINGHE	5th	8.30 a.m.	Remainder of Company left BUSNETTES by bus for POPERINGHE. Mounted Section left MORBEQUE for EECKE. Remainder of Company left POPERINGHE for BRIELEN.	
POPERINGHE BRIELEN	6th	8.30 a.m.	On a very muddy route. Mounted Section left EECKE for BRIELEN. Major Cooper proceeded on leave to England. (7½ & 21½) - Lieut. Vey took over Command of Coy.	
BRIELEN B.30.c.10.9"	6th to 18th inclusive		Company commenced work on Roads at ST. JULIEN - C.12.c. 30.15. Sheet 28.N.W.2. This week work superintended by a Corps Roads Officer - R.E.	
"	9th		1.O.R. Wounded to Hospital.	
"	11th		Capt. A.G. McMathews returned from Leave & took over Command of Coy. 1.O.R. Sick to Hospital.	
"	12th to 18th inclusive		ST. JULIEN - POELCAPELLE ROAD - Work was continued on the road - Buses - hone - lines were made splendid - props from E.R. Coys.	
"	13th		Capt. J.B. Pett found Unit (Reinforcement.) also 1.O.R. (M.T.) (Reinforcement.) 1.O.R. Sick to Hosps.	
"	18th	3.30 p.m.	Orders received for Coy. to move 19th Nov. present billets & to move to WINNEZEELE	
POPERINGHE	19th	9.30 a.m.	Company left BRIELEN & marched to POPERINGHE - arrived at 1 p.m.	
"			Coy left POPERINGHE marched to WINNEZEELE - arriving at 1-30 p.m.	
WINNEZEELE	20th	7.30 a.m.	Inspection of Kit & Coy. Equipment was made -	
WINNEZEELE J.3.c.3.3."	21st		Physical Culture drill in the afternoon - 1.O.R. (M.T.) (Reinforcement) joined Unit.	
"	22nd		Major Cooper returned from Leave & took over Command of Company.	

483/(E.A.) F.Coy. R.E.
Capt. M.S. to O.C.

WAR DIARY
or
INTELLIGENCE SUMMARY

Army Form C. 2118.

(Erase heading not required.)

463 (Kent) Coy R.E.

NOVEMBER 1917.

Place	Date	Hour	Summary of Events and Information	Remarks and references to Appendices
WINEZEELE J.3.c.3.3.	Nov. 22nd	6:0 p.m.	Orders received that Coy were to be ready to move off at 2 hours notice after Orders received. All waggons were packed.	
ESQUELBECQ	23rd		Orders received that Company was to entrain at ESQUELBECQ at 9.0 p.m. The Mounted portion of Coy. moved off at 4.30 p.m. & the Dismounted portion at 6.30 p.m. & entrained at ESQUELBECQ about 10 p.m.	
BAPAUME	24th	11 a.m.	Coy. detrained at ACHIET-LE-GRAND & marched to Huts at BAPAUME - via BAPAUME, arriving at about 4 p.m.	
DOIGNIES	25th	6 a.m.	The Company marched to a valley just south of DOIGNIES (Sheet 57C J.15.d.9.7.) & there pitched camp. Upon arrival here, the Section immediately went forward to work on the repair of DOIGNIES–DEMICOURT ROAD –	
—	26th		Work continued on DOIGNIES–DEMICOURT RD. Manning, filling up shell hole & surfacing with rubble. – 50. R.R.C. and 50. Lancs Fusrs Regt reported for duty – Work on BAPAUME–CAMBRAI ROAD was taken over from – 512 Field Coy RE.	
—	27th		3 sections of Coy worked on BAPAUME/CAMBRAI Rd – repairing & laying concrete in conjunction with 565th (Army Troops) Coy R.E. (night work). 100 2nd Lanc. Infantry were also employed on this work. 1 Sect. worked on DEMICOURT–GRENICOURT ROAD, repairing & filling in shell hole. 1.O.R. wounded & to hospital.	
—	28th		Work cont'd on Jan. 27th. – No. 3 + 4 Sections moved to Gouzard bullets at E.28.d.4.3. (Sheet 57c N.E.) For work under 99th Inf. Bde. 1.O.R. Wounded & to hospital.	
BEAUMETZ J.20.b. Sheet 57c N.E.	29th		Coy. H.Q., No. 1 + 2 Sections & Transport struck camp in valley south of DOIGNIES owing to shires being very wet, shell-fire but still heavier than to be expected – new shires were made in the sunken road at J.20.b. (Sheet 57c N.E.) Two Tronqué Tents were made by Nos. 1 + 2 Sections at E.17.d.5.3 + E.18.c.0.0. – These were also arrived by 100 Infantry all returned to their respective Units	

Archibald
Capt.
463rd (Kent) Coy R.E.

P.T.O.

Army Form C. 2118.

WAR DIARY
or
INTELLIGENCE SUMMARY

NOVEMBER 1917.

A.83 CO (E.A.) FB Coy R.E.

Place	Date	Hour	Summary of Events and Information	Remarks and references to Appendices
BEAUMETZ T20.b. (Sheet 57cN.E.)	Nov 30		Ordered Nos 1 & 2 Sections to remain in war billets ready to move at a moment's notice. No 3 & 4 Sections were put at the disposal of C.O. of K.R.R.C. but were not called upon for action. The Strong Points made by Nos. 3 & 4 Sections are reported to have proved of the greatest value in repelling the enemy attack. Nos 3 & 4 Sections worked at the construction of Trenches & the connection of Shell holes to same. — In the course of the month, many new works took place. Lorry was supplied to assist the transport which was very useful. The transport was overloaded when there was no lorry, as blanket (2 per man) had to be carried. The horses stood up to the work well; they had been clipped during the month. — Unfortunately the Tarpaulins belonging to the WDs were very worn — otherwise they would have proved of the greatest value for Company during their loose nights. The equipment amount of Tench Cooks available from the Town Major — 5 Tarpaulins could tell most part the equipment of a Field Coy, it would tell very useful as they can the erection by young Sapper of equipment such as required for Cullets are of great value for Garage & Q.M. Stores, Cookery, Smith's Shed or Workshops etc.	Enemy attacked about 8.0 a.m. on 2nd Divl front – G.O.C. 99th Infy Bde C/O 3 & 4 Sections Underlined Capt LT RE O.C.

2nd Divisional Engineers

483rd FIELD COMPANY R. E. :: DECEMBER 1917.

Army Form C. 2118.

433RD (EAST ANGLIAN) FIELD COMPANY, R.E.

WAR DIARY
or
INTELLIGENCE SUMMARY.

423RD (EAST ANGLIAN) FIELD COY RE
(Erase heading not required.)

DECEMBER 1917.

Place	Date	Hour	Summary of Events and Information	Remarks and references to Appendices
BEAUMETZ. T.20.b.	Dec 1st		Strong Point at E.22.c.9.1. Consolidated & held. L.G. Team of 10 men – The two Strong Points at E.17.d.5.3. and E.18.c.0.0. were improved and wired – Work interfered with by enemy patrols. G.O.C. 99th Inf. Bde. ordered No. 3 & 4 Sections to move into forward billets for instruction.	
"	2nd		Inspection of site for forward billets was made – Owing to lack of accommodation only No.1 Section moved forward, with material for making billets for the two Sections and advanced Coy. H.Q. at K.13.d.9.4. No. 3 & 4 Sections worked on digging trenched Cut-trench to connect up Post at E.22.d.0.5. with Front Line at E.22.c.95.50.? Also digging a trench from Batt. H.Q. at E.22.d.0.2. to Coy. H.Q. at E.22.d.35.25.	
"	3rd	8.0 a.m.	No. 2 Section moved forward to Advanced Billets – afterwards working on erection of anti-gas curtains for dug-outs at and near Bde. H.Q. No. 1 Section worked on near Coy Billets at E. 20.a.1.8.	
BERTINCOURT. T.7.d.	4th		Orders received that 2nd Division were to retire to a new line and that 183rd Field Coy. R.E. would be responsible for blowing up dug-outs and O.P.s etc. in the line to be evacuated. – H.Q. and transport moved to near billets in P.1.d. On night of 4/5. 30 dug-out entrances were blown in and 30 dug-out entrances were prepared for demolition. A body-trap was laid in the Sugar Factory. Nos. 1, 3 & 4 Sections employed on demolition of dug-out entrances, O.P.s and M.G. Emplacements.	
"	5th		No. 2 Section carried up explosives & did similar work.	
"	6th		No. 3 & 4 Sections returned to billets at T.20.b. – No. 1 Section remained in the line to complete demolition of dug out entrances, etc.	
BEAUMETZ. T.20.b.	7th		No. 1 Section returned to billets at T.20.b. – H.Q. & green billeted tent No. 2 Shelter at T.20.b. Nos. 3 & 4 Sections went to billets at P.1.d. – H.Q. (Res Transport) returned to billets at T.20.b. A Survey was commenced of all dug-outs in New Div: Front.	
"	8th		Sites for large Bde. R.E. H.Q. and Eng.r. Shelters were selected at T.36.c.8.4. & 6.3 respectively, and arrangements made to commence work next day. Rear Billets were improved. Work also commenced on dismantling 5 main Shifts.	
"	9th		Survey of dug-outs continued & making H.Q.s of Trench & Eng.r. Shelters dug into the bank employed – Dismantling standing by 6 Main Shifts Completed – Rear billets improved.	

P.T.O.

WAR DIARY or INTELLIGENCE SUMMARY

483rd (East Anglian) Field Company, R.E.

Army Form C. 2118.

DECEMBER 1917.

Place	Date	Hour	Summary of Events and Information	Remarks and references to Appendices
BERNY E.72. X.20.8.	Dec. 10th		Work continued as for 9th inst. 1.O.R. (Reinforcements) joined Unit.	
"	" 11th		Capt. A.H. Matthews & No. 522 Sergt. R. Peacock mentioned in despatches. Work on H.Q's continued with working party of 100 Sapprs. Dug-out survey & plan completed. Improvement & restoration of front billets continued. 1.O.R. Sick & Coys.	
BERTINCOURT. P.14.	" 12th		Work on H.Q's continued. Tracing of 5 Mason Huts superintended - Officers & N.C.O.'s No. 2 Section made a reconnaissance of the line - Work on rear billets continued. Also moved to rear billets.	
"	" 13th		Sapr. Hickerson killed. Jl. Cpl. Kirk, Sapr. Howe & Sapr. Hibbins wounded. Work continued as for 12th inst.	
"	" 14th		Work continued as for 13th inst. Officers No. 1 Section made reconnaissance of the line.	
"	14th/15th night		No. 2 Section erected No. 2 Post K.9.7.9. 130' double apron fence. ½ Coy. D.C.L.I. employed in carrying the material.	
"	" 15th		No. 3rd Section arrived on H.Q's.	
"	15th/16th night		Sapr. Parrack killed. (1 Officer & wounded). No. 2 Section & 20. D.C.L.I. carrying party erected No. 3 Post K.10 a.25.88. 100' double apron fence commenced. - Enemy M.G. fire interrupted the work - 1.O.R. Sick & Shops 15th.	
"	" 16th		No. 1 Section repaired screens for places on Railway 7 at K.15 c.85-15.	
"	16th/17th night		No. 3rd Section worked as for 15th inst.	
"	" 17th		No. 2 Section completed work of night before - No. 1 Section continued screening. No. 3rd Section worked as for 16th inst.	
"	17th/18th "		No. 2 Sect with 20.D.C.L.I. put up wire in front of Kellet Trench. No. 1 Section 2.O.R. Sick & 24 yrs.	
"	" 18th		Continued screening of Railway.	
"	18th/19th night		No. 3rd Section continued work as for 17th. No. 1 Section put up screening across canal at K.9.2.4.4. No. 2 " erected stops in Canal bank.	
"	" 19th		No. 3rd Section continued work as for 18th.	

P.T.O.

483rd (E.A.) Fld Coy. R.E.

WAR DIARY or INTELLIGENCE SUMMARY

Army Form C. 2118.

483rd (EAST ANGLIAN) FIELD COMPANY, R.E.

INTELLIGENCE SUMMARY. DECEMBER, 1917.
483/(EAST ANGLIAN) FIELD ONE.

Place	Date	Hour	Summary of Events and Information	Remarks and references to Appendices
BERTINCOURT P.I.d.	Dec 19/20 night		No.1 Section completed screening "Canal bank" & taped out a communication trench from WATSON TRENCH to Fort Louis. K.9.d.8.8 to K.10.a. 10.35. Complete steps to Canal bank & trench.	
"	20th		No.3 & 4 Sections continued work as for 19th inst. No.1 & 2 Sections worked on Coy billets & horse-standings. Work on forward area handed over to 57th FIELD Coy R.E. 10.O.R. (Reinforcement) joined Unit.	
"	21st		Work continued as for 20th inst. 3 O.R.s sick to Hosp.	
"	22nd		No.1 Section laced out with tape "Intermediate" line at K.14.a.c.d. + 20.a. (Sheet 57 N.E.) also marking outside belt of wire entanglement with angle iron pickets & plan wire in 50 x bays.	
"	23rd		No.2 Section worked on Coy billets & horse standings. Nos 3 & 4 Sections as for 21st inst. No.1 Section as for 22nd inst. 1 O.R. Sick to Hosp.	
"	24th		Nos. 2.3.4 Sections as for 23rd inst. 1 O.R. Sick to Hosp.	
"	25th		No.1 Section as for 22nd inst. Old Boche wire cut & placed in position for passage of troops. Nos 2.3.4 Sections as for 23rd. 1 O.R. Sick to Hosp. No.3 & 4 Sections on Canal bank & plank trench road at J.36 - No.2 Section at work on Camp P.d. huts & horse standings. No.1 Section noted.	
"	26th		No.1 Section worked on "Intermediate" line wiring - part of Section on Coy billets. No.2 Section on 36th & 49th Bdes R.F.A. (J.36.) shelters - section sent to improvement. No.2 Section at 5th R Coy R.E. Officers' Billets at K.20.c. (Sheet 57 N.E.) Sections on Coy billets. Nos. 3 & 4 Section practised to Adv. Billets at K.20.c. (Sheet 57 N.E.) Telephone was on Gotham. (1) Deepening & widening & cleaning & general improvement of trench in & leading to FORT GEORGE (K.8.9 + 14.) (2) Dug-outs at K.9.d.65.50 + K.9.d.45.1 on "all night" work) - 1 O.R. to Hosp - 11 O.R. beyond from Hosp. Work begun on FORT GEORGE & bridge	
"	27th		No.3 Section practised to Adv Billets at K.20c. LT GIVEY proceeded on Leave - & as described for 26th inst (No 3 & 4 Sect). Work continued as for 26th inst.	
"	28th		No. 1.2.3 & 4 Sections. Inspection of dug-outs at By. H.Q. WATSON TRENCH made by Major Notes Brad. Signal up for trenches, legacy T.M.BTY at line & trench emplacements - 1 O.R. Sick to Hosp. 1 O.R. joined for trip.	

Dunlop Smeet
Capt R.E.
483rd (EA) Field Coy R.E.

P.T.O.

Army Form C. 2118.

WAR DIARY
or
INTELLIGENCE SUMMARY

483rd (E.A.) Field Coy R.E.

(Erase heading not required.)

DECEMBER 1917

Place	Date	Hour	Summary of Events and Information	Remarks and references to Appendices
BERTINCOURT. P.1.d.	Dec 29th		Work continued as for 28th inst. gp. No. 1,2,3+4 Sections.	
"	"30th		Work as for 29th inst. No 1,2,3+4 Sections - Shelters for R.A.M.C (41st Bde) - And post begun at T.36.c. 5.5. (No 2 Sect.) Major W.E. Cooper took over work of C.R.E 2nd Div. - Capl. A.M. Matthews took over Command of Coy. 2/Lt Toacock + 2/Lt. Green awarded the Military Medal - 2 O.Rs. (Sprs Stumpleton + Fryning) Wounded at 48.3/6.E.	
"	"31st		Work as for 30th inst. No 1,2, 3+4 Sections. I.O.R. Sick & Hospital. The horses kept very fit in spite of having no covered standings, the difference in better ration from the Divnl Last few days was most noticeable - and probably also to portion of the oats or chaff - better were we are, a bomb-proof, the latter protection proved also useful for wind screens & getting rid of churned-up mud - Several N.C.O's went to courses of instruction, the value of these Courses was clearly shown.	

Julius Hawk

Capt Int. R.E.

O.C.

483rd (E.A.) Field Coy, R.E.

483RD
(EAST ANGLIAN)
FIELD COMPANY, R.E.
O.R.
Date 5/1/18

2nd Division

483rd Field Company R.E.

January To December
LATE 1/E ANGLIAN
1918

2nd Divisional Engineers

483rd FIELD COMPANY R. E. ::: JANUARY 1918.

WAR DIARY or INTELLIGENCE SUMMARY

Army Form C. 2118.

483 (E/A) Field Co. R.E.
JANUARY, 1918.

WM 33

Place	Date 1918	Hour	Summary of Events and Information	Remarks and references to Appendices
BERTINCOURT	Jan 1st		No 1. Section worked on "Automobile" line – K14 a,c,r,d and K20 c, wiring – also on improving billets at camp – No 2 Section on 36" v.y.pt Bdes. R.F.A. shelters at (J.36). No 3 Section – sunken road and canal bank. No 5 v.4 Sects. at forward billets K20 c. on line work. – No 4. Deepening, widening, shoring & general improvement of trenches in and leading to FORT GEORGE. 4 Bay nets at K.9.b.65.50 and K.9.d.45.04 – 2 Aid Posts at K.15.a.25.90. No Section of notice trestles for T.M.Bty. position K.9.c.15.5.35.	Refr. Sheet 57c N.E.
"	"2d		Others every carried on as 1st January. No 1 Section relieved by the 17th Div. on night 3/4th January.	
"	"3d		Work cont. as for 1st January. No 3 Section returned from line to Bivi C.	
			S.O.R.R. Joined unit (Reinforcements) from R.E. Base Depot. Work cont. Reported unit to O.C. 142 Field Cy, R.E.	
"	"4th		Nos 1 & 2 Sections worked as on 2nd January. No 4 Section returned from Hospital C. 1 O.R. rejoined unit from Hospital C.	
			Coy. rested in Camp. – Orders were received that Coy would probably move back to new billets for rest & back area work. – BARASTRE with field wagon at present.	
ACCOUIGNY	"5th		The Coy with all transport moved to ACCOUIGNY (D.27.d). – Back area and line work. Taken over from 5th Field Coy. R.E. as follows:– Repairs to cantonment billets of 9th, 5th & 6th Infr. Bdes. – some on Baths at O.28.c.7.0.	
ACCOUIGNY	"6th		Coy worked on billet improvements for 13th, 5th & 6th Inf. Bdes. – also 9th, 5th, & 6th Inf. Bdes. R.F.A. – also Line Huts for Divr Gas Officer. – Reconnaissance was made of Rifle Range (Priest at O.31.a & Co. general repairs. & c. – erection of Baths at O.28.c.7.0. and improvements 57 c N.E.) to Coy billets.	
"	"7th		Work cont. as for 6th – also improvements & billets at Dvrs Riflemen's School at N.12.b.	
	"8th		Work cont. as for 7th inst. 1.O.R. took to Hospital.	
	"9th			
	"10th			
	"11th			
	"12th			
	"13th		1.O.R. Sgt for Hospital – 4 N.C.Os joined Unit (Reinforcement) from R.E. Base Depot. Major Cope rejoined Unit on ceasing to be acting C.R.E. + took over Command.	
BERTINCOURT K.21.2.64?	"16th	10.0 a.m	Coy moved to BERTINCOURT took over billets of 226th Field Coy. R.E. C.O. made a call by 'phone to Reconnaissance of the line with C.E. V Corps & C.R.E. 17th Divn. Co.Y?	officer

A 5834 Wt. W4973/M687 750,000 8/16 D. D. & L. Ltd. Forms/C.2118/13

Commanding 483rd (East Anglian) Field Company, Royal Engineers.

WAR DIARY or INTELLIGENCE SUMMARY

Army Form C. 2118.

403rd (E.A.) FIELD Co. R.E.

Place	Date	Hour	Summary of Events and Information	Remarks and references to Appendices
BERTINCOURT (R.M.6.4.3.)	17/1/18 1916		A 5d. Work commenced on evening in front of taped front between BASS LANE & BUELLON LANE A 5d. (Sheet 57S)	
	18 Jan		Capt Mathews proceeded to course at R.E. School of Instruction at BLENDECQUES - Instructions received that Coy would work under orders of 19th Divn on nights of 20th and 25th January & that Coy would relieve the 247th Field Coy R.E. in the right sector that Coy would move to METZ on the 23rd	
"	19 "			
"	20 "		Coy worked under C.R.E. 19th Divn on clearing trench from NORTHERN Civil Boundary towards ARGYLE ROAD.	
"	21 "		1 O.R. (Sig) joined Unit on transfer from 5th H.Q. Coy. Wel. Capt I.B. PITE. struck off strength of Unit.	
METZ	22 "			
	23rd		Coy moved to METZ. One Section MTd + HQ Section at Q19.8.3.3 (Sheet 57S) + 3 Sections + Adv HQ at R19a + R13d (Sheet 57S). Work taken over from 247th Coy R.E. Work was started in LA MACQUERIE Sector. reconnd chiefly of the following: 1/ Clearing to re-laying old Duckboards in RILEY AV. - Cutting outlets & slopes 2/ levelling Le recoany and forming benns of listing + cutting drains in trenches - FIFTEEN ALLEY, HOLLY TRENCH, RILEY AV., NEWPORT TR., PRENTICE TR., CORNWALL TR. and GENERAL SUPPORT and clearing trenches at back of them in same trenches. 1 Section at work repairing billets & general improvement.	
	24th & 26 Jan		Work cont'd as for 23rd.	
	24 "		6 O.R.'s (Reinforcements) joined Unit from R.E. Base Depot.	
"	27 "		Work continued as for 26th 1 Officer + 27 O.R.'s (Sappers Mates) 1/Batt. R.BERKS Regt. joined Coy for instruction	
"	28 "		Lieut. returned to N.Q. Coy 2/Lt. W.J.M. Gillett to & fr. G.M. GARNER C.J. + S.M. GARNER C.J. Work as for 27th cont.	
"	29 "		1/Batt. Somerset Light Inf.	

Geoffrey
Commanding 403rd Field Company, (East Anglian) Royal Engineers.

Army Form C. 2118.

WAR DIARY
or
INTELLIGENCE SUMMARY.

483rd (E.A.) FIELD Co. R.E.

(Erase heading not required.)

Place	Date 1916	Hour	Summary of Events and Information	Remarks and references to Appendices
METZ (H.B. 2.g.B.3.3.)	30 Aug		Work on the 1st inst.: Surveyed dugouts at R.20.b. 53.80. regarding making new S entrance on N. side & into GAMP SUPPORT. C.S.M. GARNER, Cpl. Elliott & Pte. Baer. Depot. 1 Officer & 25 O.R.s (Sappers Males) from 1. Batt. K.R.R.C. joined Cy. for attachment. Major Cooper left for H.Q.R.E. to be 2/c C.R.E. Lieut. G. Kay took over Command.	
	31st		of Cy./Work on Sn. 30.K. – Work was commenced on dug-out entrance at R.20.b. 53.80.	

George Kay Lieut.
a/Officer
Commanding,
483rd Field Company,
(East Anglian) Royal Engineers.

2nd Divisional Engineers

483rd FIELD COMPANY R.E. ::: FEBRUARY 1918.

Army Form C. 2118.

WAR DIARY
or
INTELLIGENCE SUMMARY
483/E A FIELD Co. R.E.
(Erase heading not required.)

Instructions regarding War Diaries and Intelligence Summaries are contained in F.S. Regs., Part II. and the Staff Manual respectively. Title pages will be prepared in manuscript.

FEBRUARY - 1918.

Place	Date	Hour	Summary of Events and Information	Remarks and references to Appendices
METZ. MR. B143.33.	FEBRUARY. 1.		2 Sections living at advance billets at R19a. and R19d. Work continued in the light sector, erecting & clearing out & unblocking RILEY AVENUE, and also digging drains for various trenches & forming reed entrance & dug out in GAME SUPPORT at R.20.B. 55.60. - 1. O.R. Sick & Hosp.& I.O.R. OBlack & Hosp.	
	2.		99th Sgt. Bale relieved 6th Sgt. Bale on the line.	
	3.		The 2 sections at adv'd Billets relieved by 2 sections of the 226th Field Cy. R.E. & returned to rear billets at METZ.	
			1. O.R. joined from Hospl.	
	4.		2 Sections & hds. employed under Capt. Greenwood, M.C. (5th Field Cy, R.E.) on METZ defences at Dun's Hd. Bomb protection, Painting Village Names &c. Billet improvements & supervising digging returning the Front & Reserve line of the 2nd System - (BILHEM SWITCH).	
	5.		1. O.R. Sick to Hospital.	
	6.		Do Do Do	
	7.		Do Do Do	
	8.		I.O.R. Sick to Hospital. - 1.O.R. joined from Hospital.	
	9.		General Front R.E. organized with 3 Dugouts on the line	
	10.		1 section moved into adv'd Billets at R19a & took over work in the light sector of the 226th Field Cy, R.E. Work consisted of clearing out & reconstructing RILEY AVE GAME SUPPORT, widening and deepening HOLLY SUPPORT and the following work in dugouts viz:-	
			AID POST at R.20.a. 35.95.	
			New entrance & dugout at R. 20.d. S.P.	
			PARTRIDGE RD. R20.b.25-35 (Mess dugout).	
	12.		Connecting 2 dugouts in FREY RAVINE at R.20.a.75.85.	
			I.O.R. Sick to Hospital.	
			MAJOR N.C. COOPER. (then 2/CRE.) 53rd Cy. to take up appointment as C.R.E. 3rd Division and acting rank of Lt. Col. y command of Cy. then taken over by Lieut. G. Ver. R.E.	
	14.		1. O.R. Sick to Hospital.	
	15.		1. O.R. joined from Hospital.	
	18.		3.O.Rs. to Hospital (Sick).	
	19.		1.O.R. (Sgm) to Hospital.	
			Capt. (I/Major) C.G. WOOLNER - M.C. R.E., Junior under from 5th Field Squadron R.E. took over command of Cy.	
	21.		1. O.R. Sick to Hospital.	

Wethersong
Capt'n
483/E.A. Field Cy. R.E.

Army Form C. 2118.

WAR DIARY
INTELLIGENCE SUMMARY
1/3rd (E.A.) FIELD COY R.E.
(Erase heading not required.)

FEBRUARY. 1918.

Place	Date	Hour	Summary of Events and Information	Remarks and references to Appendices
METZ. H.Q.- Q.9.B.3.3.	FEBRUARY 23.		2.o.R's. joined Unit (Reinforcements) 1.o.R. Sick to Hospital.	
	24.		Capt. A.W. MATTHEWS returned from Leave. 1.o.R. Sick to Hospital.	
	25.		2.o.R's. Sick to Hospital.	
	27.		1.o.R. do	

[signature]
Capt.
In Officer
Commanding,
1/3rd Field Company,
(East Anglian) Royal Engineers.

2nd Divisional Engineers

483rd FIELD COMPANY R. E.

MARCH 1 9 1 8

Narrative of Operations attached.

Army Form C. 2118

WAR DIARY
or
INTELLIGENCE SUMMARY

483rd (E.A.) FIELD Co. R.E.
(Erase heading not required.)

MARCH. 1918.

Instructions regarding War Diaries and Intelligence Summaries are contained in F.S. Regs., Part II. and the Staff Manual respectively. Title Pages will be prepared in manuscript.

Place	Date 1918	Hour	Summary of Events and Information	Remarks and references to Appendices
METZ	March 1st		No. 4 Section in Adv. Billets VILLERS PLOUICH - 16 charges prepared & arrangements made to destroy dugouts in event of withdrawal. Nos. 1 & 2 Sections at Coy. H.Q. METZ. No. 3 Section under Lt. Wilson at ETRICOURT working for C.R.E.	
"	2		Lt. Wilson West. return from ETRICOURT to METZ.	
"	3		No. 1 Section relieved No. 4 in Forward Billets. Lt. Undale proceeded on Leave.	
"	4		1.O.R. reported Gen. Hosp.	
"	6		Enemy discharged gas projectors on Bde. Front. No. 1 Section reserved 2 men of Trench Mortar Battery from damaged dugout in PARTRIDGE ROAD.	
"	7		No. 1 Section withdrawn to new Billets in Second System made during the day by Coys. 2 & 4 Sections. 1.O.R. reported Gen. Hosp.	
"	8		1.O.R. Joined Unit (Reinforcement). 1.O.R. Sick to Hosp.	
"	10		No. 3 Section relieved No. 1 in Forward Billets. 1.O.R. Rgt. Gen. Hosp.	
"	11		METZ shelled. 1 Brown & 13 Horses killed. No. 1 Section moved to ETRICOURT for work on Disinfestation Chamber. 1.O.R. rgd. Gen. Hosp.	Appendix A
"	12		Sappers moved into tents outside the village. Horse Lines also moved out of the village. Work started on Second System of Wire Defence with one Batt. of H.T. Divn. daily.	
"	13		See weekly progress report.	
"	14		3.O.Rs. Sick to Hosp. 1.O.R. Sick to Hosp.	
"	15		2.O.Rs. Sick to Hosp.	
"	16		5.O.Rs. Joined to Hosp.	
"	17		No. 4 Section relieved No. 3 Section in Advanced Billets. No. 3 having lost 75% of its strength from Gas.	
"	18		1.O.R. Sick to Hosp. 8.O.Rs. transferred to Recovery Base Depot. (S.F.V.T.)	
"	19		2.O.Rs. Joined Unit (Reinforcements) 1.O.R. Sick to Hosp.	
"	20		Coys. & Billets handed over to 417th Division.	Appendix B

N. Moore Major R.E.
Commanding 483rd Field Company, Royal Engineers
(East Anglian)

Army Form C. 2118.

WAR DIARY
or
INTELLIGENCE SUMMARY

(Erase heading not required.)

448th E.A. FIELD Coy R.E.

MARCH. 1918.

Instructions regarding War Diaries and Intelligence Summaries are contained in F.S. Regs., Part II. and the Staff Manual respectively. Title Pages will be prepared in manuscript.

Place	Date 1918	Hour	Summary of Events and Information	Remarks and references to Appendices
METZ	March 21		Coy. (less No.1 Section at ETRICOURT) standing to in the open behind METZ. Gas shell of Phosgene fumes drifted across the bivouacs, causing masks to be worn. Coy. moved at 4.0 p.m. to ROYAULCOURT. Shelled in billets at 6.30 p.m. Enemy Casualties - 2 men wounded.	Appen. C,D,E.
ROYAULCOURT	22		No.1 Section Horse proceeded to ETRICOURT to move the Section to BEAULENCOURT. Coy. moved at 4.0 p.m. to BEAULENCOURT. I.O.R. sick to Hosp.	Appen. F, G
BEAULENCOURT	23		Repacking Wagons + eliminating surplus kit. 300 shovels + 250 picks collected on pontoon wagons from ROCQUIGNY + delivered to 5th Bde. Pty. sent to prepare HARLINCOURT water point - orders to Class Delegated by GS. Bde. to 117th R.F. Another party sent to prepare BEAULENCOURT water point for demolition. Orders to Class to be given by OC Bde. Company moved at 7.0 p.m. to GEUDECOURT. No. 1 & 4 Sections left at 8.0 a.m. to work on Red Line N.W. of GERM. 0.15 a 0.5. (Sheet 57C.)	Appen. H Appendix I Appendix J
GEUDECOURT	24		Orders to retire received at 9.0 a.m. - Gliderly sent to recce No. 2 + 3 Sections from LONGUEVAL where these two rear Projections at the X roads. - No. 2 & 4 Sections rejoined here. On arrival at LA BOISSELLE orders received to dig and hold a line of posts between LIGNY DAILLOT and HIGH WOOD the right of the Division being at M.24. c. 1.3 with 19th Divi on Left + 17th Divi on right. Work consisted of digging posts masking the line with wired duckboards. Insufficient infantry having been collected on this line, sappers were withdrawn at dawn to MIRAUMONT whence the transport had moved to its Bgde. of 99th Bde. Corps line on the right of 99th Bde. interrupted & guided on the Corps line on the right of 99th Bde. BEAULENCOURT water point successfully blown up at 6.0 p.m. - HARLINCOURT water point never blown owing to heavy shelling.	Appendix K

Commanding, Major W.S.
448th Field Company
(East Anglian) Royal Engineers.

WAR DIARY or INTELLIGENCE SUMMARY

Army Form C. 2118.

423rd (E.A.) FIELD CY. R.E.

MARCH 1916

Place	Date 1916	Hour	Summary of Events and Information	Remarks and references to Appendices
MAILLYMONT	March 25		Transport moved at 9.0 a.m. to AUCHONVILLERS followed at 11.0 a.m. by Sappers. Pelton remained with C.R.E. was detailed to clear three craters prepared by 2nd Coy. Tunnellg. Cy. in the BAPAUME - ALBERT road at LA BOISSELLE. At 3.30 p.m. transport moved to BERTRANCOURT carrying Sappers to assist in the defence of AUCHONVILLERS - Major Smith R.I.R. in Command of garrison - with O.C. No. 2 Coy. commanding right half, O.C. 483rd Fd. Coy. commanding left half of the village. One Coy. of 1st R. Berks. Gen'l Blake in position saved the perimeter of old trenches, 483rd Coy. N.B. in reserve behind the left of the village - 20 wired knife rests put & placed in position across the roads leaving the village. Command carried out about midnight - Sappers withdrawn to BERTRANCOURT. I.O.R. 1 Sgt. & 1 Spr.	Appendix L
BERTRANCOURT	26		Enemy reported at 11.30 a.m. advancing with armoured cars from HEBUTERNE - LEALVILLERS - Patrols sent out towards COLENCOURT and BUS. Sappers standing to - Patrols on BERTRANCOURT - ACHEUX road prepared for demolition; no water. Patrol with destroying forces in BUS. Changed position for LEALVILLERS at work.	Appendix M, N
"	27		Coy. moved to LEALVILLERS at 2.0 p.m. - Sapper Melts Reg't 99 R. Bec.	Appendix O, P
LEALVILLERS	28		Wired three hughes erected at 2.25 c.0.3 (Sketch) Water reconnaissance. Casualties. Company organised to 3 sections. (5-21.2-4)	
"	29		Nos. 2 & 4 sections working at night in AVELUY WOOD - Lewis Gun Post dug and wired at Q.34.d.6.4. - 4 holes dug outs at Q.34.a.0.0. reclaimed from Batt. S.E.Q. Whole Coy. on tasks in AVELUY WOOD. Pot dug outside main tunnel	Appendix Q
"	30		at Q35.c.7.0. - Rifle Pit improved from Q34.d.4.1 & R34.d.4.9.3/Strands of wire erected in front of these pits. I.O.R. Sick & Inj.	Appendix R, S
"	31		at Q35.c.7.0 c.p.14th section & mine shaft to AVELUY WOOD. 2 strands of wire erected in Q.31.d.4.1 front line taped East of AVELUY - HAMEL road trenches obscured and from then blocked at Q35.d.2½. at Q.35.d.7.0. improved. Stove trough erected at 7.31.C.6.3. I.O.R. 2 Sgt. 2 Sprs. 2/0	Appendix T, U

Commanding, 483rd (East Anglian) Field Coy., Royal Engineers.

Narrative of events.
483rd (E.A.) Field Company R.E.

21st March. METZ. Company standing to. Marched at 4 pm to RUYAULCOURT.

22nd March. RUYAULCOURT. Company moved at 4.0 am to BEAULENCOURT.

23rd March. BEAULENCOURT. 300 shovels and 250 picks collected on pontoon wagons from ROCQUIGNY and delivered to 5th Bde.
Party sent to prepare HAPLINCOURT water-point for demolition; order to blow delegated by 6th Bde. to 17th R.F. (Appendix A)
Another party sent to prepare BEAULENCOURT water-point for demolition. Order to blow to be given by 6th Bde. (Appendix B)
Company moved at 7.0 pm. to GEUDECOURT.

24th March. GEUDECOURT. Nos 2 & 4 Sections left at 8.0 am. to work on Red Line N.W. from Q.15a.0.5 (Sheet 57c).
Orders to retire received at 9.0 am. Orderly sent to recall Nos 2 & 4 Sections found them just starting work. Company moved to LA BOISSELLE via LONGUEVAL where there was great congestion at the crossroads.
On arrival at LA BOISSELLE orders received to dig and hold a line of posts between LIGNY-THILLOY and HIGH WOOD, the right of the 2nd Div. being at ____ with 19th Div. on the left and ____

17th Divn on the right. Work consisted of digging posts and marking the line with salved duckboards. Sufficient Infantry having been collected on this line sappers were withdrawn at dawn to MIRAUMONT whither the transport had moved. Two Brigades of 17th Divn were intercepted and guided on to the Corps line on the right of 99th Bde. (Appendix C)

BEAULENCOURT water point successfully blown at 6.0 pm.

HAPLINCOURT water point was never blown owing to heavy shelling making the charge inaccessible.

March 25th   MIRAUMONT. Transport moved at 9.0 am to AUCHONVILLERS followed at 11.0 am by the sappers. Lt Wilson remained with C.R.E. and was detailed to blow three craters prepared by

(Appendix D)   2nd Australian Tunnelling Company in the BAPAUME - ALBERT road at LA BOISSELLE. At 3.30 pm transport moved to BERTRANCOURT leaving sappers to assist in the defence of AUCHONVILLERS. Major Smith K.R.R. in command of the garrison with OC 5th Cy.R.E. commanding right half and OC 483rd Cy R.E. commanding left half of the village. One company 1st Royal Scots Regt detailed placed in position round the perimeter in old trenches. 483rd Cy R.E. in reserve behind the left of the village. 20 wired knife-rests made and placed in position across the roads entering the village. Command handed over about midnight and Sappers were withdrawn to BERTRANCOURT.

26th March. BERTRANCOURT. Enemy reported at 11.20 a.m. advancing with armoured cars from HEBUTERNE. Transport withdrawn to LEALVILLERS. Patrols sent out towards COIGNEUX and BUS. Sappers standing to. Water-point on the BERTRANCOURT - ACHEUX road prepared for demolition; no water-point worth destroying found in BUS. Transport rejoined at dusk from LEALVILLERS.

27th March. BERTRANCOURT. Company moved to LEALVILLERS at 2.0 p.m.

28th March. LEALVILLERS. Salved horse troughs erected at P.25.a.0.3. (Sheet 87d). Owing to casualties the company was organised in three sections.

29th March. LEALVILLERS. Nos 2 & 4 Sections working by night in AVELUY WOOD.

7/4/18

J. Woolley, Major R.E.
O.C. 483rd Coy R.E.

To O.C. 483rd Fd. Coy. R.E.   PAGE No. 1

(Appendix A)

Report on Preparations made for the Demolition of Bore Holes & Machinery Plant in PUMP HOUSE at HAPLINCOURT.
(5.L.2.1. SHEET LENS 11.)

Received orders from you on the 23rd March 1918 to deal with above. Took Cpl. Day & Sapr. Morrison, Heapy & Clemos. Proceeded to VILLERS AU FLOS & reported to Bde. of 6th Bde. Was told to report to 17th R.E. Batt. HQ at HAPLINCOURT where I would receive final instructions as to the time for carrying out demolition. Made arrangements with Lt Col Weston 17th R.E. & then carried out the necessary preparation at PUMP HOUSE as follows:—

WATER.

BORES. There were two; one just outside Main Engine House A. (See sketch) & one 200ˣ away. Dug down hole 4 ft deep, & about 3ft bore side & placed 10 slabs of wet gun cotton at each, with fuze &c.

MACHINERY.

In cases 1, 2, 3, 5 & 6. These were to be dealt with by sledge hammers, breaking & cracking vulnerable parts. In case of 4. Cylinders was to be destroyed by slab of gun cotton placed on same. & in case of 7. the same but with several slabs, sledge hammer also to be used for further damage.

J. Nelson 2/Lt RE
O/C No 5 Section

7/4/18.

PAGE No 2.

WELL BORES,
200ˣ APART.

YDS 0 1 2 3 4 5 6 YDS
SCALE.

⊙ D. ⊙ C.

REFERENCE.
A, MAIN ENGINE HOUSE.
B, AUXILIARY ENGINE HOUSE.
1/ COMPRESSOR SET. (PARAFFIN)
2/ 'BOOSTER' SET. (PETROL)
3/ DO. — DO. — (DO).
4/ DO. — DO — (New set only arrived)
5/ COMPRESSOR SET (New set only arrived)
6/ RECEIVER (COMPRESSED AIR)

2ʺ9ʺ
4ʹ CHARGE
WATER BORE

Note Main Engine House & Auxiliary Engine
House were about 200ˣ apart.

7/4/18.   J Wilson

Demolition of Bore-hole at (Appendix B)
    BEAULENCOURT

This water point consisted of a 4" water pipe containing a 1½" air pipe, the whole being enclosed in a 6" casing. A charge of 15 lbs gun cotton was placed 2'6" away from the pipe at a depth of 6 ft. The charge was prepared at 6 p.m. on the 23rd inst & was fired at 6 p.m. on the 24th inst. As a result the top portions of the pipes were blown off causing the water & air pipes to sink within the outer casing into the well. A crater about 8 ft wide was formed.

George Ruddle Lt
O/C No 2 Sect

Demolition of bore-hole at BEAULENCOURT

N 11.d.5.3.

Bore hole

8'0"

2'0"

2'6"

1½"
4"
2"
6'
casing

charge 15 lbs G.C.

6'0"

Bore hole

Scale ½ = 1 Foot

Key Plan

To Beaulencourt

Tole Tansley

To Bapaume

(Appendix C)

V Corps Line
night of 24th/25th March 1918

LE BARQUE
LIGNY-THILLOY
Butte de Warlencourt
Elements of 5th & 6th Bdes
LE SARS
16th D.L.I.
EAUCOURT L'ABBAYE
Bde 99th Bde H.Q.
Factory Corner
GUEUDECOURT
Seven Elms
GOC's Two Bdes of 19th Divn shown
FLERS
V Corps Line & this spot as interbde boundary

HIGH WOOD
(47th Divn was at the time supposed to be here)

Scale 1:40000
Sheet 57c.

8/4/18

To. O.C. 483rd Fd. Coy. R.E.   (Appendix D)

Report on Craters Blowing on ALBERT BAPAUME RD. X 13 d & 19 a (Sheet 57.D.)

Three craters were blown on the morning of 26th March at 6 a.m. after all our troops forward of the danger zone had evacuated.

Preparations were made on the afternoon of 25th March & during the night 25th/26th. The 12th DIV. were warned & arrangements were made as to time for blowing.

Craters A. & B. were blown from existing dug outs 200 & 250 yds respectively from C. crater which was prepared at junction of LA BOISSELLE RD with main RD: crater C. being blown from a small tunnel made under road.

VARYING FROM 10 TO 15 FT. IN A & B CRATERS
IN C CRATER: ABOUT 5 FT.

The charges were of wet guncotton & as follows

CRATER A. 320 lbs
       C. 60 lbs   } All fired by safety fuse
       B. 400 lbs. } 2 in each case.

One box in each case was opened & detonators inserted in slab.

3/4/18. J. Gibson. /RE
O/C No 1 Sec.

H.Q., R.E. 2nd DIVN.
No. 464
Date

O.C. 5th Field Co. R.E.
O.C. 226th Field Co. R.E.
O.C. 483rd (E.A.) Field Co. R.E.

      You will withdraw all your troops from forward billets and make accommodation for them in SNAP RESERVE (BILHEM SWITCH). Each Company in its own Brigade sector of the System.

      Move to be completed on night 7/8th inst.

      Work at present in hand is not to suffer.

      Please wire when move is completed, giving map reference.

H.Q.R.E.
6.3.18.

Major R.E.
a/C.R.E., 2nd Division.

CRE 2nd Divn. Appendix J.3 **A**
   Weekly Progress Report.

1. Work Forward of HIGHLAND LINE abandoned.
2. TAFF VALE AVENUE dug so far as required to 3' deep (approx.) Further deepening & firestepping has been much hampered by Gas-shelling. (see tracing attached).
3. HIGHLAND LINE. 18 small shelters in LINCOLN RESERVE south of DELL LANE completed.
Anti-bombing straights roughly excavated by Pioneers on trenches entering both lines from the East. These are being completed by Pioneers.
3 O.P.s completed.
4. SECOND SYSTEM. Further excavation of CHIP LANE. This still requires finishing off.
SNAP TRENCH. 500* deepened & firestepped. 8 shelters (six men) completed.
SNAP RESERVE. 250* deepened & firestepped. Shelters completed for 40 men (advanced section 483* by N.F.) Excavation for Aid Post completed.
5. NEW SWITCH 600* firetrench completed. 200* C.T. completed. 700* C.T. to 2'6" deep.

                                 Moorhur Major R.E.

ORDERS BY LIEUT-COLONEL P.K.BETTY, D.S.O., R.E.
COMMANDING ROYAL ENGINEER, 2nd DIVISION.

Order No. 104.   Copy No. 3

1. 47th Division will relieve 2nd Division in the line on nights March 19th/20th and 20th/21st.

2. The 47th Division will take over 3-Brigade front with 2 Brigades.

3. R.E. 47th Division will relieve R.E. of 2nd Division by mid-day 20th March as under:-

4. 5th Field Co. R.E. will hand over billets to 517th Field Co. R.E., and work to 517th and 520th Field Coys. R.E.

5. 226th Field Co. R.E. will hand over billets and work to 520th Field Co. R.E.

6. 483rd Field Co. R.E. will hand over billets to 518th Field Co. R.E. and work to 517th Field Co. R.E.

7. 5th Field Co. R.E. will take over work and billets of 517th Field Co. R.E. Dugouts in 2nd SYSTEM and work in METZ, including that supervised by Lieut. FROST with parties of 119th Labour Coy. and M.M.G.Coy. Lieut. FROST will give full particulars to and continue to assist 5th Field Co. R.E.

8. 226th Field Co. R.E. will take over billets of 520th Field Co. R.E. and work of 518th Field Co. R.E. Work on 2nd SYSTEM as far North as TRESCAULT FLESQUIERES Road, including working party of 1 Battalion from 2nd Division.

9. 483rd Field Co. R.E. will take over billets of 518th Field Co. R.E. and will do training and necessary back area work of the Division. Application has been made for 3 days off for Field Coys. and Pioneers.

10. It is hoped each Company will be given a period of training.

11. Details of relief to be arranged between Os.C. concerned. Maps &c. will be handed over and receipts obtained, to be forwarded with report of completion of relief to this office.

12. Refilling for 5th, 226th, and 483rd Field Coys. R.E. will be as follows:-

    19th and 20th as usual.
    21st and onwards:-
        BUS - BARASTRE Road, O.23.d.8.4. at 9.30 a.m. Train wagons will deliver supplies to units.

13. Tents and shelters will be left standing in their present positions, and will be handed over.
    Receipts should be obtained for tents &c. handed over.

14. Divisional R.E. Dump NORBURY will be handed over at 9 a.m. 20th. Party of N.C.O. and 25 men of 17th R. Fusiliers will

be relieved morning of 20th and on relief will rejoin their Battalion, and also the sapper attached from each Company.

R.S.M. HARRIS will rejoin H.Q.R.E. morning of 20th.

15. ACKNOWLEDGE.

H.Q.R.E.
2nd Division.
19.3.18.

Captain R.E.
Adjutant,
for C.R.E., 2nd Division.

```
Copy No. 1  to   5th Field Co. R.E.
 "    "  2  to   226th Field Co. R.E.
 "    "  3  to   483rd Field Co. R.E.
 "    "  4  to   10th D.C.L.I.
 "    "  5  to   2nd Division "Q"
 "    "  6  to   2nd Division "G"
 "    "  7  tto  C.R.E. 47th Division.
 "    "  8       Office.
```

O.C. 5th Field Co R.E.
O.C. 226th Field Co R.E.
O.C. 483rd (E.A.) Field Co R.E.

Confirmation of my wire H.E.19 dated 21.3.18.

Companies are to move to their allotted billets in ROYAULCOURT. Please notify this office on completion.

H.Q. R.E.
2nd Division
21.3.18.

"A" Form.
MESSAGES AND SIGNALS.

Appendix E

TO { } full COPE

Sender's Number.	Day of Month.	In reply to Number.	A A A
G179	21		

Brigades of 2 Divn have been ordered to GREEN LINE (BERTIN-COURT — HAPLINCOURT) move to be complete by 7 a.m. You will stand by for further orders.

You will not join your Brigade unless ordered to by Division.

From
Place   10.40 pm
Time

"A" Form.
MESSAGES AND SIGNALS.

Army Form C. 2121.
(In pads of 100.)

Prefix	Code	m	Words	Charge	This message is on a/c of:	Recd. at ... m.
Office of Origin and Service Instructions.			Sent		Service.	Date
			At ... m.			From
			To			By
			By		(Signature of "Franking Officer.")	

TO { Officer R.E. Coy.
     [illegible]
     VC 481   Appendix D

| Sender's Number. | Day of Month. | In reply to Number. | AAA |
| RE 178 | 21 | | |

You will be at one hour's notice to move receipt of this order and acknowledge by H.Q.R.E. mounted orderly

[signature]

From
Place
Time

The above may be forwarded as now corrected. (Z)

....
Censor. Signature of Addressor or person authorised to telegraph in his name.

* This line should be erased if not required.
(S198.) Wt. W12952/M1294. 375,000 Pads. 1/17. H.W.&V. Ld. (E. 818.)

"A" Form.   Army Form C. 2121.
MESSAGES AND SIGNALS.

This message is on a/c of: Appendix F

TO: OC 483 Field Coy RE

Sender's Number: RE 177   Day of Month: 21   AAA

Please send to HQ RE 6.0am 22nd inst Tool cart horses complete L.G.S. & Officer's chargers for No 1 Section of your Coy at present in ETRICOURT. Report to Section billet rations for 22nd to be brought.

"A" Form.
MESSAGES AND SIGNALS.

Army Form C. 2121.
(In pads of 100.)

Appendix G

TO: 5th Field Coy RE
OC 483

Sender's Number: RE/80
Day of Month: 22

AAA

Warning order

Field Coys of 2nd Divn will move to BEAULENCOURT 1/40,000 Sheet 57C N17. moving 22nd March. march under orders of Major E A ROBINSON M.C. RE O/C 5th Field Coy RE to reach BEAULENCOURT by 7.0 am 22nd. Detailed orders follow. OC 483 Field Coy RE will send transport order in my RE 177 at once. HQ's Divn move to BARASTRE.

Time: 12 noon

P.T.O.

If detailed orders have not arrived by the time you are ready to start — leave officer behind to receive same at 5th Field Coy. H.Q. ROYAULCOURT & bring them on.

Appendix H

H.E.25.

O.C. 483rd Field Coy R.E.
~~(...)~~ (attached Bde for Inf)

Please prepare the following for demolition
(1) HAPLINCOURT borehole and pump
    O9b 6.9.
(2) BEAULENCOURT borehole N11 b 7.3.

Boreholes should be prepared for blowing up, and pumps & engines dismantled & damaged.

These will not not be destroyed without direct orders ~~from~~ from the 6th Bde (*)
The two men, or as many as you decide, who will actually ~~blow~~ fire the charges will report to 6th Bde H.Q. CHATEAU, VILLERS AU FLOS and remain with them till work has been carried out. Suggest charges should be taken on bicycles.

23.3.18.
4.30 p.m.

W. Hartley
Major CRE 2nd Div

"A" Form
MESSAGES AND SIGNALS.

Army Form C. 2121
(In pads of 100)

Prefix......Code......m	Words.	Charge.	This message is on a/c of:	Recd. at......m
Office of Origin and Service Instructions	Sent			Date......
......By kan	At......m		...Appendix I...Service.	From......
	To			By......
	By		(Signature of "Franking Officer.")	

TO { ~~CO RE~~ ~~R Div~~ OC 48 }

Sender's Number.	Day of Month.	In reply to Number.	AAA
RE 103	23		

All Field Cos of the 2 Div
will move to GEUDECOURT
as soon as possible.

Inform forward sections
so that they will know where
to return to

HQ RE is moving to

LIGNY TILLOY

M Shaw (?)
Capt RE
OC RE 2 D

From
Place
Time 6 51 p

* This line should be erased if not required.

"A" Form
MESSAGES AND SIGNALS.

Army Form C. 2121
(In pads of 100)

No. of Message..........

Prefix.......Code........m,	Words.	Charge.	This message is on a/c of:	Recd. at.........m.
Office of Origin and Service Instructions	Sent			Date........
	At.........m.		*Appendix J*	From......
	To......		Service.	
	By......		(Signature of "Franking Officer.")	By......

TO	O.C. 483 Field Co RE		
Sender's Number.	Day of Month.	In reply to Number.	AAA
*RE 211	23		

Two	sections	of your company will	work
tomorrow	on	RED	LINE.
The	RED	LINE	runs
from	O 15 a 0.5.	N. W.	
Please	arrange	for	sections
to	go	direct	to
work	and	work	where
they	can.		

From: CRE 2nd Div
Place
Time: 11.25 pm

The above may be forwarded as now corrected. (Z)

Censor. Signature of Addressor or person authorised to telegraph in his name.

* This line should be erased if not required.

(7981) Wt. W492/M1647 130,000 Pads 5/17 D.D.&L. E1187

CRE

"A" Form
MESSAGES AND SIGNALS.

Army Form C. 2121
(In pads of 100)
No. of Message..............

Prefix........Code..........m,	Words.	Charge.	This message is on a/c of:	Recd. at..........m.
Office of Origin and Service Instructions	Sent			Date.......... K
....	At..........m.		*Appendix* ....Service.	From..........
....	To..........			By..........
....	By..........		(Signature of "Franking Officer.")	

TO { 155th Field Coy R.E. }

Sender's Number.	Day of Month.	In reply to Number.	AAA
* RE214	24		

Move on receipt of this from GRANDECOURT towards the war MARTINPUICH – AVELUY Forward sections informed to do as much repair work on roads as possible

From
Place
Time

The above may be forwarded as now corrected. (Z)
....
Censor. Signature of Addresser or person authorised to telegraph in his name.
* This line should be erased if not required.

MESSAGES AND SIGNALS.

Prefix......Code......m.	Words.	Charge.	This message is on a/c of:	Recd. at......m.
Office of Origin and Service Instructions	Sent			Date
	At......m.		......Service.	From
urgent	To......		*Appendix L*	By
	By......		(Signature of "Franking Officer.")	

TO ~~......~~ O Code

Sender's Number.	Day of Month.	In reply to Number.	AAA
* BE 225	26		

Get saddled up & stand by
to move at once. Bosche
reported in HÉBUTERNE.
When marching observe
military precautions.
Push on mounted & ground
scouts

From
Place
Time 12.15 pm

The above may be forwarded as now corrected. (Z)

Censor. Signature of Addressor or person authorised to telegraph in his name.
* This line should be erased if not required.
(7981) Wt. W492/M1647 130,000 Pads 5/17 D. D. & L. E1187

O.C. 5th ~~Field Co R.E.~~ Appendix M
" 483" " " " V.144.

All sappers mates attached to you will rejoin their units forthwith. They should report to their Bde. Headquarters, which are in or about MAILLY-MAILLET Wood, taking rations for today with them. They will be rationed by their units from 28th inclusive.

H.Q. R.E.
27.3.18.

W Shaw
for Lt. Colonel R.E.
C.R.E. 2nd Divn.

"A" Form.			Army Form C.2121
MESSAGES AND SIGNALS.			(in pads of 100). No. of Message........

Prefix......Code......m.	Words	Charge	This message is on a/c of:	Recd. at............m.
Office of Origin and Service Instructions	Sent			Date
....	At............m.		*Appendix N* Service.	From
....	To............		(Signature of "Franking Officer.")	By............
....	By............			

TO — OC 483 Field Co RE

Sender's Number.	Day of Month.	In reply to Number.	AAA
RE 230	28		

Move your company to LEALVILLERS at once somewhere near the other two Companies. D.H.Q. moves to VARENNES

P M Shaw Capt RE
for CRE 2 Dn.

2.20 pm

CRE 2nd Divn.   Appendix O

I am constructing a horse-watering point at the reservoirs at about P.25.a.5.0.

Troughs are on site in Salvage Dump.

There is supposed to be a pipe-line on the same system at about O.23.d — this is being reconnoitred.

These points are served from pumping station at U.6.a.

Until I shewd there used to be a pumping station in TOUTENCOURT.

28/3/18
2.30pm   O.C. 483rd Major RE
                        by W[...]

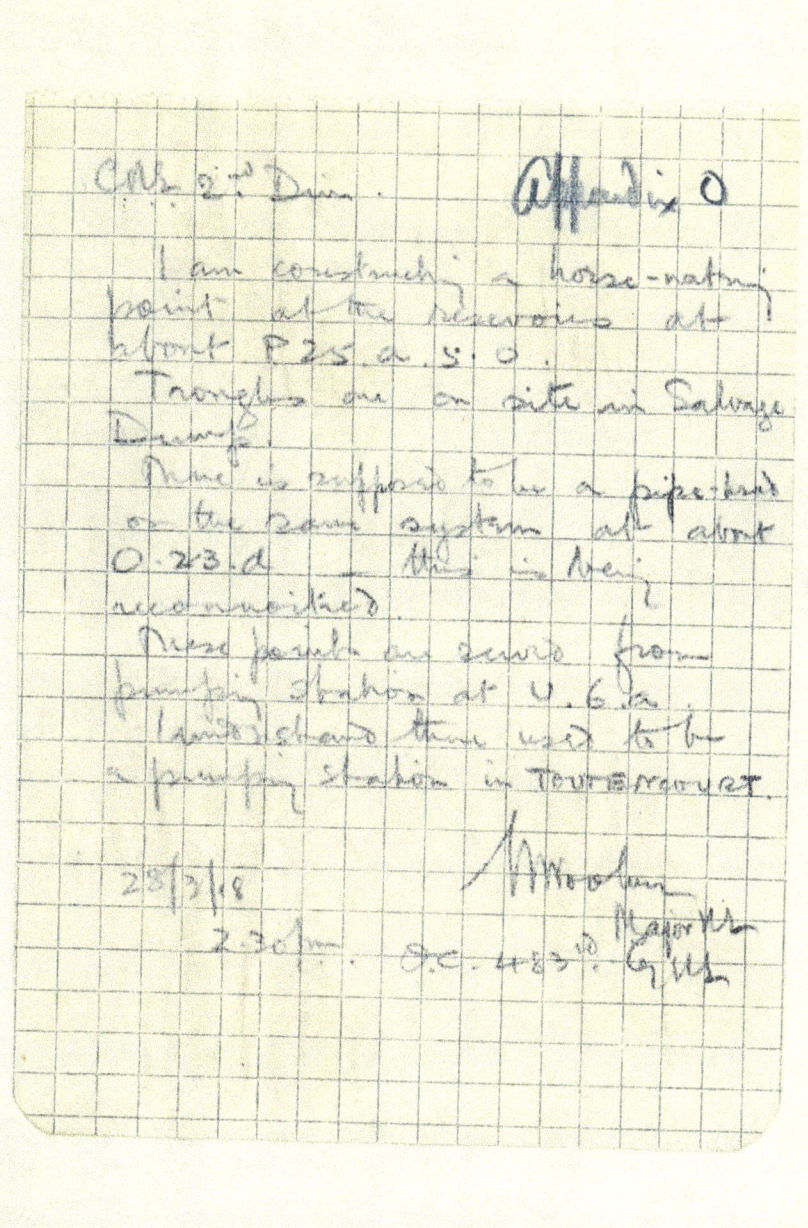

Appendix P

C.R.E. 2nd Div.

I saw yesterday an Officer & a Sergeant of 559 A.T. Coy. R.E. who installed the original water supply system in this area. The Officer promised to collect all the information he still had which he could and send it to you. Sgt G. lives at ARQUEVES. I gathered from him that there used to be a large plant at VADENCOURT SPRINGS which forced through a 6" main through the woods to U.16, crossing the CONTAY-HARPONVILLE road in U.10. Thence along this road towards VARENNES with a branch to — this point in HARPONVILLE. It turned left hand short of VARENNES and existed at CLAIREFAYE. A branch went on to the water point at the crossroads west of VARENNES. Apparently the VADENCOURT plant has been dismantled and the well at U.6.a has been T-ed on to the old rising main.

There used to be a pump at I.31.a which forced into storage about O.1.cent where there were horse troughs & water cart fillers.

There used to be a pump at LOUVERCOURT at a well in O.4.b which forced to storage in O.10.b.

Town Major ACHEUX is said to have a really excellent list of water points in this area.

Water points could be developed at the following places.
(1) CLAIRFAYE O.29.b.99
(2) P.25.a.5.0
(3) VARENNES P.31.a.7.6
(4) about O.36.d.cent
(5) HARPONVILLE.

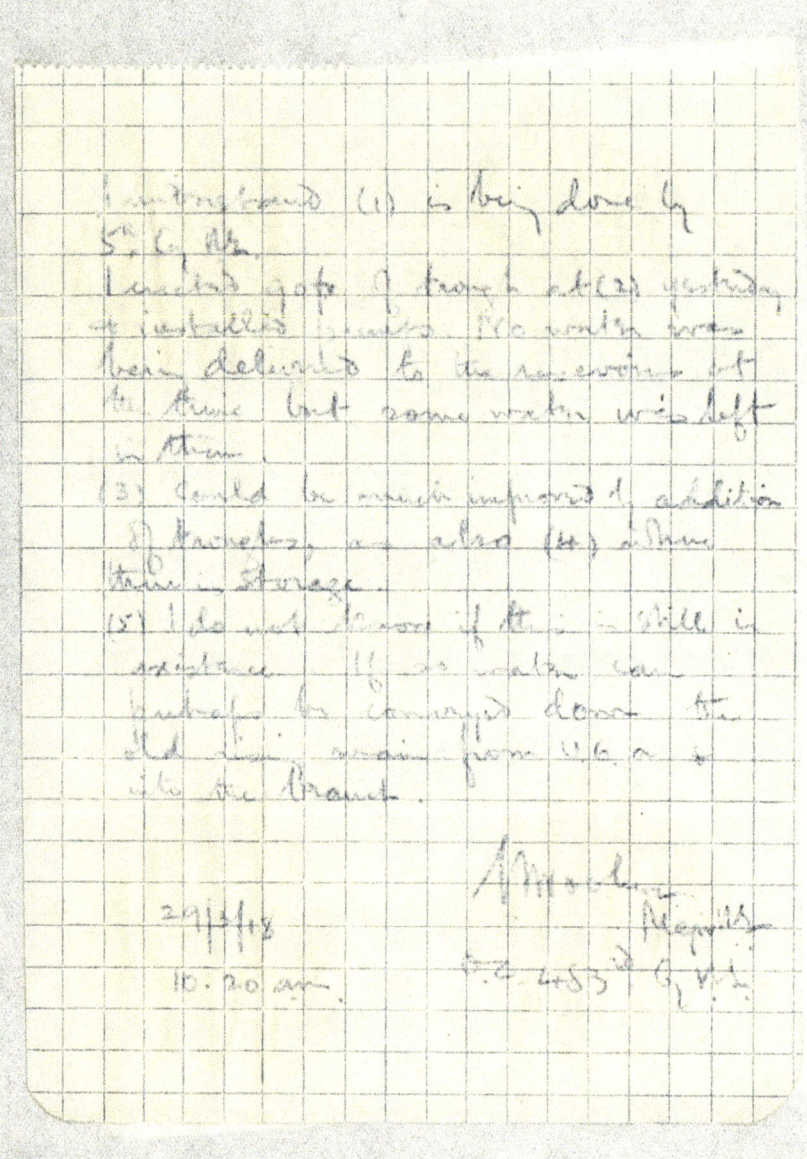

... (1) is being done by 5th Cy Mk.

Lowered gofr of trough at (2) yesterday + installed ... No water was being delivered to the reservoir at the time but some water was left in them.

(3) Could be much improved by addition of ......, and also (4) ..... them in storage.

(5) I do not know if this is still in existence. If so water can perhaps be conveyed down the old ... again from ... as ... its the branch.

29/1/18
10.20 am

J Moul...
Maj...
O.C. 483rd ...

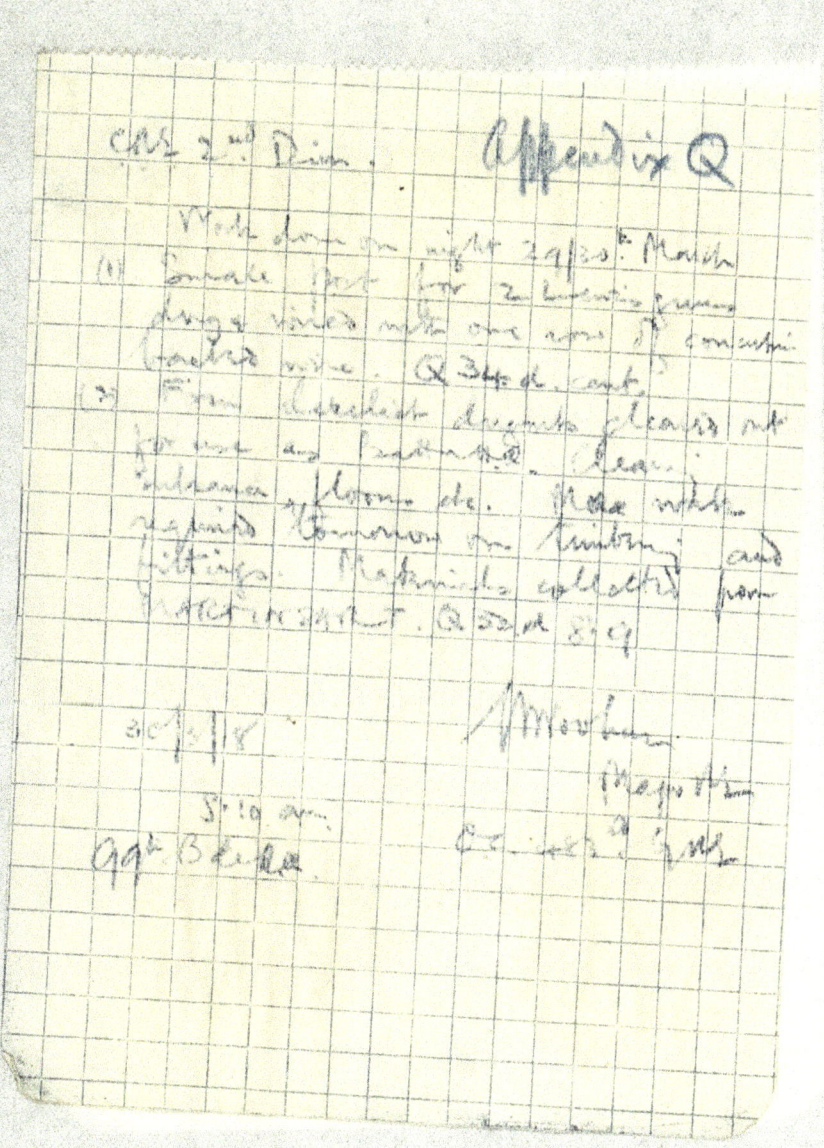

OC 5th Field Co RE
i/c 226th " " "
OC 483 " " "

Appendix R

RE 13

Ambulance
6 G.S. wagons are reporting at VARENNES dump 6.0 pm to-night (3 from 5th & 3 from 99th Bde) to carry barbed wire & pickets.

Two are for each coy.

Please arrange loading party.

OC parties to report to Bde HdQrs ENGLEBELMER not MARTINSART

J.W.Shaw (Capt) RE
i/c GRE "B"

30/3/18

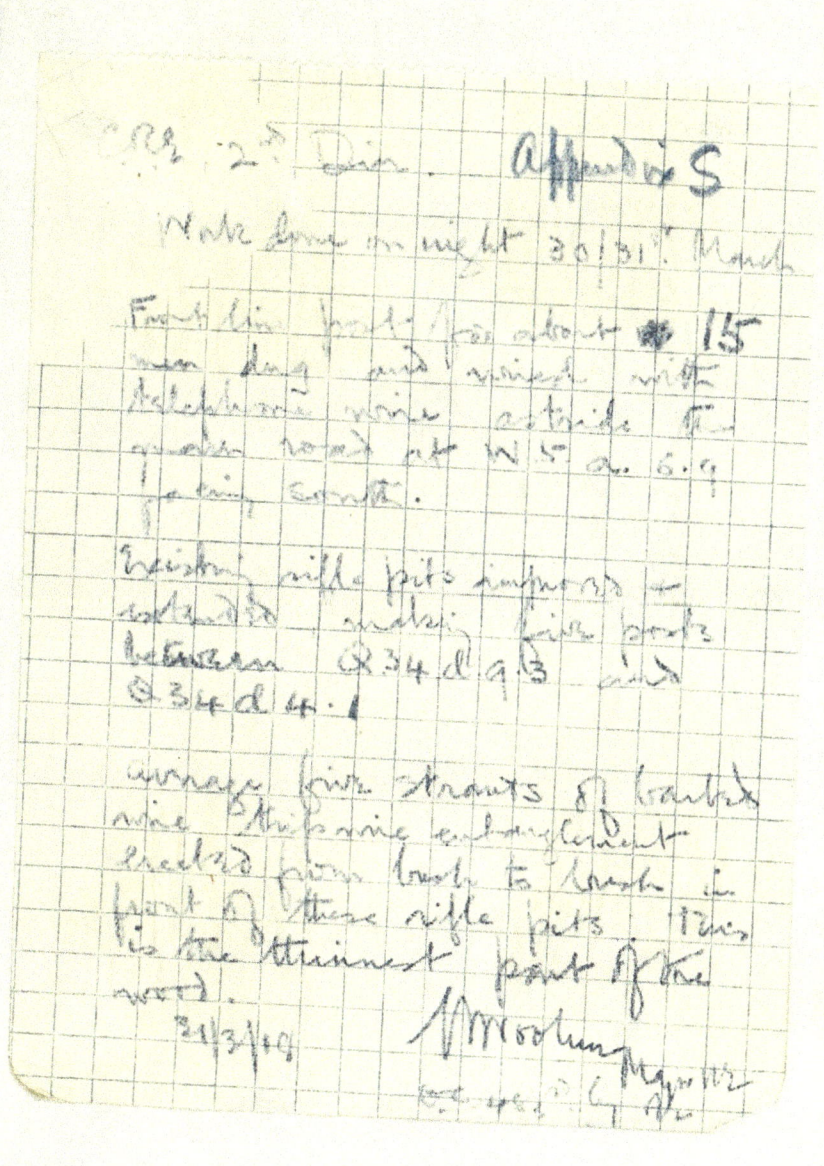

CRE 2nd Div.   Appendix S

Note done on night 30/31st March

Front line posts for about 15 men dug and wired with telephone wire astride the green road at W.5 a 6.9 facing south.

Existing rifle pits improved — selected making fire posts between Q.34.d.9.3 and Q.34.d.4.1

A very four strands of barbed wire stringing entanglement erected from bush to bush in front of these rifle pits. This is the thinnest part of the wood.

31/3/19   J Woolwin Major RE

OC 5th TYNESIDE
" "
OC M.G... — — — Appendix T RE 14

Work to night will be as follows:-

Continue work previously done last night. Companys to send 2/3 of their strength.

9 L.G.S. wagons will unload at VARENNES dump. 5.0 p.m. tonight. 3 for each Coy.

Short narrative of events will be sent on completion of work with sketches (map if possible). Each day will be treated as a separate phase.

Parties should report to O.C. Composite Battn ENGLEBELMER for any special orders. Sketches are very desirable especially on the Right Flank.

31/3/18

ANZ 2nd Divn.   Appendix U

Wiring Report for 31st/1st

Wire thickened from Q.34.d.9.3
to Q.34.d.4.1. & 2 strands
from Junction Q.34.d.9.3 to
W.5.a.9.9

Tape laid in trenches in
W.5.a. All trenches out
of this trip blocked. Thick'ps
made along tape. New
trench cut at Eastern end.
Left on main road W.5.a.6.6.
improved.

Shelters follow later.

1/4/18
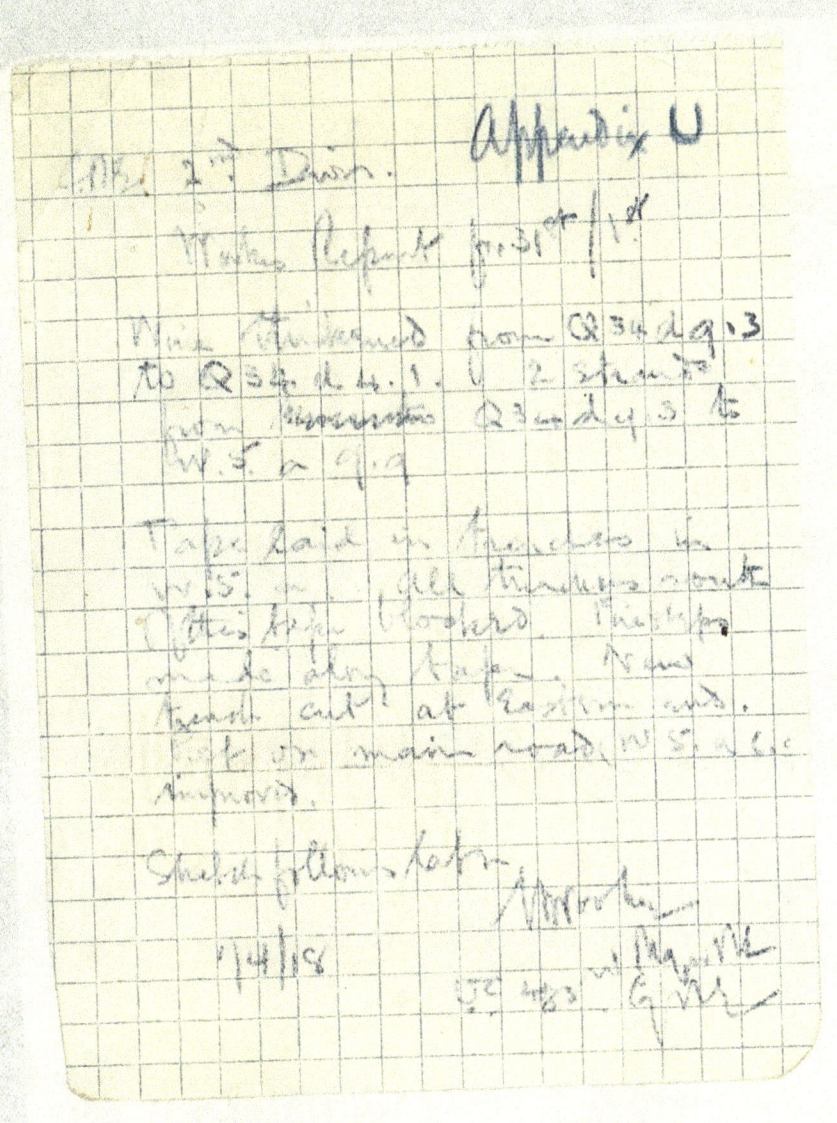

2nd Divisional Engineers

483rd FIELD COMPANY R. E.

APRIL 1918.

WAR DIARY or INTELLIGENCE SUMMARY

Army Form C. 2118.

483rd Fd Coy RE

APRIL 1918

Vol 36

Place	Date	Hour	Summary of Events and Information	Remarks and references to Appendices
MEAULVILLERS	APRIL 1ST		Nos 1 and 2 sections working by night on AVELUY WOOD. - 4 strands of wire erected over 600 yards of front astride the main ALBERT - HAMEL road. - Gully south of front line in W. 5. a. (Sheet 57DSE) filled with wire. - Posts dug at Q.34.d.9.3 and Q.35.c.1.2 - Trench dug across main road at front Q.35.c.7.0.	A
	" 2ND		Nos 3 and 4 sections working by night on AVELUY WOOD. - Trench made in trench east of main road (W.5.a) - Trench across road improved (Q.35.c.7.0) Wiring much hindered by shelling. - 2 ORs killed. - Lieut Graham wounded (at duty). 4 ORs wounded. 1 OR Sect.E.Hqrs.	B
HURTEBISE FARM.	" 4TH		Company marched to HURTEBISE FARM (N.W of FAMECHON). - Billeting party sent on to REBREUVE.	C and D.
HONVAL	" 5TH		Company marched to HONVAL. 1 OR Sect.E.Hqrs.	
	" 6TH		Training, checking tools, equipment and clothing, painting wagons.	E.
	" 10TH		Company put on 2 hours notice to move. - Wagons packed.	F.
SOMBRIN.	" 11TH		Company marched to SOMBRIN	
LA HERLIÈRE	" 12TH		Company marched to LA HERLIÈRE - Put on one hours notice. 1 OR Sect.E.Hqrs.	G and H.
	" 13TH		O.C. and Lieut Wilgar went with S.P.6.O's from sections to RANSART to take over work from 76th Field Coy RE - Guards Division. - S.P.6.O's remain for the night.	
RANSART	" 14TH		Company relieved 76th Coy R.E. - 4 sections in shelters in X.2.c (Sheet 51e). - Transport lines at BEAUMETZ.	I
	" 15TH		1 section assisting 181st Tunnelling Coy RE on shelter for new Brigade H.QRS (X.13.d.cent.) and collecting material. - 2 sections wiring N and E edges of ADINFER WOOD. - 1 section wiring E of HAMEAU FARM.	J
	" 16TH		French elephant shelters salved and erected for men at Bde H.Q. - Wiring

1.

Army Form C. 2118.

WAR DIARY
or
INTELLIGENCE SUMMARY

1/3rd E. A. Field Coy R.E.
(Erase heading not required.)

APRIL 1918

Instructions regarding War Diaries and Intelligence Summaries are contained in F. S. Regs., Part II. and the Staff Manual respectively. Title Pages will be prepared in manuscript.

Place	Date	Hour	Summary of Events and Information	Remarks and references to Appendices
RANSART	APRIL 16TH		Purple outpost line on ADINFER - BOIRY road.	
	" 17TH		Wiring VALLEY WOOD. - RE J.A. B.M.H.Q. started.	
	" 18TH		2 M.G.s at X.21.c.9.2 wired all round. —	
			60 suppers mates (1st Batt. Royal Berks.) attached.	
			2/Lieut. R.A. Fullers joined from Base. 3¼ O.R.s (Reinforcements) joined Unit. 1 OR Sect Hosp!	
	" 19TH		B.M.H.Q. mess completed	
	" 20TH		Artillery track completed from X.1.d.6.8. to X.9.c.3.9. — Lieut Bundle to	
			base on medical grounds. 3.O.R.s Sick & Hosp!	
	" 21ST		Work started on posts in ADINFER at X.21.c.5.9. and X.21.d.2.4. —	
			Artillery tramway through to HENDECOURT	
	" 22ND		Work started on posts in SUGAR FACTORY (X.24.a)	
	" 23RD		Work started on post at WINDMILL FARM. — Lieut G.M. Entwistle and	
			2/Lt. A.K. Grave, 1st K.R.R. attached as suppers males officers	
	" 24TH		Abatis inside N. edge of ADINFER WOOD started. New recce Batt H.Q.	
			(shelters) at X.14.6.0.5. — 60 more suppers males (1st K.R.R.) attached. — 1 + O.R.s	
			joined from base (reinforcements) 1 OR 292 Fd Hosp!	
	" 25TH		Bde H.Q. shelters completed. 3.O.R.s Sick & Hosp!	
	" 26TH		The K.B.s Coy 57th Mon Battery with their shelters. — Camp over COJEUL RIVER at	
	" 27TH		Viewing 2nd Mon Battery with their shelters. —	
			5.20 a.4.7. so that transport may avoid BOIRY in case of gas shelling. 1 OR Sk Hosp!	
	" 29TH		Mess at Reserve Batt. H.Q. completed — Lieut R.B. Barnard-Smith	
			joined from Base. 1.OR Sqound of Hosp!	
	" 30TH		Camp across COJEUL RIVER completed. 1.OR Sick & Hosp! 1 OR to W.L Hosp!	
	GENERAL:			
			Sections were rested in turn for one day per week.	

Commanding, M. Browne
1/3rd Field Company,
(East Anglian) Royal Engineers.

"C" Form.
MESSAGES AND SIGNALS.

Appendix E

Army Form C. 2123.
(In books of 100.)

No. of Message _____

Prefix _____ Code _____ Words _____ Received From YB By a.a. Sent, or sent out At _____ m. To _____ By _____ Office Stamp.

Service Instructions. YB

Handed in at _____ Office 18 m. Received 15 m.

TO   OC 483rd Fld Co RE

Sender's Number.	Day of Month.	In reply to Number.	AAA
N85	10		
You	should	be	prepared
to	move	at	2
hours	notice		
		Received 4pm	
		AH.	

FROM
TIME & PLACE   CRE 2nd Divn

*This line should be erased if not required.

2nd Division No. G.S. 1543/27.

483rd Field Co. R.E.

Appendix D

1. The 483rd Field Co. R.E. will move by march route to-morrow, April 5th, to the 99th Infantry Brigade Area, and will billet at HONVAL, N.E. of FREVENT.

2. Advance billeting party will proceed ahead and report to Headquarters 99th Infantry Brigade at the Chateau, REBREUVE, for details as to accommodation.

3. No restrictions as to route or time of start.

4. Arrival in billets to be reported to Headquarters 2nd Division, and 99th Infantry Brigade.

5. Please acknowledge.

4th April, 1918.

                                                            Lieut-Colonel,
                                              General Staff, 2nd Division.

Copy to 5th Brigade
        99th Brigade
        C.R.E.

RE. 19

~~O.C. 6th Field Coy R.E.~~
~~O.C. 226th Field Coy R.E.~~
O.C. 483rd Field Coy R.E.

Appendix A

Work for tonight will be in continuation of last night's. Companies to send 2/3rds of their their strength.

9 L.G.S. wagons will report as usual at VARENNES dump at 5.0pm tonight. 3 for each Company.

Parties should report at Batt. H.Q. ENGLEBELMER for any special orders.

Progress report to be sent as usual.

Work completed last night was most satisfactory please inform all ranks from M.G.C.

1/4/18.
10.50 am.

PMD

for CRE 2nd Div.

SECRET   R.E. 20.

~~O.C. 59 Field Coy, R.E.~~
~~O.C. 126th Field Coy, R.E.~~   Appendix B
O.C. 483rd Field Coy R.E.

Work for tonight will be in continuation
of last night's. Companies to send usual
parties of 2/3rds of their strength.
9 L.G.S. wagons will report at VARENNES
DUMP at 5 P.M. 3 L.G.S. wagons per Company.
The relieving division will have ~~divisional~~
officers out tonight taking over from 5th Bde.
Officers in charge of work will arrange to
get in touch with Company Commanders
of 5th Bde in the line to whom the reconnoitring
officers of 38th Division will report, and show
the incoming division the work etc that
is being done.
Companies will be rejoining their Brigade
groups tomorrow for the move, and
it is probable than an advanced party
will have to be sent on tomorrow
morning. The remainder of the Company
(including those out tonight) can follow
later in the day. Detailed orders
with regard to move will be issued later

2.15 p.m.
2/4/18   P.M. Betty
                                          C.R.E. 2nd Div. R.E.

~~OC 226th Field Co RE~~ Appendix C RE
OC 483 - - -

The following moves will take place tomorrow April 4th
226th Field Co RE ⎫
483 - - -   ⎬ from present billets

To THIEVRES, FAMECHON area
to be clear of billets by 10.0 am.

Companies to move under orders of
O.Cs.

Advance billeting parties to
report to Staff Capt 5th Bde
at the church THIEVRES for
billets on arrival.

All 1/20,000 maps to be returned
to HQ RE to night

On completion of move units
will come under orders of G.O.C
5th Inf Bde.
Acknowledge.

3/4/18   HQ RE will be at DOULLENS 4/12 & BUNEVILLE in the 5th

J H Shaw
Major RE
for CRE

SECRET.   Copy No. 5

Appendix F

99th INFANTRY BRIGADE ORDER No. 231.

11th April 1918.

Ref. Sheet 51c. 1/40,000.

1. The 99th Infantry Brigade Group will march today to the area SOMBRIN - WARLUZEL - COULLEMONT in accordance with the attached March Table.

2. Arrival in billets and location of Headquarters will be notified to Brigade Headquarters at SOMBRIN.

3. Battalions will march with 100 yards interval between Companies.

4. Transport will accompany Units.

5. Billeting parties will report to Staff Captain as under :-

   1/R.Berks.
   No. 2 Coy Train,   } Church, SOMBRIN, at 2 p.m.
   483rd Field Coy.R.E.

   1/K.R.R.C.
   100th Field Amb.   } Church, WARLUZEL, at 2 p.m.
   23rd R.Fus.
   99th T.M.Battery.

6. Brigade Headquarters will close at REBREUVE at 3 p.m. and re-open at SOMBRIN at the same hour.

Farquharson

Captain,
Brigade Major.
99th Inf. Bde.

Issued through Signals at 12.30 p.m.
to :-
23rd R.Fus.
1/R.Berks.
1/K.R.R.C.
99th T.M.Bty.
483rd Field Coy R.E.
100th Field Amb.
No. 2 Coy Train.
2nd Div. "G".
2nd Div. "Q".
A.D.M.S.
No. 2 Section, 2nd Signal Coy.
E.T.O.
5th Inf. Bde.
6th Inf. Bde.
War Diary.
File.

MARCH TABLE issued with 99th Inf. Brigade Order No. 231.

Unit.	From	To	Starting Pt.	Time of passing Starting Pt.	Route
Bde H.Qrs.	REBREUVE.	SOMBRIN	Road Junct. M.5.a.1.5.	3 p.m.	WAMIN - le CAUROY.
1/R.Berks.	IVERGNY.	do	Cross Rds N.27.a.8.9.	3 p.m.	Sus-St-LEGER.
No 2 Coy Train.	CANETTEMONT.	do	Cross Roads H.25.c.95.40	2 p.m.	ETREE-WAMIN - le CAUROY.
483rd Field Co. R.E.	HONVAL.	do	Road junction G.23.d.4.6	2.15 p.m.	CANETTEMONT - ETREC WAMIN - le CAUROY.
1/K.R.R.C.	Gnd. ECURET.	WARLUZEL.	Road junct. M.a. 9.6.	2 p.m.	REBREUVIETTE - IVERGNY - Sus-St-Leger.
100th Field Amb.	CANETTEMONT.	do	Cross Roads. H.25.c.95.40.	2.15 p.m.	ETREE-WAMIN - BEAUDRICOURT.
23rd Fus.	IVERGNY.	COULLEMONT.	Cross Roads. N.27.a.8.9.	2.30 p.m.	SUS-StLeger.
99th T.M.Bty.	REBREUVE.	do.	Road junction. M.5.a.1.5.	2.45 p.m.	IVERGNY - SUS St.Leger.

Appendix G
Copy No. 5

99th. INFANTRY BRIGADE. O.O. No. 352

Ref. Sheet 51.c 1/40000 and LENS 1/100000   13th. April 1917

1. The 99th. Infantry Brigade Group will march today to LE HAMILLE Area in accordance with the attached March Table.

2. Arrival in billets and location of Headquarters will be notified to Brigade Headquarters at LARBRET.

3. The march will be carried out with intervals of 300 yards between Units and 50 yards between Companies.

4. Transport will accompany Units.

5. Billeting parties will report to the Staff Captain at the Town Major's Office LARBRET at 11 am.
The 100th. Field Ambulance will make its own arrangements for billeting in GRINCOURT

6. Brigade Headquarters will close at SOUDAIN at 1.30 pm. and will re-open at LARBRET at the same hour.

                                                    Major for
                                                    Brigade Major.
Issued through signals at 10.30 am.   99th. Infantry Brigade.
  to :-
        23rd. R. Fus.
        1st. R. Berks.
        1st. K.R.R.C.
        99th. T.M. Bty.
        483rd. Field Coy. R.E.
        100th. Field Amb.
        No. 2. Coy Train
        2nd. Divn. "G"
        2nd. Divn. "Q"
        A.D.M.S.
        No. 2 Sect. 2nd. Signal Coy.
        L.T.O.
        5th. Inf. Bde.
        6th. Inf. Bde.
        War Diary.
        File.

March Table issued with 99th. Inf. Bde. Order No. ??

Unit.	From.	To.	Starting Point.	Time of Passing Starting Point.	Route.
Bde. Hqrs.	SOMBRIN	LA HERLIERE Area	Road Junction O.25.d.8.4.	1.30.pm.	SAULTRY - L.RENT
1st. R. ...r's.	SOMBRIN	LA HERLIERE Area	Road Junction O.25.d.8.4.	1.15.pm.	SAULTRY - L.RENT
No. 2 Coy Train	SOMBRIN	LA HERLIERE Area	Road Junction O.25.d.8.4.	1 pm.	SAULTRY - L.REN T
463rd. Field Coy R.E.	SOMBRIN	LA HERLIERE Area	Road Junction O.25.d.8.4.	1.25 pm.	SAULTRY - LAMBRET
1st. K.....C.	HALUZEL	LA HERLIERE Area	Road Junction U.3.b.7.3.	1.35 pm.	COUTURELLE GO......TZ
23rd. R. Fus.	COULMONT	LA HERLIERE Area	Road Junction U.3.b.7.3.	1.45 pm.	COUTURELLE GO......TZ
99th. T... .ty	COULMONT	LA HERLIERE Area	Road Junction U.3.b.7.3.	2 pm.	COUTURELLE GO......TZ
100th. Field Abco.	HALUZEL	GRINCOURT	Road Junction U.3.b.7.3.	2.5 pm.	COUTURELLE.

Code......... m	Words.	Charge.	This message is on a/c of:	Recd. at ......m.
Office of Origin and Service Instructions.	.		Appendix Service	Date H
	Sent At......m. To...... By......		(Signature of "Franking Officer.")	From By......

TO { 2nd R.Fus. 99th I.M.B. H.Q 2nd Field Co
     H.Q 99th No 2 Coy Train R.E.
     1/7 R.B. 100th Field Amb. }

Sender's Number.	Day of Month.	In reply to Number.	AAA
* B.M.502	12/4		

All Units will be ready to move at one hour's notice from 8 a.m. to 12 noon and three hour's notice from 12 noon to 8 a.m. until further orders are acknowledged.

From: Cel
Place:
Time: 6:45 a.m.

Rawlinson
Capt.
Bde. Major.

"A" Form
MESSAGES AND SIGNALS.

Army Form C. 2121
(in pads of 100.)

TO: OC 5th Field Co RE
OC 226
OC 483

Sender's Number.	Day of Month.	In reply to Number.	AAA
RE 16	13		

Ref my warning order this morning
Please arrange to take over work of
Field Cos Guards Divn this afternoon
as under:-
5th Field Co RE will take work of 75th
Field Co G Dvn (Builds BLAIREVILLE + road
work) in LEFT Sector Divnl Front
226" F Co RE will take over work in centre
Sector of Divnl front from 55th Fd Co G Dn
door builds (X 26 7 1)
483 Fd Co RE will take over work in
right Sector Divnl front from 76th Fd G D
builds RANSART X 8 6 5 3
Work will probably commence night
15"/16"

Time 12·10 pm

"A" Form
MESSAGES AND SIGNALS.

Army Form C. 2121 (in pads of 100).

TO: OC 5th Field Co RE
OC 483
(Appendix J)

Sender's Number	Day of Month	In reply to Number	
RE 21	13		AAA

Further to my RE 16 + warning order moves forecasted therein will take place tomorrow. Billets of Field Coys Guards Divn will be vacated by 9.0 am Field Coys of 2nd Divn will arrange to have advance parties to take over billets at that hour.

Billets of 5th Fld Co RE will be at BLAIRVILLE + Roads
" 226" " " " X 2 6 7 1.
" " 483 " " " " RANSART (x.8.6.5.3)
HQrs 11th Divl " " " X 4 6 1 5.

483" Field Co RE will please arrange to send NCO to take over dump dump BLAIRVILLE (100" S of + roads) & should lorries arrive to be offloaded after departure of personnel of Guards Divn, men will be demanded from 5th Fld Co RE for this service.

In the event of an attack Coys will stand fast in present billets & send mounted officer to HQRE.

Shaw

Distribution noted. 7 pm for CRE

Copies to:-
1. 5th Field Coy R.E.
2. 226th Field Coy R.E.
3. 483rd Field Coy R.E.
4. 2nd Divn G
5. 2nd Divn Q   } for info.
6. 10th DCLI
7. CRE Guards Divn

2nd Divisional Engineers

483rd FIELD COMPANY R.E. :: M A Y 1918.

Army Form C. 2118

WAR DIARY
or
INTELLIGENCE SUMMARY
483 (East Anglian) Field Co. R.E.
(Erase heading not required.)

MAY. 1918.

No 31

Place	Date	Hour	Summary of Events and Information	Remarks and references to Appendices
RANSART	1st		WORK CONTINUED. Re-timbering of German dug-outs for R.F.A. BRIGADE. Construction of splinter proof RESERVE BATTN. H.Q. Marking artillery tracks through VALLEY WOOD. Construction of Coy. at WINDMILL FARM. Improvements to Wire of PURPLE OUTPOST LINE. SUGAR FACTORY Tankers. Construction of mask round outskirts of BOIRY to avoid the shelled area. Stables in N. edge of ADINFER WOOD. South ADINFER Village.	
			No 522026 Sapper Robinson F. Evacuated from Hospital	
	2nd		No 292443 " Browne A.E. " " "	
	3rd		No 38301 " Lewis T. Sick to Hospital	
	6th		Divisional round BOIRY completed. RESERVE BATTN. H.Q. Ready for occupation.	
	10/5		Work started on Garrison Cookhouse (BOIRY)	
			522196 Sgt (Rod) Lynds W. Sick to Hospital	
			30163 Driver Leonard O.R. " " "	
	10th		Repair to Huts in RANSART.	
	11th		600 yds Stables completed in ADINFER WOOD.	
LAHERLIERE	12th		Company Relieved by 209th Wellington R.E. (32nd Div.) Company marches to billets at LAHERLIERE. Appendix A	
			No 23002 Sapper Randall C.N. Returned sent from Hospital	
			2nd Lieut. Little W.R. LA GAUCHE top 1st K.R.R. Shewing Centre according to programme HOPKINS B.Lt	
	13th		No 82291 Sapper Richards M. Returned home from Hospital	

[Signed] Commanding,
483rd Field Company.
(East Anglian)
Royal Engineers.

Army Form C. 2118.

WAR DIARY
or
INTELLIGENCE SUMMARY
483rd (E.A.) Field Coy R.E.
(Erase heading not required.)

MAY 1918

Instructions regarding War Diaries and Intelligence Summaries are contained in F. S. Regs., Part II. and the Staff Manual respectively. Title Pages will be prepared in manuscript.

Place	Date	Hour	Summary of Events and Information	Remarks and references to Appendices
	13th		No 519470 Spr Cook A. 21m " Druce George E. No 57941 Sapper Boott I. 511460 " Kenway F. 51859 " Allan J Mrs 99433 " Emery B " " Palm J 402405 " Smith J 21520 " William B Joined Unit (Reinforcements) from R.E. Base Depot. Authy DAG6 C.S.91. AA 11/5/18	
	14th		75 Sergt Met for 99th Royal Engineers	
	15th		522105 Sapper Baker F.H. Sick to Hospital 521908 L/Cpl Chibnall A.	
	16th		No 96303 Sapper Brown W. } Joined Unit (Reinforcements) from R.E Base Depot 402413 " Bennett N. } Authy DA35 C.8 99.	
	17th		Steam boring of northern end of La KERRIERE Mg Emplacement to Company.	
			No 522084 Sapper Bartels H } Sick to Hospital 522156 " Donovan J.S. " 425512 " River Bridge W "	
	18th		Warrant Officer under 2nd Dern S. Drug acting BASSÉE FARM	Appen. D.E.
	20th		No 523054 Sapper M Barder Resumed from Hospital	
	21st		One Lewis Gun Drill Cartridge " " "	Appen. F.
	22nd		No 522231 Sapper Eastern P.G. Sick to Hospital	

[signature]
Commanding, 483rd Field Company
(East Anglian) Royal Engineers

WAR DIARY
INTELLIGENCE SUMMARY

Army Form C. 2118.

MAY 1918

Place	Date	Hour	Summary of Events and Information	Remarks and references to Appendices
	22nd	N.652930	Major Sanderson R.E.	
		N.620368	2nd Lieut Prentice C.E.	
	23rd		Sunny	
			Cuckoo's Call	
			Gulls	
		M.22.52 Drive	Blackhawks M	
			Inspection of Brens Camp by Corps Commander	Appendix G
	24th		Inspection of R.E. 2nd Div by C.E. VI Corps	Appendix H
	25th		Inspection of R.E. 2nd Div by C.E. III Army	
		N.622233	Driver McCabe J.E.	Sick to Hospital
		N.62233a	Sapper Evans R.E.	Return Unit from Hospital
	26th	N.52040	Driver Charles R.	
		N.52026	Driver Robinson J	
		N.26534	Driver Chase D.	Returned Home from Hospital
	27th	N.90340	Sapper Lucas Bartley A	
		5Kent Rec	Lieut Cott A.D.	Sick to Hospital
		N.62057	Driver Sear S.	
		5R2133	Driver S.B.	Returned Home from Hospital
	30th		Memo sent by Lieut Drury C. West	
		N.652011	Sapper Barton F	1st R.E. Base Depot (Medical Ground) Addr: A.D.M.S. 2nd Div Notes 30/5 Appendix I.K.
		5R22 B.	Spr Lupinn R	
			283rd Depot Company	
	31st		Weather Conditions warm and sunshine	

M.Wyndham Capt R.E.
Commanding
263rd (East Anglian) Field Company,
Royal Engineers

SECRET   Appendix A

Orders by Lieut. Colonel P.K.BETTY, D.S.O., R.E.
C.R.E., 2nd Division.

C.R.E's Order No. 108.   Copy...3...

1. Should the situation remain unchanged the Division (less Artillery) will be relieved by the 32nd Division (less artillery) on the nights 11/12th and 12/13th May.

2. Details of Field Coys. reliefs will be arranged between Os.C. Field Coys. concerned.
   All Defence Schemes, maps, &c. will be handed over.

3. Field Coys. of 2nd Division will be relieved as under on 12th inst. Billets to be vacated by 10 a.m. on 12th inst.

   5th Field Co. R.E. at X.4.a.9.7. will be relieved by 218th Field Co. R.E. and move to BAILY area.
   226th Field Co. R.E. at X.2.b.7.1. will be relieved by 206th Field Co. R.E. and move to SAULTY area.
   483rd Field Co. R.E. at X.2.d.9.7. will be relieved by 219th Field Co. R.E. and move to LARBRET area.

   Any routes may be used.
   Advanced parties should be sent on to take over billets and rear parties left to hand over billets, maps, dumps &c.

4. Advanced parties of 32nd Division R.E. will be shown round all work &c. of 2nd Division morning of 10th by officers of Field Coys. This party will arrive at our billets at 9.30. a.m.

5. O.C. 10th D.C.L.I. (Pioneers) will hand over to Pioneers of 32nd Division (present H.Qs. at BLAIRVILLE) all work being carried on under orders of C.R.E. - also stone dumps and road stores.

6. 2nd Divisional Train H.Qs., Train Coys., M.V.S., S.A.A. Section and D.A.D.O.S. will not move billets.

7. Orders regarding organisation of Brigade groups will be issued later.

8. Demolition schemes will be handed over by Lieut. DAVSON R.E. to an officer of 32nd Division morning of 12th inst. This officer will be shown all jobs in hand on 10th inst.

9. Divisional R.E. Dump at BLAIRVILLE (X.4.a.8.8.) will be handed over to 218 Field Co. R.E. by 5th Field Co. R.E.

10. Reports of completion of reliefs, moves, and a copy of handing over notes will be sent to C.R.E's office, BAVINCOURT.

11. Sappers mates will return to their respective battalions on afternoon of 12th - further details will be issued later.

12. H.Q., R.E. will move to BAVINCOURT at 10 a.m. 12th inst. and re-open at noon on same day.

13. Acknowledge.

                                            E.W.Shaw
H.Q.R.E.   Captain R.E.
9.5.18.   for C.R.E., 2nd Division.

Copy No. 1 to 5th Field Co. R.E.   Copy No. 6 to 5th Bde. (for inf)
  "   2 to 226th Field Co. R.E.   "   7 to 6th Bde.   "
  "   3 to 483rd Field Co. R.E.   "   8 to 99th Bde.   "
  "   4 to 10th D.C.L.I.   "   9 to "G"   "
  "   5 to C.R.E. 32nd Divn.   "   10 Office.
            (for inf.)

O.C. 5 Field Co R.E.   Appendix B
" 226" " " ✓
" 483" " " ✓

Please submit Training Programme on attached pro-forma to this office by 5 p.m. on 11th inst. following subjects to be included:—

<u>DISMOUNTED</u>

Physical Drill
Company Drill
Rifle movements
Musketry
Use on Tool
Map reading
Siting of trenches
Lewis gun drill, gas drill &c.

<u>MOUNTED</u>

Foot drill.
Riding
Lectures on horsemanship
Gas drills &c.

H.Q., R.E. 2nd DIVN.
No. G. 5/49
Date 9. 5. 18.

Capt. R.E.
for R.E. 2nd Division

Appendix C

Day	9am – 12noon	12:15 – 12:45	2:30pm – 3:0pm
13	Section drill. Handling of arms. Gas drill. Bayonet fighting.	Physical Training	Musketry (Preliminary)
14	Company drill. Handling of arms. Bayonet fighting. Guards mounting.	do	Lecture (Map reading)
15	Section drill. Lewis Gun drill. Musketry (Prelim aim.) Fire control	do	Lecture (sites & their treatment, inventions)
16	Company drill. Gas drill. Bayonet fighting. Lewis gun drill.	do	Musketry (Rapid aim.)
17	Musketry (Ball amm.) Fire control. Lewis Gun firing.	do	Map reading (instruction of firing)
18	Company drill. Tepin Aurendue exestrade on a pipe (Section Officers). Lewis Gun drill.	do	Lecture (Gas) Aim.

Appendix D

H.Q., R.E. 2nd DIVN.
No. 35/58
Date

O.C. 5th Field Co R.E.
O.C. 226th Field Co R.E.
O.C. 483rd (E.A.) Field Co R.E.

Commencing Monday 20th inst. arrangements have been made with O.C. 2nd Divisional Wing for all dismounted men of Field Coys to be trained daily from 8.30 am to 12 Noon in physical training, bayonet practice, bombing and Rifle exercise etc.

Sections under their Officers will parade as strong as possible at 8.30 am at the Divisional Wing LA BAZEQUE FARM daily, and report to O.C. Divisional Wing representative. Horse transport and bicycles will be used to save men.

O.C. Units will visit the School daily and observe the progress of instruction.

As a few men may be required for work e,g baths, targets etc, these men should be selected from the older men who are too stiff for intensive training or who are already trained men, and daily parties kept unchanged so as to facilitate instruction.

Guards and all possible duties which interfere with instruction will be found by the mounted men during the time sappers are training, It will also be possible to include a few mounted N.C.Os and selected Drivers in the Course.

The object of above arrangements is to give the Units the best possible training under expert instructors for a short time, and to improve and select likely instructors for future use.

Haversack rations should be taken.

H.Q.R.E.
2nd Division.
17th May. 1918.

Lieut. Col. R.E.
Commanding Royal Engineer 2nd Division.

Copies to :- "G")
O.C 2nd Divisional Wing.) For information.

PROGRAMME OF MORNING WORK FOR THE TRAINING
OF ROYAL ENGINEERS AT 2nd DIVISIONAL WING.
------oOo------

Appendix E

MONDAY 20/5/1918.
- 8-30 a.m. ... ... Lecture by the Commanding Officer.
- 9 a.m. ... ... Demonstration by Young N.C.Os.

Arrangement into squads conforming with R.E. Sections.

TUESDAY, 21/5/1918 and daily after.
- 8-30 to 9-15 a.m.   P.T.
- 9-15 to 9-45 a.m.   B.F.
- 10 to 10-45 a.m.   Musketry.
- 11-1145 a.m.   Drill.

Musketry will include shooting on the Range in S.B.R's.

<u>Officers and N.C.Os.</u> For the first 4 days, all Officers and N.C.Os. will be under Sgt HADDEN during the P.T. and B.F. training, to learn the sequence of instruction.

(Signed) E. J. S A W T E L L.

Captain & Adjutant.

19th May, 1918.

OC 5th Field Co RE.
OC 226" " "
OC 483" " "

2nd Div G.S. 647/31
Appendix F

1. Orders have been issued that box respirators are to be worn for one hour daily from 21st to 26th May inclusive so as to ensure that officers and other ranks are thoroughly accustomed to work in respirators. Officers and NCOs are especially to be practised in giving orders while wearing respirators.

2. The hours of practice will be arranged as follows:-

Units	21st	22nd	23rd	24th	25th	26th	
5th Fd Co RE	5-6 pm.	On march to Div Wing.	On march to Div Wing.	On march Div Wing.	On march to Divl Wing	10-11 am	Men on Wagons + bicycles, other ranks + Drivers, Clerks etc 10-11 am
226" " "	5-6 pm	2-3 pm	2-3 pm	2-3 pm	2-3 pm	10-11 am	whole coys & the Clerks 10-11 am & Offrs
483" " "	5-6 pm	2-3 pm	2-3 pm	2-3 pm	2-3 pm	10-11 am	do

3. Particular care is to be taken that all personnel not usually on parade are practised for an hour daily with box respirators. This particularly applies to Clerks, orderlies officers servants and grooms, cooks, police, sanitary squads and other details. As far as possible the above personnel should carry on their ordinary duties in box respirators between fixed hours.

M Watt
Lieut Colonel RE
CRE 2nd Division

2175/15

H.Q., R.E., 2nd DIVN.
No. G 467/3
Date

SECRET   Copy No. 5

99th. Infantry Brigade Order No.240.

Appendix G

Ref. Map. - 51.c.S.E. 1/20,000   22nd.May 1918

1. The Corps Commander will inspect the Brigade and affiliated Field Company R.E. on the Parade Ground, LA CAUCHIE (V.17.c.5.5.) on THURSDAY, 23rd May at 5 p.m.

2. The Brigade will form up in hollow square, Battalions in close column of Companies, Field Company on RIGHT of RIGHT Battalion, Trench Mortar Battery on LEFT of LEFT Battalion.

   Ref.:-

   X. Entrance to parade ground.
   A. 483rd.Field Co.R.E.
   B. 23rd.Royal Fusiliers.
   C. 1st.Royal Berks.Regt.
   D. 1st.Kings Royal Rifle Corps.
   E. 99th.Trench Mortar Battery.

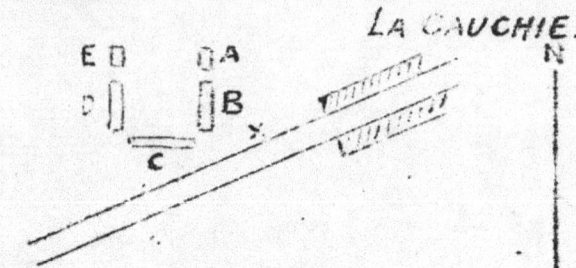

3. Dress - Drill Order without tunics - Steel Helmets will be worn - All Officers will parade dismounted.

4. The American Platoons attached for training will parade with the Companies to which they are attached.

5. Companies will not be equalized.

6. Every available man will be on parade.

7. Markers will report to Staff Captain on the Ground at 4-30 p.m.

8. After the Corps Commander has finished his inspection Battalions will close up on to their leading Companies and the Corps Commander will then address the Brigade.

9. Acknowledge.

Captain,
Brigade Major,
99th.Infantry Brigade.

Issued through Signals at 6pm to :-
23rd.Royal Fusiliers
1st.Royal Berks.Regt.
1st.Kings Royal Rifle Corps.
99th.Trench Mortar Battery
483rd.Field Company R.E.
2nd.Divn.'G'
2nd.Divn.'Q'

No.3 Battalion, 308th. Inf., A.E.F.
Staff Captain.
War Diary
File.

V 3 3

Appendix H

665th Field Co RE
Ob 226 " " "
Ob 483 " " "

The C.E. VI Corps will inspect your boys at the Divn. Wing tomorrow morning at 9:30 a.m., also the C.E. Third Army will inspect the boys at 11:30 a.m. on Saturday, 25 inst at Divn Wing.

23/5/18.

Captain RE
Adjt

2nd DIVISIONAL WING.

Appendix J

MASSED SPORTS.

There will be a Massed Sports Competition for the 3 R.E. Companies now under training with the Divisional Wing at 10-30 a.m. on Thursday next. Time allowed for the whole competition will be one hour.

INTER-SECTION COMPETITIONS:-

The following Competitions will be carried out:-

1. Bullet and Bayonet Assault - Teams of one Officer or N.C.O. and 8 men.
    Marks will be allotted as follows:-
    Control of Section in Assault.   10 points.
    Spirit of Section.   10 points.
    Fire Orders etc.   10 points.
    Each hit on Target.   2 points.
    Each disc pierced by Bayonet.   1 point.

2. Ring Course. Time allowed 28 seconds.
    2 points for each ring carried.
    No points unless correct point made at ring.
    5 points for spirit and dash.
    1 point deducted for every second over time.
    Teams of three men.

3. Points and Parries. Teams of 2 men per section.
    Three points and three parries.
    Two points for each good point or parry.
    Points to be indicated by means of blob stick ring.
    Parries made with rifle and bayonet against blob stick.

On completion of the Bayonet and Bullet Assault, each team will line up for the following events:-

A. LONG JUMP. The complete team with Commander will start in line and all jump together.
    1 point to the section for each man clearing the jump.

B. HIGH JUMP. The same as (A)

C. BACKWARD RACE of 30 yards. Time 10 secs.
    1 point to section for each man completing within the time.

D. FORWARD SPRINT of 50 yards. Time 10 secs. Same as (C)

Rifle with Bayonet fixed and scabbard, to be carried at the "On Guard" position.

JUDGES etc.

Scorer. ... ...   L/C WILLIAMS

---oOo---

BULLET and BAYONET ASSAULT.

Musketry.   ... ...   Lieut SEED.
Bayonet.   ... ...   Sgt HADDEN.
1st Line sacks. ... ...   Sgt TIDY.
2nd Line sacks. ... ...   Sgt DIX.
3rd Line sacks. ... ...   Sgt SUTTON.
Targets.   2
Lining up teams. ... ... R.S.M. CARNEY.

- 2 -

JUDGES etc. (Cont)

RING COURSE.

    Supervising Officer. ... ... Capt SANTEL.
    N.C.O. ... ... Sgt BEALE.
    10 Duty Men to replace rings.

TEST COURSE.

    Long Jump. ... ... 2/Lt. ARCHER.
    High Jump. ... ... Lieut GERT.
    Backward Race. ... ... Lieut FORESHEW.
    Forward Race. ... ... 2/Lt BARTLETT.

    Supervision of the whole Course. ... Capt. HUNTER.

All teams to be lined up at the Starting Points ready to compete at 10-30 a.m.

Teams will be numbered 1 to 16 and order of competitors will be drawn for on Wednesday at 10-30 a.m.

------oOo------

26th May, 1918.

Appendix K

2ND DIVISIONAL WING.
W.550

2nd Division "G"
Major COULON, H.Qs. P & B.T. Third Army.
C.R.E. 2nd Division.
O.C. 5th Field Company R.E.
O.C. 226th Field Company R.E.
O.C. 483rd Field Company R.E.

  Herewith result of the Massed Sports held this morning. The total number of men put through was roughly 250 and the time taken to do so, was one hour. (5 minutes being deducted for breakdown of apparatus.)

       W. Kilburn Lieut-Colonel.
    Commanding 2nd Divisional Wing.

30/5/1918.

2nd DIVISIONAL WING.

RESULT OF MASSED SPORTS.

Company.	Section.	Bullet & Bayonet.	Ring Course.	Points & Parries.	Test course.	Totals.
483rd	2	77	29	10	22	138
483rd	1	70	26	11	21	128
5th	4	86	32	12	27	157
5th	2	75	26	15	26	142
226th	4	79	31	12	20	142
226th	1	75	32	7	28	142
483rd	3	82	33	11	31	157
483rd	4	79	29	10	27	145
5th	3	73	32	16	31	152
5th	1	93	25	11	31	160
226th	3	80	18	12	27	137
226th	2	94	29	8	33	164

--------oOo--------

Winning Sections are as follows:-

```
  1st.   No. 2. Section, 226th Field Company.   ...   Total 164 points.
  2nd    No. 1. Section, 5th Field Company.     ...   Total 160 points.
( 3rd.   No. 4. Section, 5th Field Company.     ...   Total 157 points.
) 3rd.   No. 3. Section, 483rd Field Company.   ...   Total 157 points.
```

--------oOo--------

Order of Merit by Companies:-

```
  1st.   No. 5. Field Company.      ...   ...   Total points 611
  2nd.   No. 226. Field Company.    ...   ...   Total points 585
  3rd.   No. 483rd Field Company.   ...   ...   Total points 568.
```
--------oOo--------

Top Score - Bullet and Bayonet Competition:-

    No. 2. Section, 226th Field Company.   ...   94 points.

Top Score - Ring Course:-

    No. 3. Section, 483rd Company.   ...   ...   33 points.

Top Score - Points and Parries Competition.

    No. 3. Section, 5th Field Company.   ...   16 points.

Top Score - Test Course:-

    No. 2. Section, 226th Field Company.   ...   33 points.

--------oOo--------oOoOoO--------oOo--------

2nd Divisional Engineers

483rd FIELD COMPANY R.E. ::: JUNE 1918.

WAR DIARY or INTELLIGENCE SUMMARY

483rd (E.A.) FIELD Co. R.E.

JUNE. 1918.

Army Form C. 2118.

Place	Date	Hour	Summary of Events and Information	Remarks and references to Appendices
LAHEERIERE	1st		Training continued at LA BAZEQUE FARM. Owing to shelling, ropes shifted into trenches outside the village. 1 O.R. Wounded (slight) - remained at duty. 3 1.O.R. joined Unit. Reinforcement.	
	5th		O.C. and Lt. VEY. with 4 N.C.O's taken round works in new sector by O.C. 76th Coy. R.E. 1 O.R. Sick to Hosp.	
	6th		1 O.R. Sick to 39th Gen Hospital.	
	7th		2 Prs. WILSON and BARNARD-SMITH proceeded to new billets to take over works from 76th Coy. Coy marched to billets in old German line near HANNESCAMPS (E.11.c.15.43.)	Appendix "A".
E.11.c.15.43			Hors-Crim at PONNIER. No. 3 Section on detachment at BIENVILLERS. 2 Officers 9, 120 O.Rs attached from 99th Bde for instruction. 1 O.R. 99th Gen Hosp. Lieut. BARNARD-SMITH to near H.Q. with P.U.O.	
	8th		Lt. BARNARD-SMITH evacuated (Sick) 1 O.R. Wounded (slight) remained at duty. 3 O.R. (Reinforcement) 5 O.Rs Sick to Hosp. (Influenza)	
			Joined Unit - Work in Camp.	
	9th		Work on dugouts in Camp. 1 O.R. Sick to Hosp. (Influenza)	
	10th		Work in the Line. 1 O.R. Sick to Hosp. (Influenza)	
			6 O.Rs. Sick to Hosp. (Influenza) 5 O.Rs. (Reinforcement) Joined Unit.	Appendix "B".
	11th		Work started on Bde H.Q. and Cookhouse for Light Battalion.	
	12th		Retimbering old German dugout for Bde Signals. 1 O.R. Sick to Hosp. (Influenza) 2 O.Rs. Joined from Hosp. - 1	
	13th		Work started on new Coy H.Q. for Light Batt.	
	14th		Work started on wiring, deepening & widening PURPLE LINE with Infantry parties.	
	15th		2 O.R's rejoined from Hosp.	
	16th		Shelters started for rear Companies of Reserve Batt. 1 O.R. Joined Unit (Reinforcement).	
	17th		Excavation of Bde H.Q. completed. No. 3 Section moved up to forward billets.	
	18th		1 O.R. Sick to Hosp.	
	19th		Work started on Shelters for "D" Coy. 2nd M.G. Batt. 1 O.R. transferred to 565th (A.T.) Coy R.E. Bde H.Q. Mess hut dismantled, transported & re-erected in new position.	
	20th		1 O.R. rejoined from Hosp. Signal dugout completed -28 shelters completed for Reserve Batt. 40 O.R. (K.R.R.S attd) return to their Batt. 2 O.R's Sick to Hosp. 1 O.R. rejoined from Hosp.	

Commanding 483rd Field Company,
(East Anglian) Royal Engineers

Army Form C. 2118.

WAR DIARY
or
INTELLIGENCE SUMMARY

483rd (E.A.) FIELD Cy. R.E.

(Erase heading not required.)

JUNE 1918.

Instructions regarding War Diaries and Intelligence Summaries are contained in F. S. Regs., Part II. and the Staff Manual respectively. Title Pages will be prepared in manuscript.

Place	Date	Hour	Summary of Events and Information	Remarks and references to Appendices
E.11.c.15.43.	21st		Rested (Light) with in HANNESCAMPS prepared for demolition - 1.O.R. to Hosp.(Shell Gas O.E.) 1.O.R. to R. (Light) (Remained at duty). 1.O.R. Sick to Hosp.	
"	22nd			
"	23rd		Second Urgent started for Lg. Cy. H.Q. (Light Posts). Drawing Tamping of Mine. Small mines at HANNESCAMPS X roads.	
"	24th		New Bde. H.Q. Ready for occupation. 2.O.R's Wynond Yen Hosp. 2.O.R's Sick to Hosp.	
"	25th		Small mine found to be in a thoroughly unsatisfactory condition & were cancelled by C.R.E. Cap. Pattrick & Lippard awarded the M.S.M. 1.O.R. Sick to Hosp.	
"	26th		1.O.R. Sick to Hosp.	
"	28th		2.O.R's joined Unit (Reinforcements) from R.E. Base Depot. 1.O.R. rejoined Unit for Hosp. Drawing Tamping of large mine at HANNESCAMPS X roads - Duckboarding of	
"	29th		99 AVENUE Completed - 1.O.R. rej'd. from Hosp.	
"	30th		Capt. J.H. Mason, M.C. R.E. ret. O.R. Joined Unit for 247th L.Cy. R.E.	

M Morton
Major R.E.,
Commanding,
483rd Field Company,
(East Anglian) Royal Engineers.

43RD
(EAST ANGLIAN)
FIELD COMPANY, R.E.
O.R.
2/7/18

Appendix A

SECRET.   Copy No. 3

ORDERS BY Lieut-Colonel P. K. BETTY, D.S.O., R.E.
C.R.E., 2nd Division.

C.R.E's Order No. 113

1. Further to my V.398, relief of Guards Division by 2nd Division, will take place as therein stated.

2. Field Companies of 2nd Division will relieve Field Companies of Guards Division as below :-

    5th Field Co. R.E. (BARLY) will relieve the 55th Field Co. R.E. (E.11.a.3.5.) on the 6th inst. Billets to be vacated by 3 p.m.

    226th Field Co. R.E. will relieve the 75th Field Co. R.E. (W.23.c.5.4.) on the 7th inst. Billets to be vacated by 3 p.m.

    483rd Field Co. R.E. will relieve the 76th Field Co. R.E. (E.18.a.10.95) on the 7th inst. Billets to be vacated by 3 p.m.

    Companies will leave behind Billet guards until relieved.

3. Maps, Dumps, etc. will be taken over, and copies of handing over notes of Guards Division forwarded to H.Q., R.E.

4. Completion of relief will be reported to H.Q., R.E.

5. H.Q., R.E. will close at BAVINCOURT at 4 p.m. and open at LA BAZEQUE FARM at 6 p.m. on the 7th inst.

6. ACKNOWLEDGE.

Captain, R.E.
for C.R.E., 2nd Division

H.Q., R.E.
4th June, 1918.

Copy No. 1 to 5th Field Co. R.E.
      2   226th Field Co. R.E.
      3   483rd Field Co. R.E.
      4   10th D.C.L.I.
      5   "G"
      6   "Q"
      7   C.R.E., Guards Division.
      8   File.

A.119
Appendix B

O.C. 2nd Div.
Work report for 10/6/18

One Section (BIENVILLERS). Work at H.Q.RE
2nd Div. Preparing own billets
near Coy HQ.
Tamping to main charge at X roads
HANNESCAMP completed.
Tamping small charge continued.
Fixing rings to trees to ensure
their fall across the road.
Bunks repairs on houses in
BIENVILLERS (for Town Major)

One Section (very whole strength epidemic of flu)
has been in to dugouts at
F.13.a.16 and F.14.a.33. Deep
dugout in camp (excavation)

One section Assisting in making dugouts in
front line. Timber aid post
at F.15.c.0.0. Deep dugout
in camp

One section. Clearing trees for a rifle
range. Supervising work
on square. Lining well (Owens
Farm)

J. Woolley, Major RE
11/6/18   O.C. 483rd G.W.

2nd Divisional Engineers

483rd FIELD COMPANY R.E. ::: JULY 1918.

Army Form C. 2118.

WAR DIARY
or
INTELLIGENCE SUMMARY

483rd (E.4) FIELD Co R.E.

(Erase heading not required.)

July 1918

WR 39

Place	Date	Hour	Summary of Events and Information	Remarks and references to Appendices
E.11.c.15.43	1st		MAP REF. SHEET 57d N.E.	

Coy H.Q. remained throughout the month at E.11.c.15.43 and work throughout the month on

Work was carried on throughout the month on

(a) PURPLE LINE Deepening, widening, firestepping, revetting and provision of approaches, in to and from F.11.c.55 to F.23.a.4.5.

(b) PURPLE SUPPORT LINE Deepening, widening, firestepping from F.11.b.55 F.11.a.67.

(c) A Dug out for Batt. H.Qrs. in F.11.c.9.5. on the PURPLE FRONT LINE commenced 1st.

(d) Improvements to New Chards at QUESNOY FARM. Including provision of splints, Gros. Roof, new wired elevating beds and sided. In filling arrangements, concreting of floor etc. For the above work 2 Sections R.E. and parties of INFANTRY averaging 120 r.u. daily were used.

(e) Preparations for demolition of HANNES DUMPS X ROADS were complete on the 30th. Preparation for demolition of NEUFS TREES and CONCRETE STANDARDS along line of approach roads to villages were complete, and regularly detailed and inspected.

(f) Dugout for Coy H.Q. and Storeroom at F.16.d.4.5.4.3.

Army Form C. 2118.

July 19

WAR DIARY
or
INTELLIGENCE SUMMARY

(Erase heading not required)

437 (EA) FIELD CO RE

Place	Date	Hour	Summary of Events and Information	Remarks and references to Appendices
Ellis 15 43	12th		(G) BATTN COOKHOUSE was completed at F15d 2.5. m 21.a.	
			(H) Second Entrance to the Dugout at F15d 1-8. was completed.	
			(I) Shelters for 40 men were completed in area F14 a.	
			(J) Two old German Dugouts at F20 & 6.9 were destroyed all material being salved.	
			(K) All Dugouts in the area were fitted with double gas curtains.	
	14th		An Aid Post was commenced at F15d 05 m5 and worked on to remainder of month	
	15th		A Dugout for Coy HQ and garrison was commenced at F16 S.5. and worked on to remainder of month	
	13th		A Dugout for INFANTRY BDE HQ and RFA BRIGADE HQrs was commenced E4c 25 30	
			and worked on to remainder of month	
	19th		Preparation for demolition of STA VI AND reconnoitres.	

Army Form C. 2118.

JULY 1918

WAR DIARY
or
INTELLIGENCE SUMMARY
(Erase heading not required.)

ASHEA FIELD CORE

Place	Date	Hour	Summary of Events and Information	Remarks and references to Appendices
Ello 15.43	2nd		2 O.R's Sick to Hosp.	
	3rd		1 O.R. Awarded MILITARY MEDAL.	
	4th		1 O.R. Sick to Hosp.	
	"		1 O.R. Joined Unit Reinforcement from R.E.B.D.	
	5th		1 O.R. Sick to Hospital.	
	"		1 O.R. Goes Sorry to Hospital.	
	6th		1 O.R. Transferred to H/Q a R.E.	
	"		3 O.R's Rejoined Unit from Hospital	
	"		1 O.R. Sick to Hospital	
	7th		1 O.R. Joined Unit from R.E.B.D. Reinforcement	
	8th		1 O.R. Rejoined from Hospital.	
	9th		1 O.R. Sick to Hospital.	
	11th		1 O.R. Rejoined from Hospital	
	13th		1 O.R. Joined Unit Reinforcement from R.E.B.D.	
	"		3 O.R's Sick to Hospital	
	14th		1 O.R. Proceeded on 6.7.U.K.	
	15th		2 O.R's (1 Mounted) Joined Unit Reinforcement from R.E.B.D.	
	"		1 Officer Returned from Leave	

Army Form C. 2118.

WAR DIARY
or
INTELLIGENCE SUMMARY

(Erase heading not required.)

483rd (EAST ANGLIAN) FIELD CO RE

July 1918

Place	Date	Hour	Summary of Events and Information	Remarks and references to Appendices
Elle 15 ms	16th		1 OR Sick to Hospital	
	14th		1 OR " " "	
	"		1 OR Returns from Hospital	
	18th		1 OR Sick to Hospital	
	20th		1 Officer Returns Unit from REBD	
	"		1 OR " " " Hospital	
	"		1 OR " " "	
	21st		1 OR Resigning L.O. under (Passport)	
	"		1 Sgt Temp Adjt. Sent for (Passport)	
	"		Warrant Officer Sick to Hospital	
	"		1 OR Awarded BAR TO MILITARY MEDAL	
	23rd		1 OR Awarded BAR TO MILITARY MEDAL	
	24th		1 OR Returns Unit from Hospital	
	25th		1 OR " " " "	
	26th		1 OR " " " "	
	26th		1 OR Sick to Hospital	
	30th		1 OR Sick to Hospital	
	31st		1 OR Returns from leave to UK	

[Signature] Major RE
Commanding, 483rd Field Company,
(East Anglian) Royal Engineers.

483RD (EAST ANGLIAN) FIELD COMPANY, R.E.
No. 95
Date 3-8-18

2nd Divisional Engineers

483rd FIELD COMPANY R. E. ::: AUGUST 1918

WAR DIARY or INTELLIGENCE SUMMARY

Army Form C. 2118.

483 (E.A.) FIELD Coy R.E.

AUGUST 1918

MAP REFERENCES ARE FROM SHEET 57c.

Place	Date	Hour	Summary of Events and Information	Remarks and references to Appendices
E11c 15.4.3	1st to 19th		Note line at POMMIER. Company continued work on :- Dugouts at F16d 45.40, E4c 2.4, F11c 55, F11d 95 An P.O.R at F15d 50. PURPLE FRONT LINE AND PURPLE SUPPORT LINE IN F.14. Further accommodation was provided at Batt N.Q. F9d. 6.1. New Camp for two Companies of Reserve Battalion was commenced on 6th and completed on 14th.	8th 5th.
			Party of 1 NCO and 12 O.R.s of 319th Reg A.E.F. was attached to Company for instruction from 8th 5th	11th-5th-14th
			" " 3 " 24 " " 308 " E " Regt A.E.F. " " "	" " "
			" " 3 " 24 " " 308 " E " Regt A.E.F. " " "	
			Three parties worked together on work as above.	
N25b. 4.3	19th	5.30a	Company H.Q. and dismounted section moved to POMMIER at 5.30am	
E11c. 2.4	20th	4.30pm	H.Q. and Dismounted section moved to E4C 2.4.	
"	"		P.O.W. cage erected in E4C back to Gomby began at F16d. 4.5	
E11c 15.43	21st	11am	H.Q. and Dismounted Section moved to old billets E11c 15.4.3	
"	"	4pm	Company transport moved to E11c 15.4.3.	
F9a 4.5	23rd	8am	Company moved to F9a 4.5.	
"	"		Reconnaissance of COURCELLES for water. Convoy ordered one mile north through COURCELLES cleared of debris.	

Army Form C. 2118.

WAR DIARY
or
INTELLIGENCE SUMMARY

(Erase heading not required.)

AUGUST 1918

Place	Date	Hour	Summary of Events and Information	Remarks and references to Appendices
F9a.4.5	23rd		Attached Infantry working on Salvage and a party for water point at F23.46.	MAP REFERENCES ARE FROM SHEET 5/c
"	24th		Reconnaissance for water at GOMIECOURT was carried out. Work on repair of COURCELLES - GOMIECOURT - ERVILLERS Road was carried out by 1 Section R.E. and attached K.R.R. 2 Sections R.E. and attached R.BERKS working on track in area F4, F8, F14.	
"	25th		Work with 1 Section R.E. and attached R.BERKS on GOURCELLES - GOMIECOURT - ERVILLERS Road. 2 Sections R.E. and attached K.R.R. worked on improvement to track F4, F8, F14.	
"	26 and 27th		Work with 4 Sections R.E. and 10 Officers and 4/ ORs 1st R.BERKS returned to their Battalion (3/4) 1 " " " 31 " 1st K.R.R	Attached Infantry on AYETTE - ABLAINZEVILLE ROAD
A16a.4.0 A22d.4.2	28th "	4.0am 10.am	Convoy moved as follows: HQs and 2 Sections and transport 3 Section Work was carried out by all 4 Sections on COURCELLES - GOMIECOURT - ERVILLERS Road.	
"	29th & 31st		Work was carried out by all 4 Sections on GOMIECOURT - ERVILLERS Road.	

WAR DIARY
or
INTELLIGENCE SUMMARY

August 1918

/51st Field Coy
(Erase heading not required.)

Instructions regarding War Diaries and Intelligence Summaries are contained in F. S. Regs., Part II. and the Staff Manual respectively. Title Pages will be prepared in manuscript.

Place	Date	Hour	Summary of Events and Information	Remarks and references to Appendices
E11c 16 H3	2nd		2 ORs Proceeded on month Commutation of Engagement Leave.	
	5th		1 OR. Sick to Hospital	
	6th		1 OR. Returned Unit from Hospital	
	7th		2 ORs Joined Unit from R.E. Base Depot, 1 OR Accidental Injury to Hospital.	
	8th		1 OR Proceeded on Ordinary leave to UK.	
	10th		" " " " " "	
	11th		1 OR Joined Unit from R.E. Base Depot	
	14th		1 OR Sick to Hospital	
	15th		1 OR Returned from Hospital	
	19th		1 OR Proceeded on Ordinary leave to UK, 1 OR proceeded on month Special Leave.	
W26b+3	20th		1 OR Accidental Injury to Hospital	
E11c 15.H3	22nd		1 OR Returned from Hospital, 1 OR Accidental Injury to Hospital	
Fqa 4.5	25th		1 OR Proceeded on Ordinary leave to UK.	
A16a 4.0	30th		2 ORs Died of Wounds.	
			3 ORs Wounded to Hospital	
"			1 OR Slightly Wounded to Hospital	

J Munro
Commanding 451st Field Company,
(East Anglian) Royal Engineers.

2nd Divisional Engineers

483rd FIELD COMPANY R.E. ::: SEPTEMBER 1918.

Army Form C. 2118.

WAR DIARY
or
INTELLIGENCE SUMMARY

483rd (E.A) FIELD Coy R.E.
(Erase heading not required.)

Instructions regarding War Diaries and Intelligence Summaries are contained in F. S. Regs., Part II. and the Staff Manual respectively. Title Pages will be prepared in manuscript.

SEPTEMBER 1918

Place	Date Sept 1918	Hour	Summary of Events and Information	Remarks and references to Appendices
B.29d. & I.4c.3.2	1st		1. O.R. Sick to Hosp.	
	2nd	12-0 noon	Coy (Dismounted Section) moved to B.29d.	
	3rd		Remainder. Three Sections moved to I.4c.3.3. The remaining Section & Transport followed at 1-30 p.m. Transport followed at 4 a.m. 5 a.m. where it 1 Section attached to 99th Bde. Gr were & remained until 15th inst. cleared loads of Debris from MORCHIES to VAULX VRAUCOURT. 1 " on Water supply in MORCHIES. 1 " on Griding & cleaning booby-traps – over 50 were found.	
	4th		3 Sections on Water Supply in MORCHIES – pumps for wells were installed & hose	
	16th }		troughs erected. Officers made a Reconnaissance of bridges over Canal du Nord.	
	15th }		& water supply in BERNMETZ.	
	6th		An explosion occurred in Camp- believed to have been a booby trap. There were no Casualties.	
	7th		1. O.R. Sick to Hospital.	
	10th		1. O.R. rejoined from Hospital. Lieut Abbott (att'd from 23rd Battn R.Fus.) left Coy. for duty with 5th Field Coy. C.E.	
	11th		2. O.R's rejoined from Hospital.	
			Lieut J. Wilson. R.E. returned from Course at R.E.T.S. ROUEN. 2.O.R's to Hosp. (Acc injury).	
	12th		Lieut L.A Fulton Temporarily transferred to 5th Field Cy. R.E. for duty. 1. O.R. Sick to Hosp.	
	13th		1. O.R. rejoined from Hospital.	
	14th		1. O.R. ditto ditto.	
	15th		1. O.R. Joined Unit (Reinforcement) from R.E. Base Depot.	
B.24 & Y.6	16th	1-0 p.m	Coy moved to VRAUCOURT area (B.24d.76). 1. O.R. Sick to Hosp.	
	17th }		Very little training was possible as three Sections were employed on Billets	
	16th }		for Battn of 99th Inf. Bde and making billets for this Unit- also making Pack	
	22nd }		Stores in view of the coming operation. 1 Section trained in bridging	
	17th		Pack. Lieut. Seavers (1st K.R.R.C. att'd) to Hospital (Sick)	
	18th		1. O.R. Sick to Hospital.	
	20th		2. O.R's Joined Unit (Reinforcements) from R.E. Base Depot.	

Commanding,
483rd Field Company,
(East Anglian) Royal Engineers
Capt. & Officer

Army Form C. 2118.

WAR DIARY
or
INTELLIGENCE SUMMARY
453rd (E.A.) Field Coy, R.E.
(Erase heading not required.)

SEPTEMBER 1918.

Place	Date Sept.	Hour	Summary of Events and Information	Remarks and references to Appendices
B.24.d.7.6.	22nd		Major H. Mawson M.C. R.E. proceeded on Leave to U.K. Capt. A. M. Matthews R.E. took over Command of Coy. Lieut. L. A. Fuller R.E. rejoined Unit from 5th Field Coy R.E.	
	23rd 24th 26th	7.10 a.m	Three Sections remained on Work, making pack stores and advanced Dets. A.D. in Bridging	
	23rd		1 O.R. rejoined from Hospital.	
	24th		1 O.R. ditto	
	25th		1 O.R. to Hospital.	
	26th		1 O.R. to Hospital (Accidental Injury). Lieut. Barnard Smith with No.2 Section moved to 99th Bde. H.Q. at BEAUMETZ for attachment during coming operations. Lieut. Voy took Pontoons to J.34.d.7.3. & parked them over to O.C. Div. Bridging Train - 1 O.R. sick to Hospital.	
	27th		First & Third Armies attacked at 5.20 a.m. Officers made reconnaissances of forward tracks, roads & dumps &c in the area circulated by the Enemy at J.26.7.6. rejoining there 10.0 a.m.	
to	27th	6.20 a.m	Coy. moved to J.29.c.2.8. (S.W. of HERMIES station) arriving about 10.0 p.m. & bivouacked for the night.	
J.29.c.2.8.	28th	7.0 a.m	Coy. moved to K.14.a.7.8. One Section worked on approaches to bridges over Canal du Nord.	
J.29.c.2.8 to K.14.a.7.8	28th	4.0 a.m	Coy. moved to K.14.a.7.8.	
K.14.a.7.8 to L.14.a.2.6	28th	3.0 p.m	Coy. moved to L.14.a.2.6. (N.E. of FLESQUIERES) - & billeted in Dugouts in old enemy gunpits. Two Sections worked on crates supply in FLESQUIERES & erected Horse trough. 1 O.R. Wounded to Hosp. (Sgt. Holland). Lieut. Wilson proceeded on Leave to U.K. Water supply in FLESQUIERES continued. Lieut. Fuller.	
	29th	10.0 a.m	No. 1 Section went forward to put NOYELLES under bridge at L.11.b.6.6. in a state of repair in order to get Div. Pontoon Train to the Canal. Two broken trestles and 2a transom were repaired and two small trestles made & erected in 2½ hours under H.E. and gas shell fire and M.G. fire from enemy aeroplanes -	
		12 noon		

Signed,
453rd Field Company,
Royal Engineers
(A.M.Matthews)
Capt. R.E. Officer
Commanding

Army Form C. 2118.

WAR DIARY
or
INTELLIGENCE SUMMARY.
483rd (E.A.) Field Coy. R.E.
(Erase heading not required.)

SEPTEMBER. 1918.

Place	Date Sep 1918	Hour	Summary of Events and Information	Remarks and references to Appendices
L.14.a.2.6	30th		One Section continued Water Supply in FLESQUIERES. Two Sections worked on repair of bridges over river & canal at L.11.d.9.2. and L.12.c.7.2. - These could take Field Guns after 24 hours work. One Section took over maintenance of the 3 bridges mentioned above. Lieut. Barnard - Smith wounded to Hospital - Sapper Cheshire killed severely wounded - Sapper died of wounds same night. During above operations the Section attached to 99th Infy Bde did valuable reconnaissance work, all sorts of odd jobs, and erected a pontoon bridge at L.6.c.3.2. under heavy fire. -	

[signature]
Capt. R.E.
Commanding
483rd Field Company,
(East Anglian) Royal Engineers

2nd Divisional Engineers

483rd FIELD COMPANY R.E. ::: OCTOBER 1918.

WAR DIARY or INTELLIGENCE SUMMARY

Army Form C. 2118.

483 (A) FIELD COY. R.E.

October 1918.

Place	Date	Hour	Summary of Events and Information	Remarks and references to Appendices
SERANVILLERS	18th/19th		2. O.R. Sick to Hospital. 1. O.R. Sick to Hospital	
BOUSSIERES	20th	0945	Company moved to BOUSSIERES arriving 1315.	
	21st		Company working on BOUSSIERES – ST. HILAIRE roads. Lt. K.A. Faulton proceeded on leave U.K.	
	22nd		2 Sections worked on ST. HILAIRE.	
ST. HILAIRE	23rd		2 Sections worked on road from ST. VAAST to ARBRE LA FEMINE Company moved to ST. HILAIRE. Wooden Trestle Bridge over R. SELLE at ST. PHYTHON.	
	24th	0530	2 Sections assisted attack of 99th Bgde by constructing foot crossing over ST. GEORGES and 5 foot crossings over R. ECAILLON near CAPELLE under Lieut. Wilson R.E. who also carried out reconnaissance of PONT DU BUAT removing Demolition Charges.	
	25th	0900	3. O.R. Wounded to Hospital. The 4 Section with transport moved to FERME DE RIEUX near VERTAIN. Remainder of Company moved to FERME DE RIEUX. Company worked on road VERTAIN – FERME DE RIEUX – ESCARMAIN.	
FERME DE RIEUX	26th to 31st		Company employed on maintenance of road FERME DE RIEUX – ESCARMAIN and protection of bridges at ESCARMAIN and CAPELLE.	
	26th		1. O.R. Rejoined Unit from Hospital	
	27th		1. O.R. Rejoined Unit from Hospital	
	28th		1. O.R. Sick to Hospital	
	29th		1. O.R. Sick to Hospital	
	30th		1. O.R. Sick to Hospital	
	31st		1. O.R. Sick to Hospital	

522073. Sergt. Jackson M.M. 524402 Corpl. Day J.
522025. Corpl. Jefferies E.   522232 Sapr. Reed M.

Awarded Military Medal by Corps Commander. Auth. G.R.O. 3682. H.Q. 31/10/18

Signed [signature]
Major
483 Field Coy R.E.

Army Form C. 2118.

WAR DIARY
or
INTELLIGENCE SUMMARY

(Erase heading not required.)

483 (E.A.) FIELD. COY. R.E.

1st 42
October 1918.

Place	Date	Hour	Summary of Events and Information	Remarks and references to Appendices
FLESQUIERES. L.14.a.2.b.	1st to 8th		1. Sections employed in maintaining bridges over canal and river ESCAULT. 2. Sections employed in obtaining and repairing bridges to enable men to carry to-baths. 1. Section at work on Water Supply at FLESQUIERES.	
	2nd		1. O.R. Admitted to Hospital	
	4th		8. O.R. Joined Unit (Reinforcements) from R.E. Base Depot.	
	5th		1. O.R. Wounded to Hospital	
	6th		1. O.R. Killed	
	7th			
	8th		London Bridge erected over the ESCAULT canal at NOYELLES. Report received that the water was running rapidly out of the canal and flooding the surrounding country and also causing the pontoons to ground. The trestles were substituted for pontoons and completed the same day.	
	9th		A Recon: of the canal was made and the leakage located. viz. a bolt hole in a culvert running under the canal. The canal was successfully repaired with concrete under 3'0" of water. Lt. Halson (from 226 Field(s)) attached temporary for duty.	
	10th			
	11th		Lt. R.S. Gledhill be Joined Unit (Reinforcement) from R.E. Base Depot.	
	12th			
	13th		5 a de bridges over canal and river ESCAULT were dismantled and stores sorted out and packed ready for future use.	
	14th		No. 1. Section moved to SERANVILLERS.	
SERANVILLERS	15th	0830	Remainder of Company moved to SERANVILLERS, arriving at 1230.	
	16th		1 Section worked on Bgde. H.Q.	
			1. O.R. Sick to Hospital	
			3 Sections worked on road from WAMBAIX to ESTOURMEL. Major J.N. Mawson rejoined from leave and took over Command of Company. Lieut. J. Wilsher rejoined from leave.	
	17th to 19th		Company working on Road WAMBAIX – ESTOURMEL. Capt. Mathews proceeded on leave 17th.	
	17th		1. O.R. Sick to Hospital	

J.N. Mawson Major
O.E.

2nd Divisional Engineers

483rd FIELD COMPANY R.E. :: NOVEMBER 1918.

WAR DIARY.

A83rd (E.A) FIELD Cy R.E.

November 1918.

PLACE.	DATE.	TIME.	REMARKS.	APPENDIX.
FREM.-DE-RIEUX	November 1st		Coy continued work on roads –	No 43
	2nd 4th		2.O.Rs Sick & Hospt.	
to			1.O.R. do	
VILLERS POL			Coy moved to RHONELLE at 1200 hrs. Difficulty was experienced in getting up material. New Bridge was completed out night 5/6. Improvements were carried out to a heavy bridge at WARGNIES-LE-PETIT.	
VILLERS POL.	5th 6th 8th		(a) 2 Sections were employed on road from LA COISETTE (near VILLERS POL) westwards.	
	5th		3. O.Rs. Sick & Hospt	
	6th		3. O.Rs. do	
	10th		1. O.R. do	
	11th		1. O.R. do	
	12th 16th		Coy employed on road RUESNES – CAPELLE – ESCARMAIN –	
	14th		1. O.R. Sick & Hospt.	
	15th		2. O.Rs. do 4. O.Rs. Joined Unit (Reinforcements)	
	16th		1. O.R. do	
	17th		2. O.Rs. do 2. O.Rs. Joined Unit (Reinforcements)	
			1. O.R. do	
FREM-LES-MOTTE (LONGUEVILLE) to LONGUEVILLE (FREM-LES-MOTTE)	18th		Coy moved to FREM.-LES- MOTTE at LONGUEVILLE (Near BAVAI). 1. O.R. Sick & Hospt.	
	19th		1. O.R. Sick & Hospt. Lieut Jas Hopk.	

Major R.E.
O.C. 83rd/ (E.A) Field Cy R.E.

WAR DIARY.

483rd (E.A.) FIELD Coy R.E.
NOVEMBER 1918.

PLACE.	DATE.	TIME.	
LONGUEVILLE (FERM-LES-MOTTE) to VIEUX RENG.	November 20th		Coy moved to Vieux Reng.
VIEUX RENG.	23rd	3. o.R.'s	Sick & Hospt. 9.o.R's. (Reinforcements) Joined Unit.
" to RESSAIX	24th		Coy moved to Ressaix. (Mer. Binche - Bing).
RESSAIX to MARCHIENNE-DU-PONT	25th		Coy moved to Marchienne-Au-Pont arriving about 1300 hrs.
MARCHIENNE-DU-PONT	26th	1. O.R.	Sick to Hospt.
"	27th	3. o.Rs.	do
" to CHATELET	28th		Coy moved to Chatelet arriving about 1215 hrs.
CHATELET to SART-ST LAURENT	29th		Coy marched to Sart- St Laurent. Arrived about 1430 hrs.

J.M. Munro

Major R.E. O.C.
483/(E.A) Field Coy R.E.

2nd Divisional Engineers

483rd FIELD COMPANY R.E. ::: DECEMBER   1918.

WAR DIARY or INTELLIGENCE SUMMARY

483rd (E.A.) FIELD Co'y R.E.

(Erase heading not required.)

Army Form C. 2118.

483 In Coy R.E.

DECEMBER 1918.

Place	Date	Hour	Summary of Events and Information	Remarks and references to Appendices
SART. ST. LAURENT.	1st		1. O.R. Sick to Hospital.	
	2nd		2. O.R.S.	
MARCHE-LES-DAMES	4th		Coy. moved to MARCHE-LES-DAMES. (Meuse valley) arr'd about 3-0 p.m. 1.O.R. Sick to Hosp'l.	
SEILLES	5th		Coy. moved to SEILLES. (Meuse Valley) 1.O.R. Sick to Hosp'l.	
SEILLES to BARSE	6th		Coy. moved to BARSE. arrived about 2-0 p.m. 1.O.R. Sick to Hospital.	
BARSE to MONT.	7th		Coy moved to MONT. 1.O.R. Sick to Hosp'l.	
MONT to HESTROUMONT	9th		Coy. moved to HESTROUMONT. 1.O.R. Sick to Hospital.	
BERNISTER	11th		Coy. moved to BERNISTER (Germany).	
ELSENBORN-LAGER	12th		Coy. moved to ELSENBORN LAGER.	
HUPPENBROICH	13th		Coy. moved to HUPPEN BROICH.	
THUM.	14th		Coy. moved to THUM.	
THUM.	15th		1.O.R. Sick to Hospital.	
	17th		1.O.R. Rejoined Unit from Hospital.	
ELLEN	19th		Coy. moved to ELLEN - Recreation, Training & Christmas festivities.	
	20th		1.O.R. Sick to Hospital.	
	21st		1.O.R. do. 1.O.R. Sick to Hosp'l. 22nd.	
	24th		1.O.R. do. 15.O.Rs. (Reinforcements) Joined Unit from R.E. Bn. Depot.	
ANGELSDORF	27th		Coy. moved to ANGELSDORF.	
VANIKUM	28th		Coy. moved to VANIKUM. 2.O.R.S. (Balmain & Eng'r. for Demobilization.	
	29th		1.O.R. to Eng'r. (Compassionate Grounds).	
	30th		1.O.R. Sick to Hosp'l.	
	31st		1.O.R. to Eng'r. (Demobilization Staff).	

WAR DIARY
or
INTELLIGENCE SUMMARY.
483rd FIELD COY R.E.
(Erase heading not required.)

AUGUST 1919

Place	Date	Hour	Summary of Events and Information	Remarks and references to Appendices
WALD	1st		During this month the daily programme was much the same as for July, events	
	5th		essential and urgent jobs. Afternoons were given over to sport and	
			recreation, several matches in the Brigade Cricket League were played.	
			2nd Lieut R.G. GODD act attached R.R.Y. MONTEITH attached to 9th Batt London Regt for 1 mo. instruction	
			Lieut R.O. DAVIES proceeded on leave to U.K.	
	11th		11 O.R. proceeded to DAHMSTED OUTPOST to wire "Perimeter line," attached to 5200 Rifle Brigade for	
			rations. Party returned 20 Aug. and completed	
	13th		2nd Lieut R.L. THOMPSON joined from 226 Field Cy R.E.	
	16th		Lieut R.S. Bledhill rejoined from leave, and proceeded to 287th Army Troops Cy R.E. on 17th	
	18th		2nd Lieut R.Y. MONTEITH proceeded to U.K. for duty, under authy Rhine Army A.9/2/84 dated 5/8/19	
			Army Horse Show at COLOGNE, 1st Prize in "Bus: mule: team: event, R.E.(M.S Sect) Toot Cart.	
	26th		Lieut R.O. DAVIES rejoined from leave.	
	27th		Lieut R.O. DAVIES proceeded to 226 Field Cy R.E. for attachment	
	31st		Cour-Martial proceedings from GARD, all accused sentenced to 90 days F.P. No. 2.	

A J.B. Green Capt
O.C. 483rd (E.A) Field Coy R.E.

www.ingramcontent.com/pod-product-compliance
Lightning Source LLC
Chambersburg PA
CBHW080912230426
43667CB00015B/2658